THE
HISTORY OF
EGYPT

ADVISORY BOARD

THE
HISTORY OF
EGYPT

Glenn E. Perry

The Greenwood Histories of the Modern Nations
Frank W. Thackeray and John E. Findling, Series Editors

Greenwood Press
Westport, Connecticut • London

Library of Congress Cataloging-in-Publication Data

Perry, Glenn E. (Glenn Earl), 1940–
    The history of Egypt / Glenn E. Perry.
        p. cm. — (The Greenwood histories of the modern nations, ISSN 1096–2905)
    Includes bibliographical references and index.
    ISBN 0–313–32264–3
        1. Egypt—History—1798– I. Title. II. Series.
    DT100.P47   2004
    962—dc22   2004004719

British Library Cataloguing in Publication Data is available.

Library of Congress Catalog Card Number: 2004004719
ISBN: 0–313–32264–3
ISSN: 1096–2905

First published in 2004

Greenwood Press, 88 Post Road West, Westport, CT 06881
An imprint of Greenwood Publishing Group, Inc.
www.greenwood.com

Printed in the United States of America

The paper used in this book complies with the
Permanent Paper Standard issued by the National
Information Standards Organization (Z39.48–1984).

10 9 8 7 6 5 4 3 2 1

*For Nicholas, Helen, Jack, Emily, Alex, Dakota, Damian,
and Calista*

Contents

Series Foreword

The *Greenwood Histories of the Modern Nations* series is intended to provide students and interested laypeople with up-to-date, concise, and analytical histories of many of the nations of the contemporary world. Not since the 1960s has there been a systematic attempt to publish a series of national histories, and, as editors, we believe that this series will prove to be a valuable contribution to our understanding of other countries in our increasingly interdependent world.

Over thirty years ago, at the end of the 1960s, the Cold War was an accepted reality of global politics, the process of decolonization was still in progress, the idea of a unified Europe with a single currency was unheard of, the United States was mired in a war in Vietnam, and the economic boom of Asia was still years in the future. Richard Nixon was president of the United States, Mao Tse-tung (not yet Mao Zedong) ruled China, Leonid Brezhnev guided the Soviet Union, and Harold Wilson was prime minister of the United Kingdom. Authoritarian dictators still ruled most of Latin America, the Middle East was reeling in the wake of the Six-Day War, and Shah Reza Pahlavi was at the height of his power in Iran. Clearly, the past thirty years have been witness to a great deal of historical change, and it is to this change that this series is primarily addressed.

With the help of a distinguished advisory board, we have selected nations whose political, economic, and social affairs mark them as among the most important in the waning years of the twentieth century, and for each nation we have found an author who is recognized as a specialist in the history of that nation. These authors have worked most cooperatively with us and with Greenwood Press to produce volumes that reflect current research on their nation and that are interesting and informative to their prospective readers.

The importance of a series such as this cannot be underestimated. As a superpower whose influence is felt all over the world, the United States can claim a "special" relationship with almost every other nation. Yet many Americans know very little about the histories of the nations with which the Untied States relates. How did they get to be the way they are? What kind of political systems have evolved there? What kind of influence do they have in their own region? What are the dominant political, religious, and cultural forces that move their leaders? These and many other questions are answered in the volumes of this series.

The authors who have contributed to this series have written comprehensive histories of their nations, dating back to prehistoric times in some cases. Each of them, however, has devoted a significant portion of the book to events of the last thirty years, because the modern era has contributed the most to contemporary issues that have an impact on U.S. policy. Authors have made an effort to be as up-to-date as possible so that readers can benefit from the most recent scholarship and a narrative that includes very recent events.

In addition to the historical narrative, each volume in this series contains an introductory overview of the country's geography, political institutions, economic structure, and cultural attributes. This is designed to give readers a picture of the nation as it exists in the contemporary world. Each volume also contains additional chapters that add interesting and useful detail to the historical narrative. One chapter is a thorough chronology of important historical events, making it easy for readers to follow the flow of a particular nation's history. Another chapter features biographical sketches of the nation's most important figures in order to humanize some of the individuals who have contributed to the historical development of their nation. Each volume also contains a comprehensive bibliography, so that those readers whose interest has been sparked may find out more about the nation and its history. Finally, there is a carefully prepared topic and person index.

Readers of these volumes will find them fascinating to read and useful in understanding the contemporary world and the nations that comprise it. As series editors, it is our hope that this series will contribute to a heightened sense of global understanding as we embark on a new century.

Frank W. Thackeray and John E. Findling
Indiana University Southeast

Preface

As a specialist on the Middle East who picked Egypt as his main focus of interest decades ago but whose writings have concentrated less on that country in particular than originally planned, I was pleased to receive an invitation from Frank W. Thackery and John E. Findling, the editors of this series, to write this general history. Considering the central importance that the whole Islamic world—not least Egypt—has taken on in recent years as an area of global concern and also the extent to which so many, especially in the United States, lack basic knowledge, I hope to make a small contribution to public enlightenment.

With nonspecialized readers in mind, I have refrained from using fully scientific rules for transliterating Arabic words and names. There are no dots or diacritical marks. I have used regular and inverted apostrophes to indicate the letters *hamza* and *ayn* respectively when they are in the middle of words, but not at the beginning or end. I have transliterated most Arabic names based on their original spelling (e.g., *Nasir* rather than the more commonplace *Nasser*), but have opted not to be completely consistent (e.g., sticking with *Boutros* rather than *Butrus*). Also, I generally have gone along with Egyptian pronunciation in the case of Egyptian names with the letter *jim* (*j*) by using a *g* instead (e.g., *Gamal* rather than *Jamal*).

In keeping with the series of which it is a part, this book attempts to tell the story of the evolution of Egypt from ancient times until the present in a way that will be useful to the general reader or college student. Also in keeping with the series, it starts with an introductory chapter on contemporary Egypt and then proceeds to a series of chapters on particular time periods, concentrating heavily on the modern era, especially on the half century since the July 1952 Revolution. Space permits only a short sketch of the several millennia of ancient Egyptian history, including the Pharaonic age when Egypt was in the forefront of human developments in such a spectacular way. The Islamic period up to the twentieth century also gets relatively telescoped treatment. This emphasis on recent history is paralleled in the biographical sketches of Notable People in that I have included only a few medieval and nineteenth-century figures. In light of space considerations I reluctantly decided simply not to include pre-Islamic Egyptians. The list of people dealt with is necessarily arbitrary. It includes most of Egypt's modern rulers but also some people—particularly Copts and women and also some literary figures—who are not even mentioned in the main body of the book. The emphasis is on Egyptians rather than foreigners (e.g., Napoleon Bonaparte or Henry Kissinger) who played roles in the country's history, although I make room for some members of foreign ruling classes (e.g., Muhammad Ali) who became permanently established in Egypt.

For someone who is used to documenting every fact or opinion in more specialized writings in order to allow the reader to judge its soundness and to give credit to authors whose works were used, writing a general book such as this can be painful. Pages of footnotes are not an option. Needless to say, I read and consulted hundreds of books and articles on the subject while working on this book (and even more during the 40 years before starting it), many of which are not even listed in the Bibliographic Essay. In some cases—one little example being my reference to the influence of *The Prince* on two presidents that I gleaned from books by Kirk Beattie—I have used information that cannot be footnoted in this kind of survey.

Acknowledgments

I would like to thank several people for their help with this project. This includes Douglas A. Howard of Calvin College, who recommended me as the person to take on this task and whose volume on Turkey in the same series provided a valuable example for me to follow. At Greenwood Press, senior editor Kevin Ohe worked with me on the original plans for the book while Steven Vetrano served as the editor for the project once the manuscript was ready. Impressions Book and Journal Services coordinated the project. I greatly appreciate the valuable assistance provided by all of them.

I appreciate the patience shown by my wife, Eleanor, and all the other members of our family who have had to share me with this and so many other writing projects. Thanks go particularly to my eight grandchildren (seven living) to whom this book is dedicated.

Timeline of Historical Events

ca. 3200 B.C.	Unification of Upper and Lower Egypt
ca. 2687 B.C.	Beginning of Third Dynasty and of Old Kingdom
ca. 2190 B.C.	End of Old Kingdom and beginning of First Intermediate Period
ca. 2061 B.C.	Beginning of Middle Kingdom
ca. 1664 B.C.	Occupation by Hyksos, beginning of Second Intermediate Period
ca. 1557 B.C.	Beginning of New Kingdom
ca. 1200 B.C.	Attack by Peoples of the Sea
671 B.C.	Conquest by Assyria
525 B.C.	Persian (Achaemenid) conquest
332 B.C.	Invasion by Alexander the Great
323 B.C.	Death of Alexander and beginning of Ptolemaic dynasty
30 B.C.	Egypt made a Roman province

451	Monophysitism rejected by Council of Chalcedon
639	Beginning of Islamic conquest
661	Beginning of Umayyad dynasty
750	Establishment of Abbasid dynasty
868	Beginning of Tulunid dynasty
934	Emergence of Ikhshidi dynasty
969	Conquest by the Fatimids; founding of Cairo
1099	Jerusalem conquered by First Crusade
1171	Ayyubid dynasty begun by Salah al-Din (Saladin)
1187	Victory over Crusaders at Battle of Hattin
1250	Succession of Shajar al-Durr (and then Aybek), leading to Mamluk era
1260	Mongols defeated at Ayn Jalut; succession of Baybars
1382	Beginning of Burji Mamluks
1513	Defeat of Mamluk Navy by Portuguese
1517	Ottoman conquest of Egypt
1760	Takeover of Egypt by Ali Bey (the Great)
1772	Beginning of rule by Abu-Dhahab
1790s	Joint rule by Ibrahim and Murad
1798	Conquest by General Bonaparte
1801	Arrival of British and Ottoman forces; French withdrawal
1805	Muhammad Ali named governor of Egypt
1811	Massacre of Mamluks
1811–18	Egyptian expedition subduing "Wahhabis" in Arabia
1821	Outbreak of revolt in Greece, leading to Egyptian intervention
1827	Egyptian fleet defeated at Navarino Bay
1831	Egyptian Invasion of Syria and then of Anatolia

1840	London Conference demands withdrawal; Anglo–Ottoman agreement of 1838 applied
1841	Muhammad Ali made hereditary governor of Egypt and Sudan
1848	Death of Ibrahim Pasha (the effective ruler), replaced by Abbas
1849	Death of Muhammad Ali
1854	Succession of Sa'id
1863	Succession of Isma'il
1866	Fundamental Law issued, with provision for Consultative Assembly of Deputies
1869	Completion of Suez Canal
1871	Enactment of Muqabala Law
1875	Sale of Egyptian shares in Suez Canal to Britain
1876	Establishment of the Public Debt Commission and Dual Control
1879	Demonstrations led by Urabi; Isma'il dismissed and replaced by Tawfiq
1881	Urabi becomes minister of war in new government; revolt of Mahdi in Sudan
1882	Beginning of British occupation
1892	Succession of Abbas Hilmi
1898	Defeat of the Mahdi by Lord Kitchener
1906	The Dinshawai incident
1914	Egypt declared a British protectorate; Husayn Kamil succeeds and takes title of sultan; martial law declared
1917	Fu'ad succeeds to throne
1918	Delegation headed by Zaghlul meets with Sir Reginald Wingate
1919	Zaghlul exiled, igniting 1919 Revolution; Milner mission established

1920	Founding of Bank Misr
1922	Egypt declared independent, with four reserved points
1923	Egyptian Constitution goes into effect
1924	Wafdist electoral victory; assassination of Sir Lee Stack; Wafdist government forced to resign
1927	Death of Zaghlul; Mustafa al-Nahhas becomes new Wafdist leader
1928	Formation of Muslim Brotherhood
1930	Royalist coup replaces the Nahhas government
1936	Faruq succeeds to throne; Wafdist electoral victory and formation of Wafdist government (replaced the next year); Anglo-Egyptian Treaty concluded
1942	"February 4 Incident"—The British force the king to appoint Nahhas
1945	Arab League established
1948	Egyptian forces participate in the Palestine War
1949	Egyptian–Israeli armistice agreement; assassination of Hasan al-Banna
1950	Wafdist victory in parliamentary elections; Nahhas heads government
1951	Parliament abrogates 1936 Treaty; guerrillas attack British
1952	British attack police station in Ismailia, followed by "burning of Cairo"; Nahhas dismissed
1952	Free Officers coup; King Faruq exiled; land reform
1953	Three-year transition period declared; political parties abolished; Liberation Rally established; Anglo-Egyptian agreement on Sudan
1954	Nasir wins struggle with Nagib; Anglo-Egyptian agreement on Suez Base; Muslim Brothers attempt to assassinate Nasir; crackdown follows on Muslim Brothers; Israeli sabotage plot uncovered

1955	Baghdad Pact announced; attack on Gaza; Bandung Conference; arms deal with "Czechoslovakia" (i.e., the USSR)
1956	Dulles reneges on offer to help with the High Dam; Suez Canal Company nationalized; tripartite invasion; British and French pressured to withdraw; UNEF established
1957	Israeli withdrawal completed; Eisenhower Doctrine declared
1958	UAR established; Iraqi coup and subsequent clash with Egypt
1961	Adoption of Arab Socialism; breakup of the UAR
1962	Charter drawn up by Congress of Popular Forces; Revolution in Yemen; Egyptian troops are sent
1964	Provisional constitution adopted
1966	ASU official murdered, bringing renewal of antifeudal measures
1967	UNEF withdrawn; Sharm al-Shaykh declared closed to Israel; Israel attacks and Egyptian military is crushed; Gaza and Sinai occupied; Nasir announces resignation, later withdrawn on popular demand; Amir commits suicide; Security Council Resolution 242 adopted
1968	Demonstrations occur; March 30 Declaration promising reform
1969	War of Attrition declared
1970	Cease-fire accepted; death of Nasir; succession by Sadat
1971	"May 15 correction"; purge of opponents by Sadat; announcement of end to oppressive practices; permanent Constitution adopted
1972	Expulsion of most Soviet military personnel
1973	"The Crossing," beginning October/Ramadan/Yom Kippur War

1974	First disengagement agreement; attack on Military Academy
1974	October Working Paper announcing open door (infitah) policy
1975	Second disengagement agreement; renewed conflict with Arab world
1976	Separate platforms created within the ASU and later allowed to become political parties, with NDP as government party
1977	Food riots following announcement of price increases; Sadat's visit to Jerusalem
1978	Camp David meeting and agreement on framework for settlement
1979	Peace treaty concluded; Egypt suspended from Arab League; ties with most Arab states broken
1980	"Normal relations" established with Israel
1980	Law of Shame
1981	Critics arrested; Sadat is assassinated; succession of Mubarak
1982	Israeli withdrawal completed (except for Taba)
1986	Revolt of conscripts in the Central Security Services
1989	Suspension from Arab League ended
1991	"Desert Storm"; much of Egypt's international debt canceled
1994	Accelerated repression of Muslim Brothers
1996	Economic liberalization accelerated
1997	Tourists massacred in Luxor
1999	Truce between government and militants; alliance formed by Zawahiri and part of Jihad with bin Ladin

2000   Sectarian riot in Kushah

2001   Al-Qa'ida attack on U.S., intensifying Egypt's eco-
              nomic problems

2002–03   Accelerated popular anger over Palestine and U.S. in-
              vasion of Iraq

1

Egypt Today

Beginning with geography, Egypt—Misr, literally "the Settled" in Arabic but pronounced in the local dialect as Masr—demonstrates uniqueness in perhaps more ways than any other country. Although it gets scarcely any rain, its people typically would wince if they heard an uninformed foreigner call it a desert country, for the greenery of the place they inhabit is unsurpassed. In sharp contrast to life in an arid land, Egyptian agriculturalists, historically nearly the whole population, have always spent much of their lives toiling in fertile fields and wading in canals that bring the water of the Nile to them. So much did early Egyptians equate water from this river with the source of life that the thirteenth-century B.C. Pharaoh Akhenaten, in his "Hymn to Aten," found it natural to describe water falling from the sky in recently conquered Syria as "a Nile in Heaven."

Deserts on each side of the Nile Valley make up the bulk of the territory within the boundaries of the Arab Republic of Egypt (the country's official name today). In that sense, Egypt is very much a desert county. There is only an insignificant amount of rain in the winter—not enough to support even the kind of nomadism to a comparable degree that always flourished in such dry lands as, say, Syria or Iran. The number of Bedouins (Arab nomads) is miniscule in Egypt today, although Bedouin tribes (sometimes actually sedentarized) were a political force during some premodern periods (when central governments were weak). And the kind of precarious agriculture dependent on a few inches of rainfall found in much of the Middle East has hardly ever existed in Egypt, making the line between the desert and the sown much sharper than in other countries. Aridity of nonirrigated areas intensifies as one goes south, where in some places years may pass without any sight of rain. United Nations statistics show that Egypt is the only country in which 100 percent of the agricultural land is irrigated.

In the famous words of the ancient Greek historian Herodotus, "Egypt is the gift of the Nile." This river, which has no tributaries in Egypt, results from the convergence at Khartoum (in the Sudan) of the White Nile, which

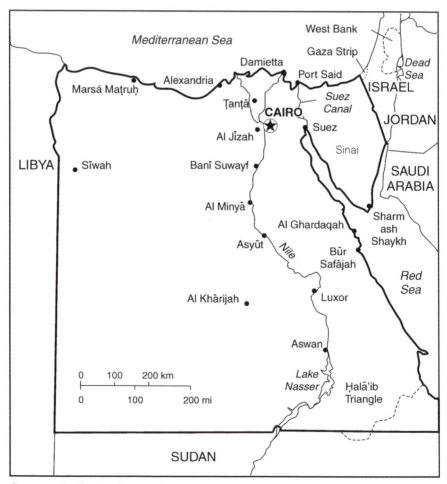

Cartography by Bookcomp, Inc.

originates at Lake Victoria in Uganda, and the Blue Nile, which flows from the Ethiopian Highlands. It swells from summer monsoon rains in East Africa to produce the inundation that Egypt experienced annually for many millennia until the High Dam at Aswan began to store the excess water.

It is this river—its Arabic name, Bahr ["sea," as opposed to Nahr, "river"] al-Nil recognizes its special status—that enables a rainless country to be perhaps the world's unique garden spot. In this semitropical climate, up to three crops per year grow on the same plot of land. According to an old fable, when God created the world He sent Wealth, along with Resignation, to Egypt. Over the millennia, the Nile made it possible for that country to constitute the "granary" or "milk cow" for empires that controlled it. The "Wealth" part of the fable was telling before overpopulation and underdevelopment negated it, but "Resignation" sometimes has been largely in the eyes of outsiders who did not know about the Egyptians' recurrent tendency to rebel against oppression.

The real Egypt is not the vast territory stretching from the Libyan frontier to the Red Sea. Projects during recent decades to "invade the desert"— even fanciful talk about building a new capital, an Egyptian "Brasilia," there—have only marginally extended the cultivated land. The inhabited area constitutes only about 6 percent of this (up from 4 percent), that is, mainly the narrow Nile Valley, which extends from the Sudanese frontier to the area near Cairo, and the fan-shaped Delta that spreads out northward (with the river splitting into two main branches before entering the sea and resulting from the accumulation of sediment brought by the annual flood over the millennia). The Delta—the "gift of the Nile" in the most literal sense—is known also as Lower Egypt, whereas the Nile Valley to the south is Upper Egypt, which Egyptians call the Sa'id (literally, "the Upland"). Rivers can, of course, run in any direction. The Nile flows from south to north, and so south is "up" and north is "down," a reality that seems strange only to people who are confused by the arbitrary conventions of most mapmakers.

THE PEOPLE OF EGYPT

Egypt is an Arab country. That is to say that its people, with minor exceptions, constitute part of a broad ethnic community—the Arabs—that extends all the way westward across northern Africa to the Atlantic coast and eastward to include all the countries—with the exception of Israel since 1948—west and south of Iran and Turkey. The Arab area also includes the northern part of the Sudan. Arab nationalists believe that this whole region really constitutes one nation (like Germany and Italy before unification in the nineteenth century) whose division into separate independent states—mere "regions" of the nation—is artificial and must make way for a unified Arab country. With attempts at Arab political unification failing, many observers have long considered the movement dead, but pan-Arabism still exists—though now often taking a religious form—in the sense that people in any Arab country become outraged when they see another Arab country as a victim.

Although Arab nationalists point to other shared cultural features, the common denominator of all who consider themselves Arabs is that Arabic is their mother tongue. Everyone, including pan-Arab nationalists, recognizes that various peoples, including those who inhabited the present Arab countries in ancient times, have been incorporated in the Arab melting pot. Using that criterion, one might argue that Egypt is one of the most purely Arab countries for it has no significant non-Arabic-speaking minorities.

In fact, it is only a literary language (basically the same as the Classical Arabic of the Qur'an, Islam's holy book), used in writing and formal speeches, that Egypt shares with this wider region. The old story of the person who landed in an Egyptian port and tried to speak the Arabic he had learned at Oxford or Princeton only to be told "Sorry, I don't speak English" is telling. The actual speech of most people—colloquial Arabic—varies greatly from country to country and indeed to a lesser extent from village to village. The everyday speech of Egypt is probably about as different from that of some other Arab countries as is Italian from Spanish. Were it not for the extent to which other Arabs have become familiar with the Egyptian cinema and radio and television they might sometimes not be able to understand the Cairo dialect.

The image of Egypt as part of a monolithic Arab people is only a half-truth. Its reality is matched by the equally true image of a mosaic of local and sectarian groups in many parts of the Arab world, and some writers prefer to reserve the term *ethnic group* for such splinters of the Arab region. Occasionally, Egyptians reject the label "Arab" altogether, and it does not sit easily on a lot of others. Although pan-Arabism sometimes has been a useful instrument for Egyptian foreign policy, it is hard to imagine many Egyptians ever accepting a unity scheme that was not dominated by their own country. Geography sets this country apart from the Arabs to the east and the west. Separated by vast expanses of desert from most of the Arab world, the populated part of Egypt is somewhat like an island in the middle of an ocean. Unlike some of today's political entities in the Arab world that represent arbitrary divisions created by Europeans in the early twentieth century, Egypt has long been a separate center of power, although in earlier centuries the authority of the rulers in Cairo normally extended to such places as Syria and western Arabia, and its modern history has often set it apart from the surrounding area.

Egyptians have been linguistically Arabized during the past millennium, but it is easy for Egyptians to look back to their distinctive ancient history and identity. Although the period since the rise of Islam has seen the movement of people from the Arabian Peninsula (the home of the original Arabs) into Egypt and elsewhere, there undoubtedly is a great deal of continuity of the Egyptian people from ancient to contemporary times. It is reported that in some villages in Upper Egypt there are "blue bloods" of alleged Arabian Peninsula origin who reserve the word "Arab" for themselves. The unique geography of the country results in many ways in the continuity of daily life in rural areas (although what superficial observers imagine as "age-old" features of life in many cases represent relatively recent innovations). But in other ways, Pharaonic culture (e.g., revealing clothes and marriages between brothers and sisters) would strike today's Egyptians as exotic and outrageous. They would find themselves more at home with ancient Arabs than with their Egyptian forebears. Occasional attempts to argue that Pharaonic culture survives are largely fanciful.

But whether one sees Egyptians as a distinct people or as merely a part of the Arab nation, what is indisputable is that they are unusually homogeneous. It is true that there is much racial variation, for although a few Egyptians—especially those who descend from the former Turkish and Circassian ruling class—could be mistaken as French or English, many others, especially in Upper Egypt, look more like typical African Americans. Afrocentrists (that is, adherents to the recent movement among African and African American scholars stressing the central role of Blacks in world history in which Greek civilization was derived from Egypt, which in turn is defined as undifferentiated from sub-Saharan Africa) proudly point to the glories of ancient Egyptian history and to the Negroid features represented in the statues of, say, the ancient Queen Nefertiti. But it is only from the point of view of Americans—who have the peculiar "one-drop rule" that defines anyone as a Black who has the slightest Black ancestry—that this outlook makes any sense. Egyptians do not have such a definition of race. The "Black Athena" Afrocentrist theory of an early Egyptian invasion of Greece that created Hellenic civilization lacks credible archaeological support, the basic debts of the Greeks to the Egyptians notwithstanding. Many Egyptians would hardly think of their country as a part of Africa except in an obvious geographical sense and are amazed (and sometimes, unfortunately, insulted) to hear Americans describing them as Black.

It is in an ethnolinguistic sense that the degree of homogeneity is so high. Linguistic minorities are quite small, including the few thousand people of Siwa Oasis near the Libyan border who speak a Berber tongue and a few others near the Sudanese border who speak Beja. Then there is the distinctive population of Nubia (not even considered part of Egypt until recent centuries), who historically inhabited the narrow valley in the extreme south and many of whose men work as servants in the cities of the north. A black-complexioned people, the Nubians, too—to the extent that they still have not adopted Arabic—speak a language that is related to Berber and other northern African tongues (and indeed are called *Barabra*). In the nineteenth and early twentieth century there were thousands of Greek and Italian immigrants as well as a Jewish minority that was partly indigenous (and Arabic speaking), but these people generally left Egypt in the 1950s.

RELIGION IN EGYPT

Notwithstanding the modern idea that all Egyptians or even all Arabs are one people without regard to religion, it recently has become increasingly evident that the older conception of communities based on religion is very much alive. Some would say that the solidarity Egyptians show with the rest of the Arab world is more a matter of religion than of ethnicity (as the Arabs as a whole are overwhelmingly Muslim), and indeed the Arab and the Islamic identities often are fused so much that one sometimes is justified in speaking of them together in contradiction to the local Egyptian one.

There is a high degree of religious homogeneity in Egypt in the sense that about 94 percent of the people are Muslims. In other words, their religion—like that of about a billion people in the world today—is Islam, literally meaning submission (to God), a faith based on what are accepted as revelations to the Prophet Muhammad in the seventh century A.D. that is similar to both Judaism and Christianity (though with its own holy book, the Qur'an). And with hardly any exceptions (other than among foreign residents), the Muslims of Egypt are Sunni Muslims, that is, members of the main sect that make up nearly 90 percent of the Muslims of the world (as opposed to the minority Shi'ites).

As in other countries, Islam in Egypt comes in varying forms. Not only is there the approach that stresses following the sacred law (Shari'ah), which includes rules for performing prayers and other rituals as well as for all areas of life, but there is also another manifestation known as Sufism. The Sufis (who can belong to any sect) are mystics who emphasize personal communion with God. They belong to various religious orders. And although the Sufi orders seemed to lose their significance in modern times, they are still important—notably the Shadhiliyyah Order that is a major force throughout the countryside.

But Christians make up about 6 percent of the population (their claim to being 10 percent or more seems to be an exaggeration). This includes perhaps a million "Uniate" Coptic Catholics who have become part of the Roman Catholic Church while preserving their own liturgy, a handful of converts to Western churches, and a few descendants of immigrants (Greek Orthodox, Maronite, etc.) from the eastern Mediterranean region.

But for Egypt the Christian community primarily means the Coptic Church. Copts are adherents to the form of Christianity that before the seventh century was the country's dominant faith. Headed now by Pope Shenouda III, the Copts represent one side of the divide in early Christian theology. As opposed to both Western and Orthodox Christianity, the Coptic Church adheres to the doctrine of monophysitism, that is, that Christ is purely divine rather than being both God and man (see chap. 2).

Religion looms large in Egyptian society. While guaranteeing freedom for all religions (specifically for what sometimes are called the three "heavenly religions," that is, Islam, Christianity, and Judaism, whereas individuals accused of "heresy" sometimes are subject to prosecution), the Egyptian Constitution proclaims Islam to be the State religion and the Shari'ah to be the "principal source of legislation." The law requires that pupils in all schools be taught their own religion, and some individuals have been sentenced to prison for "insulting a heavenly religion." As in other predominantly Islamic countries, the law that applies to a person in matters of marriage, divorce, and inheritance depends on her or his official religion, although since 1956 this has been applied by government courts rather than by separate religious tribunals.

Among both Copts and Muslims there recently has been a resurgence of religion. Muslims in particular interrupt their sleep and work to perform their five-times-a-day ritual prayers—as their faith requires—more than before, whereas women wearing clothes that only reveal their faces and hands, in accordance with Islamic rules, have become the norm rather than the rare exception. Muslim men have come increasingly to wear beards, as their religion recommends. Mosques (in which Muslim men are supposed to perform at least their Friday noontime prayers) have been mushrooming everywhere.

Islamic institutions—mosques, seminaries, and preachers and prayer leaders, as well as muftis, who issue rulings *(fatwas)* on matters of religion and law—increasingly came under governmental control from the nineteenth century on. Ironically, the principle of unity of religion and government in Islam has typically led to the domination of the former by the latter. The government dictates the content of preachers' sermons and appoints and pays the salaries of mosque officials as well as higher religious leaders, such as the grand mufti and the Rector of al-Azhar University, historically the most prominent seminary for Islamic religious learning. But now increasingly there are popular religious movements, typically led by laypeople, that challenge governmental primacy over religion. This Islamist trend (so-called by outsiders because of its use of Islam as an ideology) demands implementation of Islamic law and solidarity with fellow Muslims throughout the world. More than ever before, the main movements today calling for change pose their demands in religious terms. Some are revolutionary and violent in their opposition to what they see as an ungodly regime ruled by American quislings, whereas other, more broadly based groups, notably the Society of Muslim Brothers, want to work gradually through free elections. Although increasingly repressing these opposition movements, the government itself also is taking on more and more of a religious character by, for example, increasingly bringing unauthorized mosques under government control and getting *fatwas* (legal rulings) from subservient religious authorities (dismissed as "pulpit parrots" by radical, populist Muslims), thus legitimating governmental actions. Policies that fervent Muslims tend to oppose—ranging from promoting birth control to making peace with Israel—almost never fail to get the backing of the government-affiliated religious authorities (denunciations of the American war on Iraq in 2003 constituting an unusual exception).

The relationship between Copts and Muslims has generally been amicable. They often joined together in opposition to colonial rule. Like Muslims, Copts today range from poor peasants (especially in Upper Egypt) to wealthy Cairo families. Their level of education and wealth tends to exceed that of Muslims. But they are underrepresented in the government, the army, and other areas of life, a fact that some attribute to discrimination.

Several matters tend to set Copts apart from Muslims. Despite the secular nature of Arab identity (embracing Christian Arabs), Copts sometimes see it as Islamic sentiment in disguise, and the growth of Islamist movements leaves them particularly uneasy. There recently have been some ugly clashes between them and militant Islamists. They see themselves as purely Egyptian and, in extreme cases, fancy that Muslims are interlopers. They often allege various kinds of discrimination. For example, a law going back to Ottoman times requiring permission to build or repair churches has provided a special sore point, as Copts point to recurrent delays, but a presidential decree of 1999 extending the same limitation to Muslim places of worship purports to end this inequality. In many ways, the Coptic Church has more autonomy from the government than do Muslims (who have nothing comparable to a church), and in some cases—for example, the peace treaty with Israel in 1979—the government was able to get official Muslim authorities to support it whereas the Coptic pope expressed opposition. Of potential symbolic significance, Coptic Christmas (January 7) recently became a national holiday.

THE REGIONS OF EGYPT

Egypt's 26 governates might be grouped together in six broad (and slightly overlapping) geographic regions, starting with Greater Cairo. At the junction of Upper and Lower Egypt, this includes not only Cairo proper (population: nearly eight million) but also adjacent areas, including Shubra al-Khaymah, the industrial city Helwan to the south, and Giza on the other side of the Nile. With a population that in 2003 reached nearly 16 million souls, Greater Cairo is in many ways the core of the country. People often use the word *Masr* specifically in reference to it. It not only serves as the center of power from which this centralized state is governed, but it is also the cultural center of Egypt and in many respects of the whole Arab world. Aside from the historically cosmopolitan and "Mediterranean" Alexandria (whose metropolitan area has nearly 4.5 million people), Cairo is urban Egypt par excellence, with other cities merely rustic provincial centers by comparison.

Upper Egypt (or the Sa'id) consists of the narrow Nile Valley south of Cairo, which the river has cut deep over the millennia, leaving high granite walls on each side. Averaging four miles in width, it ranges from up to 11 miles in its northernmost (lower) reaches to a narrow ribbon in the extreme south. Upper Egypt also includes the rich Fayyum Oasis, a depression on the western side of the valley from which Egyptians began channeling water in ancient times to form a small lake (now drained). Numerous small cities dot Upper Egypt, including Helwan (which we listed also as part of greater Cairo), Qena (population: 200,000), Asyut (population: 401,000), Luxor (population: 421,000), and Aswan (population: 256,000), near the Nile's First Cataract, beyond which lies the historic land of the Nubian people. The valley above the latter city—to the country's southern border and beyond—now forms Lake Nasir, the reservoir resulting from the construction of the High Dam—completed in 1971—that made it necessary for the Nubian villages to be moved to higher ground. Many Nubian men long have worked as servants in Cairo and Alexandria.

The Delta is a rich agricultural region. It also is the location of important cities, starting with the ancient metropolis—and now the country's major port—of Alexandria at its western extreme. Other cities include Mansura (population: 561,000), Zagazig (population: 313,000), Mahalla al-Kubra (population: 462,000), and Tanta (population: 434,000).

In many respects, the Suez Canal area deserves to be singled out as a distinct region. The 101-mile waterway, including the Great Bitter Lake in the center, is an extension of the eastern part of the Delta in the sense that this also is a populated area, with the lands under irrigation extending all the way to the Canal in some places. Port Said (population: 449,000) and Suez (population: 587,000) lie at the northern and southern ends of the waterway, respectively, whereas Ismailia (population: 298,000) is roughly in the middle. Since 1977, the Sumed (Suez-to-Mediterranean) oil pipeline has paralleled the canal.

The Western Desert makes up the bulk of Egypt's territory but is largely an empty terrain of sandstone or sand. It is generally flat, the exceptions being mainly depressions rather than hills. Some of these concavities include populated, fertile areas fed by underground water, as in the cases of the Siwa Oasis near the Libyan border and the oases of Bahariyah, Dakhlah, and Khargah. In the north lies the desolate Qattara Depression. There are a few small towns on the Mediterranean coast, for example, Matruh and—famous from World War II—El-Alamein (al-Alamayn) that constitute magnets for tourists.

The northeastern corner of Egypt—considered in Asia rather than Africa—is the Sinai. This largely desolate so-called Sinai Peninsula, actually an isthmus with a peninsula protruding southward, is separated from the rest of Egypt by the Suez Canal in the north and by the narrow Gulf of Suez in the south, whereas on the east it borders a second northern finger of the Red Sea, the Gulf of Aqaba, and the territory of Palestine/Israel. The peninsula is a rugged mountainous area whose highest altitude is reached at Mount Katherine (site of an ancient monastery) and Mount Moses, where the Ten Commandments allegedly were revealed. Sinai supports a small Bedouin population. But aside from the towns along the Suez Canal and some areas on the Mediterranean coast (including the town of al-Arish), it otherwise is largely uninhabited. There are tourist resorts on the coast in the south, and some oil is exploited in the western Sinai.

Lying between the Nile Valley and the Red Sea, the Eastern Desert differs from its western counterpart in several ways. It is slightly less arid than the Western Desert. A modest mountain chain, reaching an altitude of more than 7,000 feet at the southern end, extends from north to south. Several minor ports, which roads connect to the heart of the country, dot the coastal area, as now do tourist resorts.

THE ECONOMY OF EGYPT

Egypt is in many ways a prototype for a Third World—or economically undeveloped—country. Yet it is not among the poorest. Although previously dependent on long-staple cotton exports (recently in decline), it has a long history of industrialization. More than a third of the population still depends on agriculture. At the beginning of the 2000s, the country's modest oil and gas exports ($2.6 billion in 2001) had become the second-largest source of foreign currency, following tourism. Other major sources include remittances from people working abroad and Suez Canal tolls. Long-staple cotton (mostly yarn and textiles rather than the raw product now) ranks second to oil and gas among the country's commodity exports and accounts for about a third of world trade in that product. As generally has been true for the Third World, all these sources of revenue are subject to large fluctuations from year to year. Recent World Bank figures give Egypt's per capita gross national product as nearly $1,400, putting it in the category of "low middle" income countries (along with most of the Middle East and the former Soviet Union as well as much of Latin America), ahead of almost all the countries of sub-Saharan Africa, South Asia, and much of East and Southeast Asia. The United Nations Development Programme (UNDP's) human development index (for 2001), which takes into account more meaningful criteria such as life expectancy and literacy, gives Egypt a score of 64.8, putting it in the category of "medium human development." United Nations statistics show that only 3.1 percent of Egyptians live on less than one dollar a day, compared with 11.6 for Brazil and 44.2 percent for India, whose literacy rate of 74.1, however, slightly exceeds that of Egypt (72 percent). But recent reports point to an increase in poverty since 2000.

The socioeconomic conditions of many Egyptians would be hardly imaginable even to the poor in a developed country. The traditional Egyptian village consists of hundreds of mud brick (adobe) huts—more and more replaced by fired brick that unfortunately lacks mud's insulating qualities—clustered so closely that to a newcomer it seems like one huge mud hovel. Despite medical improvements in recent decades, villagers suffer from diseases such as dysentery and from bilharzia, a condition caused by worms that breed in stagnant irrigation canals and penetrate the skin of those who wade or swim (or do their laundry) in it and gradually destroy their internal organs. According to Human Rights Watch, about a million children less than 12 years of age help support their families by working—and exposing themselves to beatings and pesticides— 11 hours a day in cotton fields for about 81 cents each. A recent study shows that rural poverty is increasing. Even in Cairo, it is estimated that 1.5 million people live in the "City of the Dead," that is, a cemetery area going back to the Middle Ages. Many of the city's apartment buildings are built in such a shoddy manner that they crumble during earthquakes such as the one in 1992 that left 400 people dead. A Western tourist on one of the main streets might momentarily forget that this is not London or New York but then walk for five minutes into narrow garbage-strewn lanes among donkey carts and imagine having gone back in time a thousand years. But strong family ties, the Islamic injunction to support charities, and perhaps features of Islamic culture and belief that reduce the occurrence of children born out of wedlock, alcoholism, and the like result in less homelessness and outright hunger—and less-violent crime—than one finds in Western cities.

Overpopulation compounds Egypt's problems. As in other less-developed countries, the death rate has decreased as a result of modern medicine whereas the birth rate remains high, although in recent years the annual population rate has come down from nearly 3 percent to about 2 percent. An estimated 3.5 million people two centuries ago—and less than 22 million in 1952—increased to 70 million by 2003 (add another 1.3 million each year). The inhabited parts of the Egyptian countryside contain more people per square mile than any other rural area in the world, and Cairo is more densely populated than Manhattan. With the amount of cultivatable land increasing slowly during the past century, the reputed age-old "breadbasket" of empires now cannot feed itself.

Under persistent pressure from international lending agencies and from the United States, Egypt has slowly been shifting toward a more capitalist economy, although the constitution still describes it as a "democratic socialist" country. Long inhibited by the danger of unleashing the fury of the poor, the government has been eliminating subsidies that made necessities inexpensive. And state enterprises are being privatized.

Hopes that Egypt would become one of the winners in a new globalized economy have so far not been realized to a great extent. A recent report of the UNDP concluded that only sub-Saharan Africa ranked lower than the Arab world in economic growth during the previous 20 years. As another dramatic indication of the lack of progress, the report also pointed out that about the same number of books are translated into Spanish each year as have been translated into Arabic during the past 10 centuries. Egypt contrasts starkly with the few economic success stories in the Third World, a case in point being South Korea, whose per capita income was about the same as Egypt in 1950 but now is five times greater.

Survival for ordinary people heavily relies on informal—unregulated, untaxed, and often illegal—activities that hardly get the notice of the state. Small-scale manufacturing and trading as well as informal savings associations make up a major part of economic activity. Networks based on family and personal friendships (*shillas*; "cliques") provide favors to individuals in need (and power for those who dole them out). Someone dubbed *wasta* ("connections," "pull") as the "vitamin W" that keeps Egyptians (and others throughout the Middle East and beyond) living. By contrast, formal organizations tend to be hollow to the extent that more personalistic ties do not permeate them.

LABOR UNIONS AND PROFESSIONAL ASSOCIATIONS

Egyptian law requires all trade unions, of which there are 23, to be members of the Egyptian Trade Union Federation, which is closely tied to the governing National Democratic Party. Under President Abd al-Nasir, workers were given favored treatment under the law, although unions lacked autonomy then as now, serving as instruments of state control. Current law threatens participants in strikes with imprisonment and hard labor, but short wildcat strikes occur from time to time. Collective bargaining is almost nonexistent. The government sometimes interferes in union elections.

Various professions (law, medicine, and the like) have syndicates recognized by the government. Some of them recently have demonstrated a strong independent streak, with opposition forces, particularly the Muslim Brothers, winning majorities on elected boards. Elections in the journalism syndicate in 2003 brought defeat for the government-sponsored candidate and a majority of Islamists and Nasirites on the board. In accordance with a recent law, the government can, under certain conditions, dismiss a board and appoint its own body to run a syndicate. Drastic official intervention repeatedly occurred during the late 1990s and early 2000s. Security forces occupied the Lawyers' Syndicate headquarters for several hours in March 2003, arresting and beating individuals who had defended protesters against the new war on Iraq.

TRANSPORTATION AND COMMUNICATIONS

The Nile (and navigable canals in the Delta) provides Egypt with a transportation system that connects the major population centers. Seaports on both the Mediterranean and the Red Sea have put this country in contact with the outside world since early Pharaonic times, and the Suez Canal makes it a crucial link in global commerce.

A network of modern roads and railroads now exists. A road parallels the Nile from Cairo to the far south. Others, including some expressways, connect Cairo to the cities of the Delta and Suez Canal. Also, there is a Mediterranean coastal road to Sallum, on the Libyan border, as well as one on the Gulf of Suez. Other roads connect the major oases in the Western Desert or extend from the Nile Valley to the Red Sea coast. Several roads cross Sinai. Railroads parallel the Nile (as far south as Aswan) and the Mediterranean coast and connect various Delta cities as well as some of the western oases. Cairo was the first city in Africa or the Middle East to have a subway system. Started in 1982, the Cairo Metro has been progressively extended to connect parts of Greater Cairo as far south as Helwan. The country has several airports, and EgyptAir (formerly United Arab Airlines) connects Egyptian cities; Cairo International Airport handles millions of passengers each year.

Cairo is a hub for other kinds of communication that extend beyond the country's borders. It is the major center of book publishing for the Arab world. There are 18 main newspapers, the best-known being *al-Ahram* ("the Pyramids"), and many magazines. The cinema has a long history there, with three-quarters of the Arab world's movies made in Cairo and widely shown throughout the region. Egypt has many domestic radio and television networks, and its broadcasts to the outside world in Arabic and other languages have been highly influential. It has two television broadcast satellites, and its Media Production City aspires to be the "Hollywood of the East." Although the Internet has been slow to catch on in the Arab world generally, Egypt had four Internet providers and more than 1.5 million users by 2001.

EDUCATION

The law requires that Egyptian children attend school between ages 6 and 14. But this is not fully enforced in practice, notably in the case of girls (whose ratio to boys in primary school in 2000 was 85 percent).

Classes are large, and there is much emphasis on rote memorization. Many people spend much of their income to pay for private tutoring.

Egypt has 14 state-run universities, including Cairo University and the University of Alexandria. For a less-developed country, it has a high proportion of university graduates, more in fact than can find appropriate employment (a government job with minimal pay was guaranteed for all graduates in the past). It attracts students from throughout the Arab world and various countries in Africa. Considered the world's oldest and leading training ground for Islamic scholars, al-Azhar now also offers a wider range of studies, drawing students from throughout the Sunni Muslim world. Admission to universities is based on examination scores required to graduate from secondary school. Classes are large (as many as 500), with emphasis on memorizing the professor's lectures. Lack of funds makes for inadequate resources, and professors are overloaded and underpaid, often moonlighting at other institutions or supporting themselves by driving taxicabs. All reports point to declining quality. There is no tuition, but expensive (and illegal) private lessons provided by professors tend to be the only way many students can pass. The small, exclusive American University in Cairo, modeled on liberal arts colleges in the United States, provides an exception to the general picture.

SPORTS

Football (soccer) is known as Egypt's national game. There is intense rivalry between teams such as Zamalek and Ahali. The national team, the Pharaohs, participates in international competition, with victories in the quadrennial World Cup qualifying matches bringing thousands of fans to the street to blare their horns and cheer. There was much disappointment (and even talk of a jinx) in June 2001 when the Algerian team defeated the Pharaohs, followed by a draw in the game with Morocco, eliminating them from participating in the 2002 World Cup competition in South Korea. Egyptian teams have been winners in African Cup competitions several times during recent years.

Egyptian youth participate in numerous other sports. Notable successes in the Olympic Games go back to the 1920s. Though not winning any awards, Egypt barely lost in the handball competition (a game that in recent years has become the country's second most popular game) in the 2000 Olympics in Sidney, Australia. Egyptians were less successful that year in swimming, table tennis, fencing, rowing, shooting, gymnastics, and volleyball.

THE GOVERNMENT OF EGYPT

In characterizing the government, one must distinguish between the democratic principles the Constitution proclaims and the authoritarian reality. Its governmental institutions—a popularly elected president and multiparty parliament whose votes of no confidence can force the prime minister to resign (unless canceled by a popular referendum) and a professional judiciary that upholds the law—typify those of modern democracies in general.

The Judiciary

The court system is based on the French model. The law itself, aside from the areas left to religious law, is codified, as in France and other continental European countries. There is a separate hierarchy of Administrative Courts, with the Council of State at the apex, that deal with matters relating to the authority of governmental bodies. The regular criminal court system is made up of District Tribunals that try minor cases, Tribunals of First Instance that deal with more important cases, Courts of Appeal, and a Court of Cassation, which is the highest appellate tribunal with general jurisdiction. At the top is a Supreme Constitutional Court that has authority—which it exercises fairly often—to decide on matters of constitutionality of laws. Also representing French influence, the judiciary is a distinct profession for which one is specifically trained. Each court (except for the District Tribunals) is made up of a panel of judges (and no juries). Judges have life tenure and are appointed by the president on the recommendation of the Higher Judicial Council.

The judiciary sometimes plays a significant role in guarding the rule of law. Repeatedly during recent years, courts forced new parliamentary elections on the ground that the previous elections had been illegal. Some deem this a bright spot for constitutionalism in an otherwise authoritarian and repressive regime, although Ministers of Justice sometimes apply financial pressure on judges.

The other side of the story is that Egypt has been in an official State of Emergency since 1981, which parliament renewed for another three-year period in 2003. This allows individuals, including civilians, deemed to constitute a threat to national security to be tried by special military courts, whose decisions cannot be appealed. People can be detained without charge. Rules of evidence are lax, and convictions often are based on confessions obtained through torture that is so severe as to result in dozens of deaths.

The Legislature

Aside from a largely decorative advisory Consultative Council (144 members, two-thirds of them elected and the others appointed by the president), there is an elected People's Assembly. The country is divided into 222 districts, each of which chooses two members. The president can appoint 10 additional members, which sometimes allows him to rectify the underrepresentation of Copts and women. Various parties—8 of 15 legal parties in the most recent (1999) general elections—compete for seats. But the Muslim Brothers, who represent the most substantial opposition, are excluded, although sometimes they have participated in electoral coalitions with other parties or as independents.

Again and again, opposition parties are allowed to get a few seats, but the lion's share goes to the entrenched National Democratic Party (NDP). In part this is a result of the patronage—favors that can be doled out to supporters—in the hands of a party that is in power. But from the accounts of all impartial observers, it is clear that the perpetuation of the NDP in power is also in large part a matter of outright fraud in the way elections and vote counting are conducted. In a recently widely publicized cause célèbre, a well-known Egyptian sociologist, Sa'd al-Din Ibrahim, was sentenced to seven years in prison—though eventually this was overturned—partly for making a video (supported by European Union funds that he was falsely accused of embezzling) portraying such corrupt practices ("intended to harm Egypt's image abroad"). In any case, the huge majorities in parliaments resulting from such elections are always tame, providing no limitation in fact on the power of the president.

The Executive

Real power is concentrated in the presidency. Following nomination each time by a parliament controlled by his party, referenda held every six years recurrently give Husni Mubarak another six-year term. The "yes" vote never drops far below 100 percent. There is never an opposition candidate. The president designates a prime minister (with approval by parliament a formality), who heads the Council of Ministers or cabinet. There are 32 ministries—for example, Foreign Affairs, Justice, Education, Interior, and Defense and Military Production. Unlike his predecessors, Mubarak has not named a vice president.

The Military

Today's Egyptian government in many ways is an outgrowth of the revolutionary government established by the July 1952 military coup d'état led by Gamal Abd al-Nasir. Mubarak, was an air force commander who owes his position to being appointed vice president by his predecessor, Anwar al-Sadat, one of the members of the military junta in the July Revolution. Similarly, it was Nasir's choice of Sadat as vice president that enabled him to become president. Egypt has had four presidents (including General Muhammad Nagib, the titular head of the junta, in 1953–1954) during the past half century, all of them coming from the military. However, the government long has ceased being a military regime per se. Still, top military officers find themselves in positions of influence. Support from key military leaders was a key factor enabling both post-Nasir leaders to consolidate their power, and recurrently only a loyal army has enabled them to suppress mass uprisings.

With an annual military budget of $4.4 billion (4.6 percent of its GDP) in 2001, Egypt's active armed forces consist of the Army, Navy, Air Force, and Air Force Command. They total 443,000 men (and no women), including 320,000 in the Army. In addition, there are a quarter million reserves. This does not include the 330,000-strong paramilitary forces, particularly the quarter million members of the Central Security Forces (in the Ministry of Interior and responsible for guarding public places and generally thwarting threats to the regime), the National Guard, Border Guard, and Coast Guard. Since the 1970s, American weapons have increasingly replaced those of Soviet origin. In addition Egypt has its own arms industry, which is run by the military, as are various nonmilitary industrial and agricultural activities, including land reclamation.

2

Ancient Egypt

Egypt's history is as remarkable as its geography. The Egyptians' claim that their country—its capital city in particular—is "the mother of the world" contains much truth if that means it is where history and civilization began. Its early history is the heritage of the whole world to an extent that is not true of, say, Japan, India, or England. The historian Philip Hitti once stated that everybody has two countries, his or her own and Syria (defined to include Lebanon and Palestine), but arguably he should have added the Land of the Nile to his list.

The sheer length of Egyptian history makes it unique, as does its pioneer role in human development. The historian Arnold J. Toynbee pointed out that ancient Egyptian civilization endured longer than any other and that the country also has played a disproportionate part in Islamic civilization. In response to criticism that some of his works had six times as many references to Egypt as to England, Toynbee asserted that the former's role in history has been more like 60 times greater than that of the latter and blamed his own Western and English bias for the failure to give it the attention it deserved.

EGYPT'S EMERGENCE

The country took on its present form as a result of climatic changes in northeastern Africa. After the end of the Ice Age about 10,000 years ago, which turned northern Africa into a desert, the swamps along the Nile provided a refuge for tribes in the region. By ca. 5,000 B.C., settled agricultural life was established. The people probably were diverse, representing racial strains similar to those found south of the Sahara to some extent, as well as others who were typically "Mediterranean." They often are classified, along with related northern African peoples such as Berbers and Nubians, as Hamitic. Properly speaking, this relates to a family of languages and has no racial significance. Actually, most linguists today classify these Hamitic tongues, alongside the Semitic languages (e.g., Arabic and Hebrew as well as now-defunct tongues such as Akkadian), which in ancient times were mostly limited to southwestern Asia (although their roots are believed to be in Ethiopia), as separate branches of a Hamito-Semitic family of languages.

The Egyptian people and their language apparently were influenced by an early influx of Semites, probably by tribes from Palestine and Syria. If so, this provides an early example of the migration of Semitic peoples, who periodically—at least according to a widely accepted theory—overflowed from the increasingly desiccated Arabian and Syrian deserts into the Fertile Crescent (that is, the relatively well-watered lands of the Eastern Mediterranean littoral and the Tigris–Euphrates Valley) and Egypt. But although the Fertile Crescent was fully Semitized at an early date, Egypt retained its non-Semitic identity and language until the process of Arabicization began in the seventh century A.D.

THE BIRTH OF EGYPTIAN CIVILIZATION

There is basis for disagreement on whether civilization began in Egypt or in another Middle Eastern river valley, Mesopotamia (today's Iraq). For a long time, it was thought that the civilization of the Sumerians, in southern Mesopotamia, preceded that of Egypt. But recent discoveries showing that writing—at least one crucial test of civilization—in Egypt apparently began to evolve earlier than previously thought puts that in question. The truth is that innovations accelerated in both river valleys at about the same time. Indeed, writing probably developed independently in both Sumer and Egypt, and Egyptian ships that sailed to the Phoenician city of Byblos (in today's Lebanon) as well as Sumerian vessels landing on Egypt's Red Sea coast may have brought innovations of Sumerian origin at an early date. By the mid-third millennium B.C., there was an advanced civilization in Syria, too, centering on the city of Ebla, which must have been in contact with Egypt, thus facilitating civilizational diffusion.

By the fourth millennium B.C., such a phenomenal flowering of civilization emerged in Egypt as to evoke pseudoscientific speculation in some circles today that this was the work of advanced travelers from another planet. The amazing accomplishments of the Egyptians do not require such explanations, for the Nile Valley and Delta provided the uniquely fertile and regularly watered soil necessary for this burst of progress. And it was the challenge of controlling the Nile that led to such innovations—not just digging irrigation ditches but also keeping records and organizing a centralized government. Greater specialization also brought a division into social classes, for although the overwhelming majority of the people tilled the soil, there were now leather workers, carpenters, basket makers, potters, weavers, brick makers, and metalworkers practicing their crafts, not to mention the powerful merchants, priests, and scribes. With its artistic hieroglyphs that resemble a sequence of real pictures on Egyptian tombs and temple walls or even the more simplified hieratic script written on parchment, Egypt had a distinctive civilization from the start.

Egypt possessed many advantages that other early civilizations lacked. The Nile flows gently and provides a waterway connecting almost every inhabited part of the country as far south as the First Cataract (rapids), near modern Aswan. North winds enable ships to sail upriver as easily as down. The Nile Valley and Delta lacked many things, but they were accessible close by. The plentiful limestone (and, in some places, sandstone) in the cliffs at the Valley's edge and the granite in the extreme south resulted in a civilization whose monumental stone structures contrasted sharply with the mud brick buildings of Mesopotamia. Egypt had accessible gold mines in the Eastern Desert and, to the south in Nubia, also the source of ebony and ivory. The copper mines of Sinai provided another relatively secure foundation of Bronze Age Egyptian civilization. Timber was (and is) almost wholly lacking in Egypt, but with a surplus of grain to offer in exchange, Egyptian ships could bring it back from Byblos from the earliest historic periods. By the end of the third millennium B.C., Egyptian ships were sailing southward through the Red Sea to the land of Punt (today's Somalia), with its spices and incense, and also obtaining perfumes, spices, and ebony from the coast of Arabia. The peripherality of such imports helped make it unnecessary for Egypt to control other lands in the early millennia, although the introduction of iron in the late second millennium, with the need for large quantities of wood required for smelting, seems to have posed a new challenge, evoking a period of expansionism but eventually reducing Egypt's relative status in the world.

Other geographic factors promoted greater stability in Egypt than in other places. Instead of being surrounded by populated mountain and steppe regions that served as reservoirs for potential invaders (as in the case of Mesopotamia), the extreme dichotomy between Egypt's solid block of densely populated land and its desert hinterland allowed Egyptians to enjoy long periods of splendid isolation. Although the upper Nile provided a route for its people to bring materials to sell at the Egyptian frontier, the Cataracts also had great defensive value. Only during periods of internal decay was Egypt invaded from upriver, from Libya, or even from the somewhat more vulnerable northeastern frontier.

The Nile floods, which brought fertile silt as well as water, were not destructive and capricious like those in Mesopotamia. The first swelling of the river each year was so regular that Egyptians could invent a 365-day calendar early in the third millennium B.C. by averaging the number of days in the interval over a 50-year period. The level of the Nile flood varied from year to year. But unlike Mesopotamia's perennial fragmentation, this induced the Egyptians to create one government that could maintain grain for bad years.

The challenge of controlling the Nile was not too great, and so Egypt experienced long periods of unity and prosperity. It is customary to divide such a long history, not on the basis of individual kings, but rather, by using a system derived from a fourth-century B.C. priest, into 30 dynasties. Some dynasties ruled for centuries, and a new one often represented only a shift to another branch of the family. Also, Egyptian civilization was characterized by massive stone structures that such conditions permitted. And both political stability and the durability of building materials conveyed the feeling that structures should endure forever. The mood of Egypt was characterized by security, optimism, and joy. Egyptians were preoccupied with preparation for the afterlife, not because of a morbid fear of death, but because they looked forward to more good times in the next world.

FROM THE OLD KINGDOM TO THE MIDDLE KINGDOM

Egyptian civilization first rose in separate centers. The multiplicity of warring princes was matched by the diversity of local gods with their own temples and priesthoods. Eventually two kingdoms, Upper and Lower Egypt, emerged. The Delta seems to have defeated the south at one point, but King Narmer (or Menes) finally prevailed over Lower Egypt in ca. 3200 B.C. Unity would last uninterrupted for a millennium, with the capital moved to Memphis, 20 miles inside the Delta. This approximate location at the junction of the two former kingdoms (near the modern city of Cairo) would, with a few exceptions, forever remain the center of political power. But the kings of unified Egypt continued to wear the white crown of the south and the red crown of the north to symbolize two lands.

The struggle for unity was reflected in the Egyptian version of the widespread story of a mother goddess and the god who dies and is resurrected. Of the many religious cults in ancient Egypt, that of the god Osiris—son of the Sun god Re or Amon-Re, whose priests at Heliopolis became increasingly powerful—remained the truly deep-rooted and popular one (and, some would argue, survives today in the form of the somewhat parallel Christian doctrine of the resurrection of Christ and in reverence for the Virgin Mary as well as in the Judeo-Christian-Islamic idea of the Last Judgment). According to the legend, the evil god Seth murdered his brother Osiris, but the latter's wife and sister, the loving Isis, found his body in faraway Byblos. When Seth tore it apart, Isis located the pieces and put them together again but could not completely restore its life. Thus Osiris became the god of the underworld, the home of the dead, where he subsequently weighed the souls of the deceased in order to admit only the righteous. Isis and Osiris's son Horus, represented by a falcon and possibly symbolizing Narmer, finally got revenge by killing Seth and became the earthly ruler.

The beginning of the Third Dynasty in ca. 2687 B.C. ushered in a period of incredible splendor, the Old Kingdom. Accepted as gods, these monarchs ruled a centralized realm through their viziers (prime ministers) and nomarchs (governors of nomes, i.e., provinces). The kings were considered to be owners of all the land and its produce. Even the people were theoretically the king's slaves (but a notable aspect of early Egypt was the rarity of actual slavery in comparison with other ancient civilizations). There were not even any private merchants to compete with state commerce. Each god–king identified himself with Horus and is sometimes pictured with a falcon head, whereas his dead predecessor was always called the "Osiris king."

Believing that the survival of the soul depended on the preservation of the body, Egyptians focused much of their energy on building massive tombs to preserve the king's mummified remains. In the Third Dynasty, King Zoser began the practice of having pyramids, and a great engineer, the genius Imhotep, oversaw the construction of the step pyramid at Saqqara, near Memphis. Greatness climaxed under the Fourth Dynasty with the construction of perfect pyramidal structures at Giza. The largest, that of King Cheops, reached 481.4 feet above its 13.1-acre base. Its granite blocks, which range up to 15 tons and average two and a half tons, are fitted together without mortar so tightly that a knife blade cannot be inserted between them. Contrary to the myth perpetuated by the Greek historian Herodotus, it does not seem that slaves built the pyramids. The predominant view of Egyptologists today is that vast numbers of people found employment when the annual flood covered their farmland and that fervent devotion to a national cause inspired them to toil for many years on these amazing structures.

But by the twenty-third century B.C., Egypt was in decline. Building the pyramids and the cost of maintaining the temples attached to each of them exhausted the country. The poor rose in revolt at one point. Among the literature of this "first intermediate period," the *Prophecies of Ipuwer* bewailed the fact that the formerly rich were starving while the poor had gained wealth. Semitic nomads entered the country from the northeast and ruled large parts of the Delta. Ipuwer describes the cessation of voyages to Byblos and the breakdown of law and order that enabled robbers to prey on travelers. "Laughter has disappeared forever," he says. Of the various arts, only a literature of pessimism that was atypical of Egypt flourished at this time.

A powerful ruling house eventually emerged in the Upper Egyptian city of Thebes and began the Middle Kingdom. King Menthuhotep, of the Eleventh Dynasty, reunited Egypt in ca. 2069 B.C. Amon, the Theban god, now came to the fore and merged with the Heliopolis deity as Amon-Re. Built of small blocks, the Middle Kingdom temples have not survived, and large pyramids were no longer the fashion, but in many ways the greatness of the Old Kingdom resumed. Egyptian literature reached its zenith, with works such as the *Story of Sinuhe,* concerning an exiled Egyptian who became a nomadic chief but was overjoyed to return home in his old age, and the *Tale of the Shipwrecked Sailor,* not to mention medical, mathematical, and other scientific writings. In the early nineteenth century B.C., King Senwosret III, of the Twelfth Dynasty, extended his frontiers both northward into Palestine and southward to Nubia. The Fayyum Depression, west of the Nile Valley, became a rich agricultural oasis that greatly enhanced Egyptian prosperity after King Amenemhet III built a canal to divert Nile water there.

CATASTROPHE AND REVIVAL: THE NEW KINGDOM

Egypt's Middle Kingdom's glory had run its course as the Twelfth Dynasty, which ended in 1786 B.C., made way for weak rulers and civil war.

Pressure from the movement of Indo-Europeans from central Eurasia pushed other peoples ahead of them like dominos; Semitic nomads infiltrated into the eastern part of the Delta in increasing numbers. The "second intermediate period" of Egyptian history was beginning, as southwestern Asian rulers established their capital at Avaris, in the eastern Delta. These Hyksos (literally, "rulers of faraway lands") continued to push into Egypt, taking Memphis in 1664 B.C. The strangeness and seeming invincibility of the nomads to Egyptians increased when the former started bringing in horses. Even the princes of Thebes sometimes had to pay tribute to the invaders but again kept the country from being entirely overrun.

To Egyptians, this "barbarian" invasion was an intolerable affront to their great civilization. Egyptians long afterward looked back on the Hyksos as the epitome of cruelty and destructiveness. Still, there was no shortage of collaborators with these rulers, who in many ways became Egyptianized. But it was inevitable that Egyptians would learn to drive their own horse-drawn chariots and turn them against the Hyksos.

Indeed, it was Egypt that led the way in the resurgence of the old civilizations against the "barbarian" tribes. King Sekenenre of Thebes began the process of driving the Hyksos out in the early sixteenth century B.C. His son, Kamose, continued to batter the occupiers with chariots, and King Ahmose, founder of the Eighteenth Dynasty, finished the job in 1557 B.C. This ushered in the New Kingdom and another period of Egyptian greatness.

Culture flourished in the New Kingdom. Queen Hatshepsut started as the regent for her infant stepson, Thutmose III, but then put on a fake beard and declared herself king. As the world's first known female ruler, she built a temple on the side of the mountain across the river from Thebes that has been deemed the best piece of Egyptian architecture. Although the temple is strikingly beautiful, it is the massive ruins of the temples of Luxor and Karnak, some of whose columns rise 78 feet high, that leave the visitor most in awe. The discovery in 1922 of the tomb of the boy King Tutankhamun, which had eluded robbers, revealed a bewildering treasure of fine statues and other pieces of art. The sheer amount of gold in the tomb bespeaks the riches that were flowing into the royal coffers.

The Hyksos conquest broadened Egyptian perspectives. It was no longer possible to think of Egypt as a self-contained world and so superior that its security could be taken for granted. Egyptian security called for control of Syria, especially at a time when other potential conquerors were emerging in the north. With a professional army that eventually grew to 20,000 men, Egypt embarked on a policy of expansion. Scarcely had Egypt itself been liberated when King Ahmose pursued the Hyksos into Palestine, and his successors pushed on to conquer the Canaanite cities. King Thutmose I reached the Euphrates, but then the king of Mitanni (later known as Armenia) felt threatened by the Egyptian colossus and fomented a Canaanite revolt in the mid-fifteenth century B.C. King Thutmose III led his armies back into Palestine, where he defeated the Canaanite coalition at Megiddo (Armageddon). This time, the Egyptians went on across the Euphrates, where they routed the Mitannian army. Egyptian naval forces took control of the copper- and timber-rich island of Cyprus. On its southern flank, Egypt also conquered Kush and pushed the frontier to the Fourth Cataract, deep in present-day Sudan, now increasingly significant as a source of gold, copper, and wood.

Even now, the Egyptian concept of empire differed from that of the Mesopotamians. For the latter, the world extended out without a break, awaiting a ruler who could make its "four quarters" into one kingdom. To the Egyptians, Egypt was what counted, and the rest of the world, particularly Asia, was peripheral. The whole upper Nile Valley appeared to be a simple extension of Egypt, and so Kush was completely annexed and progressively Egyptianized. But in Asia the local rulers, though subjected to paying tribute to their overlord in Thebes, were left to rule over their own peoples with as little interference as possible. Egyptian garrisons remained only at strategic points.

Still, in many ways Egypt became a part of a wider world. Egyptian kings married foreign princesses. Egyptian and foreign rulers exchanged letters in which they addressed each other as "brother." Diplomatic missions became common. An international script of Mesopotamian origin, cuneiform, and a diplomatic *lingua franca*, Akkadian, facilitated all this. Even the letters from the king of Egypt to Canaanite vassals were written in Akkadian.

The new cosmopolitanism inspired the world's first recorded vision of world unity on a spiritual level. Although a wider world view had initially driven Egyptians from isolationism to imperialism, the gentle King Amenhotpe IV, who ruled from 1372 B.C. to 1355 B.C., provided an opposite manifestation in championing a universal religious doctrine. He showed so little interest in his empire that he left it in disrepair. He proclaimed the existence of one "sole god, like whom there is no other." This one God—represented by the sun's disc—was called Aten, who had created the world and whose rays emitted life.

The reforming king forbade the worship of other gods. He had the name "Amon" removed from temples and tombs and deleted from his own name, calling himself Akhenaten (the spirit of Aten) instead. He built a new capital city, also called Akhenaten, about midway between Thebes and Memphis, which kept the now suppressed priests of Amon away from the center of power.

The reformation was all-pervasive. In his pursuit of truth, the king patronized a realism in art that portrayed himself and his family in the ungodlike poses of ordinary people—for example, children sitting on his lap and the king and queen embracing. Truth dictated that Akhenaten's statues portray him as ugly, deformed, and effeminate, and some historians believe he was undergoing a sex change. But Atenism found little popular support, and Akhenaten's death ended the movement, as the old gods and their priests regained favor.

Egyptian power now met a match in the north. Although King Akhenaten's reforms were distracting Egyptian attention from the empire, the ambitious and able military commander, King Suppiluliumas of the Hittites (centered in Anatolia), went on the offensive, and large parts of northern Syria came under his control. The Mitanni became Hittite vassals for a while. The whole Egyptian empire in Asia was falling apart, as Akhenaten failed to respond to the pleas of Egyptian commanders for reinforcements when Canaanite cities asserted their independence or came under the rule of nomadic Habiru invaders.

Egypt came back after the Atenist interlude but never restored its supremacy. King Ramesses II met the Hittites in the Battle of Kadesh in 1285 B.C. There was no conclusive victory. If anything, Egypt lost the battle and thus failed to break the Hittite challenge. Meanwhile, Assyria (in northern Mesopotamia) overthrew the lordship of the weakened Mitanni and was emerging as a new threat. To forestall this danger, Egypt and the Hittites realistically opted for détente and to what amounted to joint hegemony and coexistence over the world they knew. A peace treaty concluded in 1270 B.C. by Ramesses II and Hattusilis II of the Hittites provided for the mutual renunciation of force and even for the extradition of fugitives. The two superpowers partitioned Syria into a Hittite-ruled north and an Egyptian-ruled south. Hattusilis II's daughter became the pharaoh's "Great wife."

THE "BROKEN REED"

The Egyptian-Hittite arrangement for world order could not last. Soon there were signs of mutual suspicion, and the permanence of Hittite power was being threatened by separatist efforts of the empire's diverse peoples. But in any case, a totally unexpected assault from the west brought an end to the era. Perhaps representing the continuing domino effect of the movement of Indo-European peoples or maybe fleeing from a natural disaster, the "Peoples of the Sea"—shiploads of men, women, and children as well as others moving overland through Anatolia in ox-carts—descended on the whole eastern Mediterranean region. The Hittite Empire, in which the secret of forging iron had been developed but long kept secret, completely succumbed to the onslaught. Not only was a major pillar of the international system now missing, but the Peoples of the Sea found the Hittites' secret, and now their desperation combined with iron weapons to make them invincible for a while.

The Peoples of the Sea—notably the Philistines, apparently fleeing from the Aegean region—soon reached Egypt. Even during the last years of Ramesses II's long reign, a few seafarers had made a futile attack on the coast. In 1227 B.C., during the reign of King Merenptah, a coalition of Sea Peoples and Berber tribes struck overland from Libya but were defeated. King Ramesses III repelled a similar incursion a half century later but acquiesced in the settlement of large numbers of Libyans in the western Delta. The Egyptians faced a greater threat in 1194 B.C., when the Philistines attacked their outposts in Syria, and a Philistine fleet sailed from Cyprus to the Delta. Philistine ships entered the Nile but were trapped in large nets and the invaders annihilated. Frustrated in Egypt, the Philistines settled on the coast of Palestine (and indeed gave the country its name).

Although Egypt survived, the empire in Asia disintegrated. Resisting the Peoples of the Sea had exhausted the country. Trade routes through Palestine were disrupted. Even expeditions to the mines in Sinai stopped, although Egyptians did manage to get some copper from Cyprus. Internal conflict pitted kings against priests; corruption abounded, and the authority of the ruler weakened. Egyptians had become unsusceptible to innovation, scarcely bothering to use iron for several centuries. The epithet "broken reed" now came to be applied to a country whose longevity seemed to have brought senility. The *Story of Wenamun* tells how the central character met contempt for himself and his country when he embarked on a trip to Byblos to acquire cedar wood. For a while, Egypt broke into two kingdoms and then, beginning in 975 B.C., fell under the loose rule of Libyan mercenaries (the Twenty-Second through the Twenty-Fourth dynasties). Kush's Egyptianized ruler overthrew the Libyans and established the Twenty-Fifth Dynasty in 715 B.C., initiating a minor cultural renaissance, but nothing compared with the accomplishments of the past.

The period following the invasions by the Peoples of the Sea is sometimes dubbed the era of small powers. With Egyptian hegemony gone, such peoples as the Phoenicians, Aramaens, and Israelites flourished in the western Fertile Crescent.

But an ancient (and always extremely militaristic) people, the Assyrians, were becoming a new superpower. Access to iron ore enabled them to adapt well to the Iron Age, and they were able to equip armies of unprecedented size. Further advances in horse breeding and the development of saddles, bridles, and bits enabled the Assyrians to introduce cavalry warfare, and they invented portable siege towers. Assyrian expansionism reached new heights in the eighth century B.C. throughout the Fertile Crescent region. In 691 B.C. King Easerhaddon moved the Assyrian forces on to Egypt and rapidly conquered it. Egypt was then under a weak Kushite dynasty and was no longer a challenge for a real army. However, with some help from troops sent by the semi-Hellenized kingdom of Lydia in western Anatolia, an Assyrian-appointed governor asserted Egypt's independence and became King Psamtik I, the founder of the Twenty-Sixth Dynasty. Following a period of disintegration, the Assyrian Empire fell in 612 B.C. before a coalition of Medes, Chaldeans, and others. King Necho of Egypt, who apparently saw that the Assyrians' complete destruction would make way for a more powerful threat, sent an army to help them, but to no avail. The Chaldeans' New Babylonian Empire defeated Egyptian armies at the Battle of Carchemish in 605 B.C.

Egypt had shown few signs of vitality since the time of the Peoples of the Sea. However, King Necho II was able to carry out a great feat in constructing a canal to connect the Nile with the Red Sea, although it is not clear whether this first "Suez Canal" was completed at this time. He sent an expedition around Africa, but the ships were Phoenician. Both the cultural creativity and the military prowess of the past were gone, and the country would not be able to resist the next powerful conqueror.

The Persian Cyrus II ("the Great") founded a new dynasty, the Achaemenids, in Iran in the mid-sixth century B.C. and soon swept across southwestern Asia. Cyrus's successor, Cambyses, attacked Egypt in 526. With his troops transported on Phoenician ships and supplied overland by camel caravans hired in Arabia, he quickly overwhelmed the land of the Nile, extending his rule even into Nubia. Egypt now was part of a cosmopolitan empire that for a while extended to the Indus and was increasingly connected commercially by royal roads (and a royal postal service), established sea routes, and coined money. Egypt was an important link in all this, as shown by the Emperor Darius's renovation of Necho II's canal. Like other peoples generally, the Egyptians enjoyed a degree of autonomy, and their culture and religions were respected. The rulers at the top were Persians, although this in many ways was a multinational empire. But Egypt was a backwater in a world dominated by the Phoenician alphabet and the use of Aramaic as the language of government.

EMERGENCE OF HELLENIC DOMINATION

By this time, the Greeks were demonstrating a new kind of vitality. Greek commerce was increasingly dominating the area, and the Persian "kings of kings" were relying increasingly on Greek mercenaries, as was the Twenty-Sixth Egyptian Dynasty, which restored the country's independence for a while. Greek commercial colonies (settlements) came into being throughout the Mediterranean and Black Sea regions, including one at Naucritis, near the Egyptian coast. The eventual rout of Persian forces attempting to conquer Greece early in the fifth century B.C. started a downhill trend for the Achaemenid Empire and portended increased Greek ascendancy. With Greek aid, Egypt revolted against Persian rule and established its independence twice. Two successive short-lived indigenous dynasties—the Twenty-Ninth and the Thirtieth—ruled after the rebellion in 404 B.C. and, by using Greek mercenaries, were able to ward off several attempts at reconquest. Only with the help of his own Greek mercenaries did the Achaemenid King Artaxerxes III finally manage to restore Achaemenid control over Egypt in 334 B.C.

It was the turn of another conqueror to take the place of the Persians when Philip II of the partially Hellenized kingdom of Macedon established his rule over the Greeks to the south during the 330s B.C. His 19-year-old son Alexander II ("the Great") began a whirlwind conquest of the Achaemenid Empire and beyond in 334 B.C. After driving the shah's forces out of Anatolia and Syria (and before marching on eastward in 331 B.C.), Alexander's armies entered Egypt in 333 B.C. and quickly took control. As Persian rule had long been unpopular there, the Macedonians were greeted as liberators and Alexander as "Horus" and the "son of Amon-Re," among other titles, indicating that he was the new pharaoh. The new ruler was becoming receptive to such titles and to the spell of Egypt as he detoured from his military campaign to cross the desert to Siwa Oasis to consult with the oracle of Amon, whom he considered to be the same as the Greek god Zeus under a different name. Of all the Alexandrias he founded and named for himself, the city on the western edge of the Egyptian Delta would have no real rival during the following centuries.

THE PTOLEMAIC KINGDOM

The Macedonian conquest began an era, known as Hellenistic, when Egypt and the Middle East generally were subordinated to Macedonians and Greeks and eventually by another offshoot of Hellenic civilization, the Roman Empire. The unity of Alexander's realm did not survive his untimely death in 323 B.C., but that did not end Macedonian rule over most of the area. Instead, the generals divided the spoils, creating separate Hellenistic kingdoms. Ptolemy became the ruler of Egypt, beginning a dynasty that sometimes also controlled parts of Syria, Anatolia, and even the Aegean region. The struggle for succession hardly involved Middle Eastern peoples except that their countries provided bases for the rival Macedonian generals and their Macedonian and Greek troops. Egypt was now part of a new cultural whole in which ideas and commerce flowed freely across frontiers, all facilitated by a new *lingua franca,* Greek, thus relegating the Egyptians' native tongue to a subordinated role. Only gradually were many Hellenized Easterners able to participate in the dominant culture, and indeed Eastern elements eventually began to infiltrate it.

Egypt provided a flourishing seat for Hellenistic civilization. With a population that reached 300,000 during this period (and perhaps a million in Roman times), Alexandria—a major entrepôt for trade that extended overland and by sea throughout the Mediterranean and the Red Sea— emerged as the great city of the age. With its famous museum and 700,000- volume library, it had no rival as an intellectual center, although this was the expression of a cosmopolitan civilization that scarcely involved creativity in the local language and by the subordinated indigenous people. Despite the existence of a large Egyptian population that inhabited its own quarters, it was a Hellenic city, not Egyptian, and was aptly described at the time as "by [not in] Egypt." It was also the home of immigrants from throughout the Hellenistic world, many of whom, with the notable exception of the large Jewish community that emerged there, became completely Hellenized. Even the Jews adopted Greek—as opposed to their native tongue, Aramaic, in the case of those who came from Palestine— as their language of everyday life.

With their gymnasia and theaters, the Hellenes in Alexandria and Egypt maintained a style of life that was foreign to the country. Yet it was a paradox for the cultural capital of the Hellenistic world that Alexandria as a whole lacked the self-government that Greek cities generally practiced (even when no longer independent city–states) but was governed autocratically by the king, although particular sections of the city did have autonomous government. And this was virtually the only Greek city in Egypt, joined by the now relatively minor Naucritis and a small new settlement, Ptolemais, in Upper Egypt. Thus the country with the largest Hellenic city was in some ways the least Hellenized of all.

Egypt's Macedonian rulers had no loyalty to the country as such, which served as a gigantic plantation for their own enrichment. Reversing Alexander's practice, the Ptolemies did not employ Egyptians as provincial governors, and the state was run by a complicated Greek bureaucratic system. Except for the Hellenic cities, all the land was considered to be the king's property, directly run by royal officials or, in other cases, granted to military settlers and other favored persons. A fixed payment in kind guaranteed a regular flow of agricultural produce, especially wheat, to the "King's Barn" in Alexandria. In a bad year, the peasants were left barely enough to survive, and then only by increasingly turning to the practice of leaving newborn babies to die. The Ptolemies improved Egyptian agriculture by introducing new varieties of plants and by adopting the Archimedes screw to draw water from the Nile, in addition to the water wheel turned by oxen that probably had recently come from Iran, but they had no thought of helping Egypt.

The whole economy was under the tight grip of the king, solely for his enrichment. Many business activities, ranging from mining to manufacturing papyrus, were royal monopolies. Other businesses required annual licenses. High import duties protected the king's products from foreign competition.

The Ptolemies increasingly were Egyptianized. The tight control of the economy was a continuation of the ancient Egyptian pattern. And it was necessary to present an Egyptian face to the Egyptians. The Egyptian religion was fostered, although royal possession of the temple lands constituted a blow to the priests. The rulers were not averse to calling themselves the sons of Amon-Re. More remarkably, Ptolemy II fell into the Egyptian royalty's pattern of brother–sister marriage as early as 275 B.C., and his energetic and capable sister-wife, Queen Arsinoe, provided needed leadership that prevented defeat in the ongoing war with the Seleucids. During another "Syrian War" in 217 B.C., the Ptolemies resorted to the recruitment of Egyptian soldiers, who turned the tide of conflict in their king's favor at the Battle of Rafia (near Gaza). More than anything else, this was symptomatic of the state's Egyptianization. Reflecting the declining flow of Greek soldiers to the East, the use of indigenous troops gave the Egyptians a sense of importance and, at the same time, made them less amenable to foreign exploitation. And although Hellenization was spreading, it was increasingly superficial, and the line between the Hellenes and the natives was becoming less distinct. By the time of the last Ptolemies, Memphis was a second royal capital, and kings were crowned there in the millennial Egyptian style, making them in some ways simply the Thirty-First Dynasty.

By the end of the second century B.C., the Ptolemaic state was in an advanced condition of decay. Continuous wars, particularly with the Seleucids of Syria, sapped the country's energy, as had internecine conflicts within the royal family. Even the orientalization of the dynasty did not make it less oppressive, and popular opposition increased. Peasant strikes became common, and sometimes people fled the land to join bands of brigades. Large-scale revolts occurred from 216 B.C. onward and sometimes disrupted trade and access to Nubian gold supplies. One revolt ended in 85 B.C. with the destruction of much of Thebes.

Non-Egyptian territories were gradually being lost, and only the intervention of Rome saved control over Egypt for a while. After ca. 200 B.C., the Romans played the rulers of the Eastern Mediterranean off against one another to prevent anyone but themselves from gaining preeminence. Thus when the Seleucid king, Antiochus IV, invaded Egypt and besieged Alexandria in 168 B.C., a Roman envoy appeared and literally used his own sword to draw a circle in the soil, ordering the ruler not to move outside the line before agreeing to withdraw. Antiochus IV had no alternative but to comply.

Then the Romans gradually took over various lands in the region until only the decrepit Ptolemaic kingdom remained outside the empire. Cleopatra VII ("the Great") and her teenage brother-husband, Ptolemy XII, were struggling for the throne. The story hardly needs to be recounted. Julius Caesar went to Egypt in pursuit of his rival, Pompey, and then married Cleopatra. After Caesar's death, Mark Antony came to Egypt and also married her. Caesar's nephew, Octavian (later the Emperor Augustus), defeated this last Hellenistic queen and her latest Roman husband at Actium in 31 B.C. At least in the beginning, the country had a special status unlike the rest of the empire as the emperor's veritable private plantation.

In many ways, the Roman period was an extension of the Hellenistic age. Greek remained the language of the ruling elite in Egypt as generally was true in the eastern part of the empire. A change of rulers did not basically undo the Ptolemaic pattern. And Roman emperors tried to legitimize themselves in ancient Egyptian terms as new sons of Amon. Outside Alexandria, the country remained largely rural, with few autonomous cities. Perhaps the empire's most exploited province, Egypt was still a great plantation for the benefit of the rulers, the only difference being that its grain now flowed to Rome, where it provided about a third of the food supply, instead of to Ptolemy's Barn. Forced labor and the requisitioning of property made life hard for the peasants, who periodically went on strike or fled the land when the yoke became too great. The indigenous people of the country bore the brunt of oppressive taxes. Peasant uprisings were endemic to Egypt, but the very geography of the country made it easy for Rome to suppress rebels. One change from the Ptolemaic pattern was the introduction of some private ownership of land, resulting in absentee landlords. Although some estates were broken up during the rule of Emperor Marcus Aurelius, the lot of the peasant remained hardly improved.

Its stagnation notwithstanding, Egypt's ancient culture proved beneficial to its upstart conquerors. Julius Caesar's new calendar, which most of the world uses today in modified form, was based on the 12-month Egyptian year system. And despite the Emperor Augustus's attempt to impose something like it, there was no clear-cut apartheid. Some Hellenized Egyptians joined the elite class, and there were cases of intermarriage.

CHRISTIAN EGYPT

Subordinated politically and culturally, Egypt and other Middle Eastern lands provided religious inspiration that spread throughout the empire. The worship of Isis, for whom Roman emperors built temples in the capital city, may long have pervaded the Mediterranean area more than any other such faith.

Then came Christianity, which, following sporadic persecution that perhaps was more intense in Egypt than anywhere else in the early fourth century under the Emperor Diocletian, became the official religion of the empire. Egypt remained an important province of this Christianized Roman Empire until the seventh century, a realm now reduced to its eastern half with its capital in Constantinople and so different from that of the early Caesars that in recent centuries it has come to be known as the Byzantine Empire. Indeed, the old division between Romans and subject peoples had grown less distinct, as all the free population, including Egyptians, gained citizenship in the empire by the early third century, something that by that time admittedly may have been of little value, considering the autocratic nature of the state. Citizenship—as well as military service, which would have provided an avenue for gaining citizenship—is something that Egyptians in an earlier period had mostly been excluded from. There now were even emperors of Middle Eastern origin, though not including any Egyptians. Greek, as opposed to the spoken tongues of countries such as Egypt, continued as the basis of elite culture.

Egypt was one of the first countries in which the new faith took root. Christianity seems to have spread rapidly in rural areas as a way for people to differentiate themselves from the then–still pagan Hellenistic ruling class. According to legend, it was Christ's disciple Mark who founded the Egyptian church. Clearly a majority of Egyptians had accepted Christianity by the late fourth century. By the fifth century, the old religions had largely disappeared, although some would point to the popular identification of the Virgin Mary with Isis (whose old statues throughout the empire allegedly were sometimes simply renamed) in order to argue that it was the spirit of ancient Egypt that now was permeating the world. Egypt is where major Christian practices, notably monasticism, emerged.

But Egypt's Christianization left it set apart from the version of the faith that dominated the empire. A great issue was whether Christ is Divine or human or both. The answers that the Hellenic-dominated church adopted generally failed to find acceptance among the long-subordinated peoples of the Middle East, particularly in Egypt, as though their positions were manifestations of a broader alienation. Indeed, it was an Alexandrian church leader, Arius, for whom the doctrine of Arianism, that Christ was created by and therefore lesser than God, was named. Proclaimed heretical at the Council of Nicea in 325, Arianism eventually vanished, leaving the debate over the nature of Christ to take a new form.

The prevalent doctrine in Egypt was Monophysitism, that Christ has only one nature, the Divine, that has completely displaced His human aspect. Thus emerged a distinct branch of Christianity that soon also spread to Ethiopia. This was the Coptic Church (which today is headed by its own pope), using the Coptic language, based on Demotic (an outgrowth of the country's most ancient tongue) but with the Greek alphabet substituted for the older script. The word *Copt* (in Arabic, *Qibt*) is derived from *Aiguptioi*, Greek for Egyptian. Reversing the victory of Alexandrian church leaders at the Council of Ephesus (419), the Fourth Ecumenical Council, meeting in Chalcedon (across the Bosporus from Constantinople) in 451, rejected Monophisitism in favor of what henceforth would be the orthodox (or Chalcedonian) position (shared today by Orthodox, Catholic, and Protestant churches), namely that Christ is both God and man and that the two natures are inseparable.

A decision that represented the predominance of the Hellenistic world in the expanding faith was not the end of the matter. Monophysites, who included almost all Egyptian Christians except the Hellenic ruling class, stood their ground. Emperors found themselves in a quandary, for by supporting Monophysitism, they were in danger of antagonizing orthodox Church opinion in Constantinople and farther west (as well as in parts of heavily Hellenized Anatolia). But by favoring Chalcedonianism, emperors were certain to alienate the east, notably Egypt. During the late fifth century, the Emperor Zeno tried to walk a tightrope by issuing an evasive "Act of Union" but succeeded only in antagonizing both sides. His successor, Anastasius I (491–518), won Egyptian hearts by espousing Monophysitism, the followers of which, however, found themselves persecuted by his successor, Justin I. Though influenced by his pro-Monophysite wife, Theodora, Justinian was also devoted to restoring the orthodox western provinces. His policies wavered, but he became pro-Monophysite before his death in 565. But after Justinian, the Monophysites knew only persecution from Constantinople and were ready to welcome a foreign deliverer.

It may have seemed that the nemesis of Hellenism had appeared as recurrent warfare between the Romans and the Persian Sassanians resumed in 602. A Persian invasion had already temporarily penetrated the Delta about a century earlier. Now Sassanian forces marched on to almost reach Constantinople. They quickly occupied Egypt in 616. After a decade of Persian rule, the Romans, though almost as exhausted as their foe, returned as part of an amazing offensive that appeared to bode the end of the Sassanian Empire. It indeed was on its last legs, but the power that would topple it as well as end Constantinople's control over the east, particularly Egypt, was incubating elsewhere.

3

Islamic Egypt to 1798

Both the Coptic-speaking population of Egypt and the Hellenic Orthodox Christian ruling class could hear echoes of momentous events occurring beyond their province's eastern frontier during the 630s. But no one could have understood that a great transformation was erupting that not only would provide Egypt new rulers but would also bring a nearly total change in its religion and its language and identity. Indeed, Egypt was to become such an integral part of a new civilization that even when it eventually provided a seat for independent rulers, its history cannot be understood outside the broader context.

A new prophet, Muhammad, had arisen in western Arabia by ca. 610. A distinct religion, proclaiming itself a revival of the true monotheism that recurrently had been corrupted, unfolded as he received revelations from the Angel Gabriel. The Prophet's followers would collect these messages, which make up the Qur'an, the holy book read and memorized by Muslims, that is, those who submit to God in accordance with the religion of Islam (literally *submission*). For Muslims, Muhammad was the final messenger or prophet in a series going back to Adam and conveying the message of God ("Allah" in Arabic, the same word used by Arabic-speaking Christians and Jews). Islam was much like Judaism except for stressing that it is a message for the whole world. It was like Christianity in accepting Jesus as the Messiah as well as the doctrine of His Virgin Birth but rejected His divinity and the idea that God had a son.

Persecuted in his home city of Mecca, Muhammad found acceptance in Madina and established an Islamic state there that soon expanded into much of the Arabian Peninsula. After his death in 632, the caliphs (literally, "successors or deputies") who took on the mantle of his political leadership sent out armies that soon conquered the Persian Sassanid Empire and drove the Romans/Byzantines out of Syria and Palestine.

THE ARAB/ISLAMIC CONQUEST OF EGYPT

The Arab conquest of Palestine cut Egypt off from overland contact with the rest of the Roman Empire. Conditions in that country left it an apple ripe for an energetic newcomer to pluck, although it had revived as a vibrant commercial center following the end of the Persian occupation. The bubonic plague in the sixth century had reduced its population of perhaps five million by about two-thirds.

An Arab force moved on from Palestine at the end of 639 to attack Roman garrisons in Egypt. Led by Amr ibn-al-As, who acted on his own without seeking the approval of the Caliph Umar in Madina, Amr's troops at first numbered no more than 4,000. The patriarch of Alexandria, the emperor's appointee, already was paying tribute to the Muslims in the hope of averting an invasion. The Arabs proceeded to besiege the Roman garrison in the fortress of Babylon (not to be confused with the more famous ancient city on the Tigris), within today's Cairo, near the edge of the desert. The fortress fell after a little more than a year had passed, leaving the Egyptian Delta cut off from Upper Egypt. Reflecting a decision to concentrate on defending Anatolia from the new conquerors, the Romans concluded a treaty with Amr that turned over Alexandria to him but allowed their troops to withdraw. With the failure of an attempt by naval forces to retake the city two years later, the Arab conquest of Egypt was secure, although Byzantine raids on the coast occurred during subsequent centuries.

Popular dissatisfaction with Roman rule facilitated the conquest. The country suffered from much internecine conflict that was intensified by the Emperor Heraclius's sponsorship of a compromise theological position known as Monothelitism. This caused disaffection among many Chalcedonians (orthodox) as well as among the supporters of the rival Coptic patriarch. It would be an exaggeration to suggest that all Copts welcomed the invaders with open arms, but they sometimes collaborated with—or simply did not resist—them. And the Jewish minority, whose forced conversion to Christianity Heraclius decreed and for which the rise of Islam provided the beginning of a new golden age, were at least as ready as the Copts to accept Muslim rule.

EGYPT AS ONE OF THE CALIPH'S PROVINCES

Preferring throughout most of their conquered territories to settle at such points (*amsar*, plural of *misr*, "settlement" or "colony") instead of in major local population centers, the Arabs set up camp at Fustat (literally, "the Tent"), near the conquered Babylon. It was from Fustat—and the much later city of Cairo that now has grown to include the sites of both Fustat and Babylon—that Amr and his successors would govern this new province of an Islamic state that soon extended from India and western China to the Atlantic. The monumental Mosque of Amr stands today where the conqueror established the rudimentary beginnings of the structure in Fustat.

From simply being a military encampment, Fustat eventually evolved patterns much like other Islamic capital cities. In close proximity one found the ruler's or provincial governor's residence, a grand mosque, a bazaar (*suq*), and a public square (*maydan*). Various communities, usually differentiated by religion and sometimes by ethnicity or the area from which they originated, typically lived in their own quarters, each walled off from one another. In each quarter, a shaykh (headman) collected taxes and generally was in charge, with the homes and workshops for various crafts were found along the narrow, winding streets. Each Islamic city as a whole lacked the corporate existence found in Europe.

The Arab troops formed the local ruling class of the province. Governors, starting with Amr, theoretically were the proconsuls of the caliph, who was seated at first in Madina and then for a while in Basra during the caliphate of Ali, then in Damascus after the beginning of the Umayyad dynasty in 661 and in Baghdad or nearby following the establishment of the Abbasid dynasty in 750. Governors typically came from the capital but sometimes emerged from the local Arab elite, among whom top offices—the commander of the police and the chief judge as well as governor—often long remained in the same family.

The troops in Fustat represented the interests of their men in the wider Islamic state, particularly in defending their right to much of their province's revenue. And they repeatedly played a major role in the politics of the caliphate. Indeed, it was their dissatisfaction with an attempt to centralize the government made by the third caliph, Uthman ibn Affan of the Umayyad family, that precipitated the first Islamic Civil War. This conflict started with Uthman's murder by troops from Fustat in 656. Ironically, it was Amr, who, as rival parties fought each other in Egypt, now formed an alliance with Uthman's nephew Mu'awiyah and retook the country again two years later—this time for the Umayyads in their struggle with the fourth caliph, Ali, which led to the rise of the Umayyad dynasty. In another struggle for the succession (the Second Civil War), the Umayyad Marwan's rival, Ibn Zubayr, gained control of Egypt, but Marwan led a force that regained it in 684. He appointed his son, Abd al-Aziz, as governor, who seems to have ruled the province pretty much on his own for two decades and proceeded to send troops to help defeat Ibn Zubayr in Mecca and thus to consolidate the Umayyad dynasty, but this left the old elite in Fustat generally intact. With civil war pitting various Arab tribes against one another throughout the Islamic realm in the 740s, Egypt again provided an important theater of conflict, with the last Umayyad caliph, Marwan II, sending a governor who tried to stamp out opposition. Coming from the east, the advancing revolutionary armies of the Abbasids found much support in Egypt, where Marwan II met his death when he fled there in 750 with the victorious Abbasids on his heels.

It was the Arab forces in Fustat who took the initiative in pushing the Islamic frontiers westward to the Atlantic. The Umayyad governor of Egypt chose Musa ibn Nusayr as the commander of the force of Syrians tribesmen who crossed into Spain in the early eighth century. As for the south, wars with the Nubians led to stalemate and the failure to extend the Islamic realm farther than Aswan. The Nubians, who remained Christian for centuries, would sometimes constitute a military threat to Egypt.

The emergence of the Abbasid dynasty in 750 brought tremendous change to the state. In line with the universalist principles underlying the Islamic religion, newly converted peoples gained true equality. Admittedly, the new dynasty was Arab, but now it was no longer the "Arab kingdom" of the Umayyads. Persians in particular came to play a leading role in the central government. At first this seems to have made little difference in Egypt. The governors sent by the caliph could rule only by working with the local Arab elite of Fustat as they faced sporadic revolts. But other Arabs were settling in the country and clashing with the old Fustat elite, whose entrenched domination was uprooted by about 820. After the Caliph Ma'mun sent another general, Abdullah ibn Tahir, to Egypt to end a period of disorder and to act as the new governor, a new pattern emerged whereby a series of "super-governors" ruled Egypt without even residing there. Instead, they sent forces, heavily consisting of Persian and Turkish Muslims that kept the province under control. The large degree of autonomy that Egypt—particularly the elite in Fustat—

enjoyed for nearly two centuries following the initial Islamic conquest made way for oppressive rule. This evoked a revolt of both Muslims and Copts in 831 that ended when Ma'mun visited the country and stopped the abuse.

A NEW IDENTITY ARISING

This incorporation into the Islamic empire began slowly to turn Egypt into an Arab Muslim country. The predominant stock would always remain the same as in ancient times. The number of Arabs who settled in Egypt at the time—growing to perhaps 40,000 by the end of the century—was relatively small, and the tribes from the Arabian Peninsula that eventually moved into the country, particularly the south, would not dislocate the indigenous majority. Slavery would bring new blood to the Nile Valley over the centuries, with descendants of enslaved Turks and others coming to make up the ruling class. The importation of black slaves—sometimes also for military purposes—and also some settlement by individuals from various parts of Africa (coming, for example, as pilgrims and as students to Egypt's Islamic educational institutions) must also have added a further Negroid element to the population's makeup, as did the eventual incorporation of Nubia as part of the country and a considerable movement back and forth from the Sudan in modern times. And the prosperous and culturally fluorescent Middle Ages pulled immigrants from many parts of the world, with Arabic the language of the melting pot.

Arab culture in general and the Arabic language in particular slowly took hold. At first, government officials—that is, scribes, who were mostly Copts—continued to keep records in Coptic. Greek, too, remained in use for a while. Sometimes Copts used the Greek alphabet for writing Arabic, just like the Judeo-Arabic that used Hebrew letters. It was not until the early eighth century that orders came from the caliph that the registers of soldiers entitled to a share of the revenue be written in Arabic. Copts—and also Jews—remained heavily represented in the bureaucracy. Coptic persisted as the main tongue of the indigenous Egyptian for centuries but ceased being spoken by the majority by the eleventh century. It was largely extinct by the fourteenth century except as the liturgical language of the Coptic Church, and some say that Coptic religious music has preserved influences of the Pharaonic culture. Also, there seems to be some Coptic influence on the colloquial language.

The change in religion also came slowly. There are reports of a few conversions at an early date, but the conquerors did not impose their religion on what they considered "People of the Book," including Chris-

tians and Jews. These non-Muslims were supposed to be "protected people" *(dhimmis)*, allowed to live under their own religious law and practice
their faith subject to certain restrictions that only sometimes were enforced.
The *dhimmis* also had to pay a head tax that Muslims were not subject to,
but that usually was not onerous, at least not compared with what they had
endured under Roman/Byzantine rule, although by the eighth century on
a few occasions increased taxation did evoke revolts (but none that seriously threatened Islamic rule). All this relative tolerance of the Arabs notwithstanding, there were advantages to being a Muslim, and so by the tenth
or eleventh century, a majority of Egyptians had converted to Islam. Popular anti-Christian feelings during the thirteenth century Mamluk Sultanate—paradoxically caused by the overrepresentation of Christians in
governmental offices and apparently directed specifically against such officials at a time when Cypriot crusaders launched a devastating attack on
Alexandria—may have brought more conversions to Islam.

The Egyptian peasants now were subject to Arab overlords, but these
were replacements for other overlords. The peasantry remained on the
soil pretty much as always, though they were apparently less exploited
than before the Arabs came. They were not technically owners of the land,
which in Islamic jurisprudence mostly was classified as *miri* (princely, that
is, formally owned by the state, but with customary rights of usage that
were much like private ownership as well as rights to common lands for
pasture). The replacement of one set of rulers by another may sometimes
have been barely noticed.

A further word on land in Islamic Egypt (and the Islamic world generally) is in order, particularly as practices developed over the centuries.
Rulers established a pattern of giving land grants (*iqta*, literally, "appor-
tionment") to various people, particularly military commanders. This was
similar in some respects to the feudalism of Europe during roughly the
same period, but one should be wary of equating the two. Land grantees
in Egypt basically were given the right to collect the land tax, often used
to support troops (again like European feudalism), but these overlords
usually did not either live in manors on the land or pass on their grants
to their heirs. The grants sometimes consisted of disconnected plots, unlike the compact domains of vassals in European feudalism. Although
some overlords undoubtedly were arbitrary and oppressive, this did not
belie the usage rights of the peasantry to *miri* land. Much the same is true
of another pattern that prevailed in Egypt during the Ottoman period
(unlike the *iqta* in other parts of the empire), whereby land was allotted
as "tax farms" (*iltizam*, literally "concession").

The kind of freehold land ownership—called *mulk* in Islamic jurisprudence—that most readers today are familiar with did exist. This was the exception in the case of agricultural land, although cases of large *mulk* estates were known in medieval Egypt. Much more common was the phenomenon of endowments (*waqf*, plural, *awqaf*) for charitable purposes, as to support a mosque or a school but sometimes actually for use by members of one's family. Much land was tied up in the *waqf* system, as many individuals chose it as a way of protecting holdings from confiscation by arbitrary rulers.

INDEPENDENCE FROM BAGHDAD: THE TULUNIDS

The gradual spread of both Arabic and Islam to the people of Egypt as well as the emergence of an independent regime there ironically failed to end the dichotomy between a tiny ruling class and the ethnically distinct masses. A new ethnic group, the Turks, not only were converting to Islam but were also gaining primacy as soldiers and de facto rulers in the Islamic world. With the erosion of the role of the Arab tribes as the foundation of military power, other ethnic groups—such as Berbers and Kurds—also were helping fill the vacuum in various places. In Egypt in particular, it was not until the mid-thirteenth century that Turkish mamluks fully predominated in the military. But in many respects, the Egyptians, however Arabized and Islamicized, would remain a subordinate people.

The Turks—related linguistically to the Mongolians and Manchus— were indigenous to Central Asia. (This is roughly the region made up of such Turkish peoples as the Uzbeks and the Kazakhs in the former Soviet Union today.) It was only during the eleventh century that Turkish tribes began to invade Anatolia, resulting in the eventual creation of today's Turkey. As they conquered Central Asia in the seventh and eighth centuries, the Arab Muslims soon came into contact with the Turks, who eventually converted to Islam. In the meantime, many Turkish children were for sale in the slave markets.

Muslim armies started using enslaved Turks, whose military qualities stood out, as soldiers. The Abbasid Caliph Mu'tasim began to depend on such troops in the 830s. Although the term is better known in relation to Egypt in the period starting in the late thirteenth century, the new soldiers were called *mamluk*s (literally, "owned people," i.e., slaves). It was not long before Turkish commanders—typically mamluks, although some never were enslaved—sent to various provinces began to rule more or less independently of central authority and to create dynasties of their own while formally declaring their loyalty to the caliph. Eventually, indeed, caliphs themselves became formalities as their Turkish sultans (literally "power holders") became the real rulers. Although the mamluks were purchased as slaves, they were legally manumitted after a period of military training. They developed an intense loyalty to their owner that survived as long as he lived. As such mamluks advanced to become generals, they bought more mamluks, and the process repeated itself from generation to generation. Throughout the Islamic world one observes a unique pattern in which the soldiers and rulers typically were Turks who arrived as slaves.

The caliph ended a period of disorder in Egypt by transmitting a Turkish general, Ahmad ibn Tulun, there as the new governor in 868. Ibn Tulun quickly established his rule, but the caliph—now occupied with the need to wipe out rebellions closer to home—could not control him. Like other generals who created seats of independent power in various provinces, Ibn Tulun and his successors in Egypt formally recognized the authority of Abbasid caliphs by having their names mentioned in the Friday sermons and stamped on coins. Alternatively, Ibn Tulun intervened in caliphal politics and even aspired for a while to move the seat of the Abbasid caliphs to Fustat. Ibn Tulun and his successors often warred with their nominal superior in Baghdad. In reality Egypt now was independent (and would be most of the time for several centuries) and even extended its control to other regions. Syria in particular was normally united with Egypt under the various independent dynasties. But this was the same sort of "independence" that we saw under the Ptolemies, that is, rule by a non-Egyptian military class over the indigenous people. The major difference between dynasties established by the Ptolemies and that of Ibn Tulun (the Tulunids) is that in the latter case, the ruler shared the faith of an increasing proportion of his subjects. In addition, the seat of power remained, as under the caliph's subordinates, at the center of Egypt in Fustat, not off in a Hellenistic city on the country's periphery, as was the case with the Ptolemies' capital of Alexandria.

In one sense, even this overstates the alien nature of the government under the Tulunids and subsequent dynasties. It was the military—"the men of the sword"—that the foreign elite made up, with rulers rising from its ranks. But the life of the general Muslim population went on in ways that the rulers did not ordinarily interfere with. Lives were governed by Islamic law, and the ruler could not always disregard that with impunity, although there were cases of, say, taxes being imposed that Islamic law did not provide for. Top judges who applied Islamic law, as well as muftis (jurisconsults who issue legal rulings or *fatwas*), were appointees of the ruler, but they were bound by Islamic principles. Such religious functionaries—"men of the turban"—came from the ulama (the learned scholars), who generally represented the indigenous people. Much the same is true of the preachers and the prayer leaders. Even if sometimes dependent on the ruler for office, such ulama often acted as spokespersons for the Egyptian population. And ulama, merchants, and others formed a subordinate part of the ruling class through a process of patronage whereby they received favors from the ruler and provided favors for their own followers among the populace. This is aside from the fact that the bureaucracy—"the men of the pen"—was filled with Copts (and perhaps sometimes people of Coptic background who had converted to Islam).

The alien character of the rulers needs further qualification. With the ruling class constantly being renewed by the importation of new mamluks, the descendants of the mamluks tended to melt into the general population. They married Egyptian women. Sometimes sons of mamluks were soldiers too, but generally not in the elite units.

On his death in 884, Ibn Tulun's son Khumarawayh succeeded him and even enlarged his realm. A series of ineffective rulers from the Tulunid house made way for the weakening of the Tulunid state and its reconquest by the Abbasids in 905. The next 30 years proved tumultuous, as the diversion of large amounts of revenue to Baghdad bred resentment among the local troops, with different units clashing among themselves.

A new threat was rising from the Fatamid dynasty, which had established itself in North Africa. The Fatimids raided Egypt, temporarily occupying Alexandria three times before finally being driven back by forces under a general of Central Asian origin whose father had been a Tulunid soldier. His name was Muhammad ibn Tughj Abu Bakr, whom the caliph awarded the title *al-Ikhshid* ("the servant"). Deciding that Egypt was too difficult to rule directly, the caliph allowed ibn Tughj to establish another local dynasty in Fustat, known as the Ikhshidis. With troops of different ethnic backgrounds recruited to check on one another, a Black eunuch, Abu al-Misk al-Kafur, eventually took power. Kafur's death in 968 left the country leaderless and in a weakened condition that allowed Fatimid armies under Jawhar, a Sicilian slave general, to conquer the country the next year.

THE FATIMIDS

From the point of view of most Muslims, the Fatimids belonged to a heterodox form of Islam. But here we need to stop our discussion of events in tenth century Egypt to make sense of religious developments since the time of the Prophet Muhammad. Two main sectarian divisions had begun to emerge at an early date, as some Muslims insisted that Muhammad had designated his cousin and son-in-law, Ali ibn Abi-Talib, to succeed him as the leader of the community. This Alid faction—or party (Shi'ah) of Ali—insisted on a hereditary series of imams (literally, "leaders") starting with Ali. But most of the Muslim community—what would eventually emerge as Sunni Islam—accepted a series of caliphs (successors)—but also called imams—starting with Muhammad's companion, Abu Bakr, who theoretically were elected, although with the establishment of the Umayyad dynasty it in fact became hereditary. For the Sunnis, however imperfect these caliphs were, they were legitimate rulers. Although there were Alid factions (as well as a third, and eventually largely extinct, group of less concern to us here, known as Kharajites) in early Fustat, the Sunni form of Islam predominated in Egypt. Whether subservient to the caliph or autonomous, none of the rulers of Egypt had been Shi'ites until the time of the Fatimids.

Even calling the Fatimids Shi'ites may cause confusion. Many people are aware of Iran as a predominantly Shi'ite country (although this was not the case until the sixteenth century). The Shi'ism of Iran and adjacent countries is the Twelver variety, so-called from the acceptance of a series of 12 imams, the last of whom disappeared from view but will return as the Mahdi (guided one), a sort of messianic figure. The Fatimids, named in honor of Muhammad's daughter Fatima, the wife of Ali, belonged to a different branch of Shi'ism, one whose line of imams diverged from those of the Twelvers. This is the Isma'ili subsect (not very numerous today, represented mainly by the Nizari branch, the followers of the Aga Khan), sometimes also called Seveners because of their belief in a different line of succession that passed through Isma'il to his son, who was the last. For Isma'ilis, the imams are infallible, and they believed that one—the seventh or one of his successors—would appear as the Mahdi. Notwithstanding the rarity of Isma'ilis today, they were important in early Islamic politics, organizing a famous missionary movement—the Da'wah—to spread their message and establishing several states in Arabia and the Fertile Crescent at different times. It was one Isma'ili leader from the east, calling himself "al-Mahdi" (the Mahdi) who gained the backing of Berber tribes and established the Fatimid dynasty, with its seat of power in al-Qayrawan, near today's Tunis, in 910 and came to dominate much of North Africa (as well as Sicily) before conquering Egypt.

Jawhar established a new capital city, Cairo (al-Qahira, "Mars"; "the Victorious"), about two miles from Fustat. And from now on this was not just a seat of provincial power but of the Fatimid Empire, headed by a caliph that challenged the authority of the Sunni Abbasids. Thus for the first time Egypt was the center of a state that claimed to be the legitimate authority for the whole Islamic world and aspired to conquer Baghdad. It was at least the equal of any other Islamic empire, and Cairo emerged as one of the great centers of Islamic civilization as reinvigorated commerce and industry created an era of property. The newly founded al-Azhar mosque/university—in post-Fatimid times destined ironically to become the greatest institution of Sunni learning—had the purpose of inculcating the Isma'ili doctrine into missionaries who would spread it in all directions. With Cairo the center of the great missionary movement, the Fatimids sometimes gained the loyalty of various factions in Arabia and Iraq, and briefly during the 1050s one of their supporters took control of Baghdad and had their imam/caliph's name mentioned symbolically in the Friday sermons.

Ironically for a state that was so devoted to spreading its own sect, few Egyptians ever converted to Isma'ilism. They seem in general to have accepted the Fatimids, but essentially in the manner of Sunni caliphs rather than the infallible authorities that Isma'ilis proclaimed. Perhaps explained by the Fatimids' tendency to concentrate their religious activities on areas still to be added to their rule, they generally demonstrated great toleration toward their own Sunni subjects as well as toward non-Muslims. Christians sometimes were veziers (*wazir*, "minister"). The Fatimids ushered in the great heyday of the Jews in Egypt (ended in later centuries by economic decline and the plague), with one becoming the "man behind the throne" under Caliph al-Mustansir in the mid-eleventh century. The one notable exception to this tolerant policy in the early eleventh century was the Caliph Hakim, who apparently was mentally deranged. His erratic policies included sporadic persecution of one religion after another (see the "Notable People" section).

Struggles over succession helped to weaken the Fatimids as well as cause rivalry among the missionary movement in the east. Ethnic conflict in the military posed another problem, with newly organized Black slave units rivaling both the Turkish mamluks and the Berber troops that the Fatimids originally depended on. During the later Fatimid period, powerful viziers emerging from the military sometimes reduced caliphs to figureheads.

CRUSADERS AND AYYUBIDS

We have seen that the unity of the Islamic state began to splinter at an early date. The Fatimids were not the only example of a dynasty that rejected even the nominal legitimacy of the Sunni Abbasid caliphs in

Baghdad. Several Shi'ite dynasties rose in the east, with one controlling Baghdad itself after the mid-tenth century (but oddly in that case not challenging the nominal authority of the Abbasids). There was an upsurge of Sunni dynasties by the mid-eleventh century, with a general from the Turkish House of Saljuq conquering Baghdad in 1055 and assuming the new title of Sultan. The Saljuqs, who restored the unity of much of the Islamic world east of Egypt for a while, clashed with the Fatimids on many occasions in Syria. But the Saljuks also eventually splintered into petty local dynasties at a time when the Fatimid state in Egypt also was in decline.

This weakness of the Islamic world made way for the Crusades. These Western Christian holy warriors took control of most of Palestine and Syria at the end of the eleventh century. Egypt was not the focus of the Crusaders, although it was the Fatimids who lost Jerusalem to them in 1099. The Fatimids retained a foothold in southwestern Palestine for a long time. Egypt provided a secondary terrain for the European intruders, while the struggle against them was the backdrop for power struggles within Egypt that brought about the Crusaders' defeat and the establishment of a new dynasty.

The rise of a new Islamic power in Syria and northern Iraq is closely tied to events in Egypt. The Zangids, a Kurdish dynasty establishing itself in Mosul (northern Iraq), began to inflict blows on the Crusaders in 1144. A new Zangid ruler, Nur al-Din, won further victories when, in response to the Crusaders' setback, a Second Crusade was organized. But the Crusaders now raided the Egyptian Delta as the country was wracked by internal conflict, evoking intervention by the Zangids. At the request of a former vizier, Shawar, Nur al-Din sent a force headed by the Kurdish general Asad al-Shirkuh to Egypt, but after Shawar was restored to power, he turned on his benefactor to make an alliance with the Crusaders. After Shirkuh returned to Syria (and following an unsuccessful attempt by him to take Egypt), Shawar called on him again as the Crusaders were invading Egypt. After Shirkuh returned with a large force, he drove the enemy out of the country in 1169 and as a result was appointed vezier by the Fatimid caliph. Although a Sunni, Shirkuh now was the dominant figure in the Fatimid regime, as would be his nephew, Salah al-Din al-Ayyubi (known in the West as "Saladin"), upon the strongman's death shortly afterward.

Saladin, the founder of the Ayyubid dynasty that had its seat in Cairo for nearly a century (extending its sway to parts of Libya, Syria, Arabia), was to be one of the great figures in Egyptian—and world—history. After beating back further Crusader invasions, this new sultan terminated the feeble Fatimid dynasty's titular authority by having the name of the Abbasid caliph mentioned in the Friday sermon in 1171, thus symbolically heralding the restoration of Sunnism as the official religion. In a renewed conflict with the Crusaders, his forces decisively defeated them at the Battle of Hattin in 1187 and restored Jerusalem to Islamic rule. His magnanimity toward the Christians there, so much in contrast to the brutality they had inflicted on the Muslims and Jews when they first took the city, made him the object of much reluctant admiration in Christendom. A Third Crusade, organized to reverse their defeats, left the Crusaders with only a narrow strip of land in northern Palestine and southern Lebanon and with Saladin still in control of a Jerusalem that according to a peace settlement in 1192 Christian pilgrims could visit only if unarmed.

Although the Ayyubid dynasty lingered until 1260, it declined after its founder's death in 1193. Little Ayyubid principalities in Syria tended to fall away from Cairo's control. But the attempts by the Fifth and Sixth Crusades (1219 and 1249) to occupy the Delta failed.

THE MAMLUK SULTANATE

As a new threat to the Islamic world emanated from Mongolia, the Ayyubids organized a new military force that not only would defeat the Mongols but also would replace Saladin's dynasty. The new regime was known at the time as the Dynasty of the Turks, but we call it the Mamluk Sultanate because it consisted of a series of sultans—at first of Turkish origin—that had been brought to Egypt as mamluks, with those who rose to power—as we already have explained—continuing the same process on and on over the generations. Although rule sometimes passed from father to son (either nominally or in reality), this was not a dynasty in the usual sense of the word, for rulers recurrently arose from the newly imported mamluks.

It was the last Ayyubid sultan, al-Salih, who laid the groundwork for his dynasty's replacement by beginning to rely on mamluk troops rather than the diverse units previously favored by his dynasty. Because these mamluks were stationed on the island of Rawdah in the middle of the river (*bahr*, the word ordinarily translated as "sea"), they came to be known as the Bahri mamluks. Representing a common practice of the ruling class in the Islamic world over the centuries, al-Salih also took a Turkish slave woman, Shajar al-Durr, as his wife. There was a tendency for women in the harem (forbidden, i.e., private, quarters) of palaces in the Islamic world to wield great influence, often to become the real rulers, and Shajar al-Durr proved to be a case in point, as shown when the sultan died in 1249, and the Mamluk Sultanate began to emerge through a series of events that might not seem credible if a fiction writer were to invent them.

Shajar might be considered the first Mamluk sultan. She took over effective power by keeping her husband's death a secret, waiting for her son Turanshah to return from a military campaign. Once he was back in Cairo, it was not long before the mamluks murdered him because they formed an alliance with his mother. It was then that Shajar took the title "sultan." This was so unusual that she then allowed a mamluk commander, Aybak, to wed her and take the title while she continued to rule. Shajar's jealousy when her husband married another woman led her to have him assassinated, followed by her own murder soon afterward by a group of mamluks. A mamluk general, Qutuz, then occupied the throne in 1250.

The early Mamluks were fierce, skilled cavalrymen who made a name for themselves as the defenders of Islam. One of their generals, Baybars, foiled the attempt of the Sixth Crusade to invade Egypt in 1249. They also defeated an Ayyubid in Syria who tried to subdue them, effectively ending that dynasty's goal of restoring its power in Egypt. But the real threat came from farther east, as armies from Mongolia overwhelmed most of Eurasia. The Mongols conquered Baghdad, still the seat of the Abbasid Caliphate, in 1258 and appeared invincible. The Mamluk armies, led by Baybars, met them at the Spring of Goliath (Ayn Jalut) in Palestine in 1260 and dealt them their first defeat. Various Mongol-ruled successor states—notably the Il-Khans of southwestern Asia—long continued to cover large areas, but Mamluk rule extended to Syria and parts of Arabia. With the assassination of Sultun Qutuz soon after the victory over the Mongols, Baybars ascended the throne, an event that marks the end of the consolidation period for the Mamluk regime. He and his successor, Qalawun (who ruled from 1310 to 1341), continued to war with the Il-Khans and other enemies, including the Crusaders, and the Mamluks finally drove the latter from their last stronghold on the mainland, at Acre, in 1293.

The Mamluk period intensified Cairo's role as a major center of the Islamic world. Indeed, to legitimize their rule, the Mamluks set up a member of the Abbasid family who fled from the Mongols as the nominal caliph in Cairo. This was a burgeoning center of trade that involved Italian merchants in the Mediterranean and commercial connections eastward via the Indian Ocean and overland through Asia, as well as the importation of gold and slaves from sub-Saharan Africa. The economy prospered, and the coffers of the state swelled, thus facilitating the importation of more mamluks. But by the middle of the fourteenth century, the bubonic plague was devastating the society. According to one interpretation, the defeat of the Mamluks' major external enemies paradoxically led to the decline of a state whose raison d'être had been warfare.

The ethnic composition of the mamluk class changed with the rise of Sultan Barquq in 1382. Qalawun had begun importing members of the Circassian ethnic group from the Caucasus region, perhaps to balance the power of other mamluks. Because these mamluks were stationed in the tower *(burj)* of the citadel in Cairo, they came to be known as the Burjis in contradistinction to their predecessors, the Bahris. This was a period of brutal internecine struggles for power, with sultans rapidly succeeding each other.

A NEW FLOWERING OF CIVILIZATION

For a while after the Islamic conquest, Egypt remained somewhat peripheral to the new civilization that rapidly was taking shape in Damascus and Baghdad. The Arab garrisons in Fustat and elsewhere in the country were small amid a populace that only slowly was adopting the culture, religion, and civilization of the conquerors. It is notable, for example, that early developments in Islamic theology and jurisprudence occurred largely in such cities as Madina, in the Hijaz, and Basra, in Iraq. We hear little about the role of Egypt in such matters, although the important jurist, al-Shafi'i, died there in 820.

With Fustat/Cairo becoming the capital from which new dynasties ruled Egypt and other lands from the ninth century on, it also emerged as a major center of Islamic civilization. According to one estimate, the population of Egypt in the thirteenth century was about three million, with perhaps a tenth of that concentrated in the capital city. Rulers became the patrons of religious and cultural activities. Preserved better than those in many other places, Cairo's mosques occupy a prominent place among the great monuments of Islamic civilization. It was notably under the Mamluk Sultanate that Islamic Egypt's glory reached its zenith, as the devastation caused by the Mongols farther east left it as arguably not just the seat of the symbolic Abbasid Caliphate but also the center of Arabic Islamic civilization (as opposed to the largely Persian-based high culture that would also flourish for centuries farther north from the Balkans to India). Cairo acted as a magnet, attracting skilled artisans and scholars from throughout the Islamic world. As a case in point, the great fourteenth–fifteenth-century historian Ibn Khaldun—a Tunisian by birth whose career as a scholar and government official in various lands, including Egypt, epitomizes the ease with which people moved throughout the Islamic world—was dazzled by this "mother of the world" for which he found no comparison elsewhere.

The civilizational flowering grew out of a flourishing economy. Though this hardly compared with its former role as the "granary" of the Roman Empire, Egypt remained an important source of grain for other parts of the world. In the pre-Industrial Revolution age, that is, before industrial production emerged on a large scale but concentrated in a few countries, Egypt was a center of industries, centered mostly in small workshops in which skilled craftspeople produced fine fabrics, glass, and metalwork for local use and for export. Most of all, Egypt's location made it a key point on the trade routes connecting the Indian Ocean region (and, indirectly, China) with the Mediterranean region and even northern Europe as well as the sub-Saharan region. In fact, there generally existed a correlation over the centuries between the fluorescence of Egypt and the extent to which the major trade routes passed through it. And the late medieval period (ending in the fifteenth century) was one of the times when that route enjoyed preeminence. Business practices were extremely sophisticated, with partnerships and patterns of credit facilitating them. Economic benefit motivated such commerce across the boundaries between rival dynasties and even across the divide between Islam and Christendom to a remarkable degree. Merchants from Venice and other Italian states actively engaged in trade with Egypt and generally provided the commercial link to Europe during this period. Such trade, best epitomized by the spices from the Indian Ocean region, provided the basis for the prosperity of the country and financed its great architecture and the stipends that supported scholarship.

OTTOMAN EGYPT

By the early sixteenth century, two great Islamic powers had arisen to the north of the Mamluk realm. Both were ruled by Turkish dynasties (each of whom patronized a form of civilization in which Persian was the main language of high culture). The Ottoman Empire, whose origin goes back to the thirteenth century, embraced Sunnism and dominated most of the Balkans and Anatolia by this time, whereas the great power that united Iran in 1501, the Safavids, was committed to Shi'ism. Known by today's historians as the "Gunpowder Empires," both (the Savavids, however, more slowly) embraced artillery as a means of warfare, putting at a severe disadvantage such forces as the mamluks, who were wedded to older methods of cavalry warfare and thought the new weapons to be designed for unchivalrous sissies. As they struggled ferociously with each other, the Mamluks looked on with apprehension, and when the Ottomans won a decisive victory over the Savavids at the Battle of Caldiran in 1514, the former gained predominance. The Mamluks inevitably would succumb to the Ottoman colossus, who could field armies larger than anybody in Egypt could imagine.

A development of great world historical significance, the Portuguese "discovery" of a route around Africa to the Indian Ocean in 1498 undermined Egypt and contributed to its weakness vis-à-vis the Ottomans. The Mamluks sent a naval force to confront the Portuguese but were defeated in 1513. The Red Sea route through which spices passed westward from Asia withered in importance—and with it Egypt's entrepôt role.

The Ottoman Sultan Salim the Grim may have had special reason to dislike the Mamluks. The Ottomans accused them of backing the Safavids, although the facts about that are debatable. Neither was Salim's destination clear when he marched eastward in 1516, but Mamluk Sultan al-Ghawri sent a force to Syria just in case he did not move on to strike at the Safavids. Whatever Salim's original intent, his army crushed the Mamluks at Marj Dahiq in 1516. With al-Ghawri dying in the battle, another commander, Tumanbay, took his place and desperately tried to save Egypt—even by acquiring guns for use by low-ranking units—but was crushed in several engagements during 1517.

At first, the Ottomans tried to exterminate the mamluks but soon adopted a more pragmatic policy. The mamluks remained in place alongside the Ottoman forces. Continuing to recruit troops through the old enslavement process, the mamluks remained a major component of the ruling class and during succeeding centuries would sometimes reduce Istanbul's rule to little more than a formality. Whether ruled by Ottoman governors or by mamluks, the indigenous population thus remained subordinate to a foreign military class. In that sense, little had changed, but in another way the change was fundamental, for now Egypt had become a mere province of an empire centered in Istanbul. No longer could Cairo claim to be the seat of the caliphate, for the conquerors took the last Abbasid caliph with them to Istanbul (later Ottoman sultans would claim that he had turned over the office to them). The prosperity brought by its former location at a key point on a major artery of world commerce was gone, and with it the greatness of its cultural achievements.

The eighteenth century saw recurrent anarchy, with factions of mamluks, Ottoman Janissary units, and tribes often fighting one another. A mamluk commander, Ali Bey ("the Great"), gained the upper hand after the middle of the century and established a personal empire that extended for a while to Syria and western Arabia, much like the Mamluk Sultanate's old realm. Another mamluk, Abu-Dhahab, overthrew him in 1772. The 1790s saw joint rule by two mamluk commanders, Ibrahim and Murad, as a new threat emerged.

4

From Bonaparte to the British

For the first time since the Crusades, a European invasion of Egypt was in the offing in the 1790s. A long period of European imperialism—at first French and then British—was beginning, while intervening efforts to revive the country floundered. Along with this emerged a clash between the forces of cultural authenticity and those who saw the need to Westernize, if only to ward off further Western domination.

By the eighteenth century, Christian Europe was the main center of power in the world. It had begun to dominate the seas three centuries earlier and took control of the Americas and various coastal areas, although powerful indigenous land empires continued to prevail in the Middle East and Asia. Europe enriched itself through this early expansion, and the subsequent explosion of its scientific and technological capacity by the 1700s gradually enabled it to threaten the now generally declining non-Western empires. From the beginning of the century, the Islamic world—the Ottoman Empire in particular—had ceased to constitute a military threat to Christendom, and by the 1770s the Ottomans were losing territories to Christian Europeans, particularly to Russia.

BONAPARTE IN EGYPT

Egypt awoke to these new realities when General Napoleon Bonaparte (later to become the Emperor Napoleon) suddenly appeared off the coast near Alexandria on June 29, 1798, as the commander of a seaborne French force of 36,000 troops. This was in the context of a struggle between the great powers of Europe since the French Revolution of 1789 (and earlier). For Bonaparte, an invasion of Egypt provided a substitute for a now-discarded project of invading France's main enemy, Britain. French control of Egypt would constitute a major blow to the British Empire, considering the country's strategic location along the "road to India." Britain had displaced the French in India during the Seven Years War that ended in 1763. The ruling Directory in Paris—as well as Bonaparte, who dreamed of re-enacting Alexander the Great's conquest of "the East"—saw Egypt as a stepping-stone to India. But some argue that the motive was to gain commercial advantage in Egypt itself, where the British and the French already were competing for trade.

The French army soon vanquished the mamluks, at least in Lower Egypt. Murad Bey's forces were crushed at the Battle of the Pyramids in July and Ibrahim Bey's troops met defeat in the eastern Delta soon afterward. The French were in control of Cairo in less than a month following their landing. The mamluks remained entrenched in much of the south, and Murad Bey continued to resist efforts to take control there. Ibrahim Bey fled to Syria to join forces with the local strongman, the Bosnian soldier Ahmad al-Jazzar Pasha.

The French forces stayed for only three years, but their defeat was more at the hands of their British rivals than by mamluks or Ottomans. Though previously allies of France, the latter nevertheless could not put up with an invasion of this important, if recently uncontrollable, province. A new coalition of Britain, Russia, and the Ottomans emerged. Facing the prospect of a two-pronged attack by Ottoman forces, one by sea and another by Jazzar Pasha across Sinai, Bonaparte went on the offensive by invading Palestine in February 1799 but, failing to conquer the city of Acre, returned to Egypt after four months.

Despite an attempt to present themselves as liberators from tyrannical mamluk rule, the French met strong local resistance. Few Egyptians were impressed by the proclamation prepared in stilted Arabic by scholars Bonaparte brought with him claiming that the French were better Muslims than the mamluks, even that they were "true Muslims" who worshiped God and respected the Prophet Muhammad and the Qur'an. By October 1798, the people of Cairo and the Delta rose in revolt, with the French engaged in brutal suppression of the uprising and often unable to control the countryside. Although some ulama at al-Azhar cooperated with the French, particularly by participating (along with merchants and village and tribal shaykhs) in appointive advisory administrative councils they set up on local and national levels and some admired the scientific experiments that the French scholars carried out, they now took the lead in the resistance movement.

British power on the seas endangered Bonaparte's project. From the beginning, it was partly a matter of luck that his expedition evaded the British navy. And the French barely had arrived on Egyptian soil before the British fleet defeated them off the coast in the Battle of Abuqir on August 1, leaving them isolated from their own country while they proceeded to pacify Egypt and war with both the British and the Ottomans. After a little over a year, Bonaparte slipped out of the country to return to France, leaving General Kléber (and later General Jacques Menou, who converted to Islam) in command. With Ottoman forces penetrating Egypt by the end of 1799, Kléber's main concern was to negotiate terms for withdrawal. The French were faced with an even more massive uprising in Cairo and the Delta during the summer of 1800, but they brutally suppressed it. In March 1801, a large British force arrived at Abuqir Bay and soon was joined by Ottoman troops arriving by sea and—initially under the command of the grand vezier, that is, the sultan's chief minister— overland from Palestine. With Cairo soon surrounded by British and Ottoman forces, the French agreed to the terms of an earlier abortive evacuation agreement, and their forces were out of the country by the end of summer. Not interested in permanently occupying Egypt at this time, the British withdrew within two years, leaving the mamluks, various Ottoman units, and the local people to compete for power.

It has been conventional to consider Bonaparte's invasion a fundamental turning point in the history of Egypt and the Middle East generally. Many authors treat this arbitrary date as the beginning of "modern" Middle Eastern history, the implication being that the Middle Ages had lingered there for three centuries after the beginning of the "modern period" in Europe and that the presence of Europeans provided the sort of enlightenment necessary for Egypt to start the "modernizing" process.

The French invasion indeed was important in many ways. It enabled the West to know much more about Egypt, notably its ancient history. Some Egyptians also became acquainted with aspects of modern science from the scholars that General Bonaparte brought with him. With its demonstration of the country's weakness, the invasion began a process of "defensive Westernization" in order to ward off future threats—a process that, however incomplete, has often evoked the apprehension of those who believe that this has been at the expense of Egypt's own Islamic traditions. The short-lived occupation began a long-term French influence on the country. And the aftermath of the invasion created a vacuum in which an Ottoman commander, Muhammad Ali Pasha, emerged as a centralizing, modernizing ruler who in many ways transformed the country, even if the eighteenth-century precedent of Ali Bey the Great diminished the new ruler's uniqueness.

EMERGENCE OF MUHAMMAD ALI PASHA

The French withdrawal made way for a struggle among several contenders for leadership. Much decimated by this time, the mamluks were divided into factions led by Bardisi Bey and Alfi Bey (both of whom were mamluks of the now ill and aged Murad Bey). There was an Ottoman governor whose influence was quite limited. Also, there were several Ottoman military units that had come to evict the French, notably a small, fractious Albanian battalion that was destined to predominate. The troops were unpaid and hungry and hard for anybody to control as they roamed the country robbing and raping. They expelled one governor from Cairo. Bedouin tribes sometimes entered the fray. The people of Cairo, led by the ulama and merchants, were another crucial ingredient of the situation. They strongly disliked both the Ottomans and the mamluks. Even after their withdrawal, the British remained potentially influential because some factions were eager for their support, and they temporarily reoccupied Alexandria for a while during 1807.

It was the Albanian battalion that soon came under the command of the wily, illiterate Muhammad Ali Pasha, who eventually established his primacy through a series of tactical alliances that defeated one contender after another. At first, he allied himself with Bardisi Bey against the governor but then discarded the mamluks in favor of the popular leaders of Cairo, headed by Umar Makram. With Muhammad Ali winning strong support from the public against the mamluks and a new Ottoman governor, who turned out to be especially unpopular, Sultan Salim III named him governor (wali) of Egypt in 1805, a reluctant recognition of the dominant, if still precarious, position he already had managed to achieve, at least in Cairo. Now the new governor was able to discard the popular leaders whom he had used to come to power. Growing opposition in Istanbul to the Sultan's reforms—that is, his attempt to establish more centralized, autocratic control over the empire by establishing a modern ("new order") military force—led to his overthrow in 1807 and thus to the absence during this crucial period of any effective Ottoman influence over developments in Egypt. Already in 1806, a replacement sent by the sultan, who had decided to move Muhammad Ali to a province in the Balkans, backed down when he got to Egypt and sized up its de facto ruler's strength.

Muhammad Ali's Egypt had an anomalous relationship to the Ottoman Empire. He remained technically a viceroy of the sultan in Istanbul—to whom he paid a small annual tribute and whose name symbolically was mentioned in the Friday sermons and stamped on coins. Muhammad Ali was very much an Ottoman; that is, he was conscious of being part of the empire's elite. He and most of his successors in Egypt did not even bother to learn the local tongue, and Turkish long remained the official language. But with the central government of the empire unable to strengthen itself, it was the governor of Egypt who now found himself independent enough to carry out the kind of modernization that had brought Salim III's downfall in 1807. It was not until 1826 that the new Ottoman sultan, Mahmud II, felt secure enough in the face of conservative opposition to resume his predecessor's modernization scheme. And by that time, the governor in Cairo had grown so powerful that he seemed ready to take over the whole empire.

Muhammad Ali bided his time with the mamluks, the last local threat to his power. He made use of them for a while, allowing them to run most of Upper Egypt, but their failure to pass on taxes to him evoked another military campaign in 1811 that established his direct authority there and caused the mamluk leaders to move to Cairo. On March 1 of the next year, as hundreds of mamluks that Muhammad Ali had invited to an important event at the Cairo Citadel proceeded through a narrow passageway, his artillery opened fire. Within the next few days, his forces had massacred several thousand of them. Nearly a millennium in which mamluks had dominated Egyptian politics finally was over, although many mamluks remained in the army and, more generally, the ruling class. Indeed, the continuing subordination of indigenous Egyptians—dismissed as "peasants" but slowly moving into important posts—to a Turkish and Circassian elite points to a major element of continuity against which protests would be directed in the latter part of the century.

Muhammad Ali's armies began a series of conquests. His first adventure outside Egypt was in Arabia. With the militant "Wahhabi" Sa'udi dynasty of central Arabia, which represented a militant puritanical movement, occupying Mecca and Madina, the sultan called on the pasha soon after his appointment as governor to send troops to restore Ottoman authority, and although Muhammad Ali at first refused to do so, he eventually dispatched an expedition to Arabia in 1811 that finally, under his able son, Ibrahim Pasha (who replaced the first commander, his brother Tusun), occupied the Saʿudis' capital and ended the Wahhabi threat for the time being. Although the Saʿudis made a comeback in central Arabia within a few years, the pasha continued to rule the coastal area of Arabia as far south as Aden until 1840. Even as late as 1813, when the pasha traveled to Arabia before putting Ibrahim in command, Istanbul sent someone to Cairo to unhorse him in his absence, but Muhammad Ali's lieutenant there was able to squash the plot.

A major priority of the ruler was to build a powerful army. Some of his Albanian troops were caught conspiring against him, and they rioted when the scheme was uncovered. In any case, it was proving impossible to transform them into the kind of modernized force that Salim III had wanted to establish—and which Muhammad Ali now aspired to emulate. Following the completion of Ibraham Pasha's mission in Arabia, his father decided to invade the Sudan, mainly to obtain slaves to be used as soldiers (and also hoping to find gold and to capture mamluk fugitives who had taken refuge there). The campaign turned into a nightmare, as his troops and most of the newly enslaved men succumbed to disease. Perhaps the most important long-term effect of the invasion was the emergence of the idea of the "unity of the Nile Valley," with the Sudan as a natural southern extension of Egypt.

With the failure of the plans for a Black military force, Muhammad Ali came up with a previously unthinkable solution: the use of Egyptian peasants as soldiers. He began to conscript them. The process often resembled catching wild animals, as peasants fled or tried to maim themselves to avoid this horrible prospect. But eventually he was able to turn them into an army of 30,000—commanded, of course, by mamluks and other officers of foreign origin. Only gradually would "peasants" gain admission to lower officer ranks, and ultimately their demands for upward mobility helped create a new crisis.

To strengthen his military capabilities, Muhammad Ali made major transformations in Egyptian society that would allow for maximum extraction of the country's resources. Taking up a project that Bonaparte had started, he began gradually in his early years as governor to abolish the *iltizam*s and to have the taxes collected by government officials. He also took control of the *waqf*s (religiously endowed property) and undermined the influence of the *ulama*, who had provided the popular leadership. He brought religious institutions, including al-Azhar, under his control, initiating the kind of state-over-religion pattern that twentieth-century Islamists would revolt against. Eventually, he turned the country into essentially his own plantation, with more being siphoned out of the peasants' production and coming directly to the central government. The pasha would later begin to parcel out land grants to various members of his family and other favorites among his officials, and eventually this evolved into purely private ownership, consequently creating a new landlord class engaged in commercial agriculture and wielding the whip against the peasantry.

A related development was the introduction of high-quality long-staple cotton as the country's specialization. This was grown for export to the textile industries of Europe and thus to provide tax revenues to pay for the pasha's army. It was bought from the producers at low fixed prices for profitable sale abroad. Bled mercilessly by taxes and conscripted to engage in public labor, the peasants repeatedly—but unsuccessfully—rebelled. The pasha also suppressed the people of Cairo when they revolted under the leadership of Umar Makram in 1809.

Muhammad Ali believed that building an effective military machine necessitated major changes in the country. He made major improvements in agriculture by brutally conscripting peasants to dig new irrigation canals—and to restore an old one connecting Alexandria to the Nile—that allowed more and more of the land to be cultivated through perennial irrigation (that is, throughout the year, as opposed to the former "basin" agriculture that allowed crops to grow only after water was collected following the annual inundation). There were major strides in the amount of land under cultivation. He set up a wide range of industries (all government monopolies), ranging from textiles and food processing to a naval arsenal, bringing in French and other European experts to help.

Further transformations went beyond increasing agricultural and industrial production. Muhammad Ali set up a modern hospital under the direction of a French physician, Clot Bey, as well as a medical school. A school for army officers emerged, also with French instructors. He introduced vaccination for smallpox. The need to produce candidates for these specialized schools caused him to establish preparatory schools, the beginning of a state-run, secular educational system (a first for the Islamic world, as opposed to the old-style Qur'anic schools and al-Azhar). An official printing press, a school for surveying, and the like came into being. He sent student missions to Europe and set up a translation bureau (headed by the imam of one of the student missions to France, Shaykh Rifaʻa Rafi al-Tahtawi) to produce Arabic versions of important books. A new educated class—largely made up of Arabic-speaking Egyptians— was emerging. Most of all, this ardent modernizer set up a more autocratic rule (the Consultative Council established in 1829 and made up of high officials and ulama, was an appointive body), centered on members of his family but with a trained bureaucracy and centralized control over the provinces, although other Western ideas that were infiltrating the country ultimately would challenge this. Tahtawi in particular, though loyal to the ruler, wrote approvingly about French concepts of liberty as well as expressing his love of the Egyptian homeland.

Meanwhile, the pasha's military campaigns rolled on. When the sultan's Greek subjects revolted in 1821, he called on him for help. Muhammad Ali managed to build a fleet to transport his troops, commanded by Ibrahim Pasha. By 1827, they had taken Athens. So successful were they that the sultan again was apprehensive about the power of his nominal subordinate, who sometimes dared to make impossible demands on him.

But ultimately, the Egyptians failed in Greece. The European navies intervened and destroyed much of their fleet in 1827 at the Battle of Navarino Bay, and the pasha worked out an agreement with the European powers allowing his forces to return to Egypt. With the sultan offering him only the island of Crete for his services, the latter was resentful and determined more than ever to act independently. In 1826, the sultan massacred the Janissaries (originally slave troops) who stood in the way of his own modernization plans and resumed the process interrupted two decades before of building a modern military machine. However, he was far from catching up with his nominal vassal in Cairo.

Syria always was of supreme strategic importance for the rulers of Egypt, and in 1831 Muhammad Ali sent forces there under the command of Ibrahim Pasha. The invaders moved into Anatolia the next year and crushed Ottoman forces in a battle near Konya. With the Egyptians having almost reached Istanbul, it seemed quite possible that Muhammad Ali was about to take over the Ottoman Empire, although Ibrahim's goal was the more modest one of occupying Istanbul and demanding recognition of Cairo's independence. But again the European powers proved to be the decisive hindrance, for the sultan was so desperate in the face of the Egyptian invasion that he concluded a treaty with the Russians that seemed about to put him under their protection. The other European powers could not tolerate that, and so they intervened to save the sultan at the pasha's expense, but not before Muhammad Ali's armies inflicted another serious defeat on his overlord in 1839 at the Battle of Nizib, resulting in the Ottoman fleet coming over to his side. In the London Conference of 1840, the main European powers demanded that Muhammad Ali withdraw from the territories he had occupied outside Egypt, and the British and Austrians backed this up by sending a force to defeat Ibrahim in Syria amid a popular insurrection evoked by the high taxes Ibrahim had imposed.

Though Muhammad Ali's wings were clipped, the new arrangement left him and his family firmly in control of Egypt and the Sudan. In 1841, the sultan recognized his lifetime tenure as governor as well as the principle of hereditary succession for his heirs. Limits were put on the size of the Egyptian army. The rest of Muhammad Ali's life was anticlimactic. He was too ill to govern even before his death in 1849. Ibrahim Pasha became the effective ruler for a few months but died before his father.

Muhammad Ali's scheme to make Egypt an industrial power fell apart. An Anglo-Ottoman agreement of 1838 banning monopolies in the sultan's domains was made applicable to Egypt after 1840. According to one interpretation, the consequent inability of Muhammad Ali to protect his new industries nipped them in the bud and prevented Egypt from becoming the first modern industrialized country in the non-Western world (preceding Japan by several decades). Others argue that the pasha's industrialization already had failed due to the inadequacy of supplies of wood and coal that dictated dependence on animal and human muscle power to run machines. In any case, both the undermining of traditional craft industries and the failure of modern industrialization left Egypt in the classic Third World role as an importer of expensive manufactured goods and producer of cotton and other cheap raw materials, vulnerable to drastic shifts in prices, for European markets.

MUHAMMAD ALI'S SUCCESSORS

Muhammad Ali's immediate successors extended his policies of autocratic centralization and modernization. Even his nephew, Abbas I, who ruled from 1848 to 1854, was not, as once portrayed, the reactionary ruler who tried to undo his predecessor's legacy but rather continued to send students abroad and to promote the development of railroads and the like as well as to start another military school. Muhammad Ali's son Sa'id (1854–1863) was greatly enamored of Europeans and eagerly cooperated with foreign schemes to develop the country.

Under Sa'id's successor, Isma'il (1863–1869), Egypt experienced a transformation that—until the bubble burst—convinced the exuberant ruler (whose status his overlord in Istanbul in 1867 promoted from mere "governor" to the lofty Persian title of "Khedive [lord]," unlike the head of any other province in the empire) that Egypt now was "part of Europe." He spent lavishly on palaces as well as schools, including the Dar al-Ulum

(House of Sciences), for teacher training, although at least 95 percent of the population still was illiterate by the 1880s. A Europeanized educated class proficient in French occupied top positions. New sections of Cairo looked like modern European cities. Although Egypt still was overwhelmingly a country of villages and peasants, there was increasing urbanization. Cairo's population had grown from a quarter million in 1800 to over a half million, and Alexandria, which had declined over the centuries to little more than a village during the previous century, could boast a population—much of it European—that was approaching a quarter million by the 1880s. There were more improvements in agriculture, including the completion of the Nile barrage—started under Muhammad Ali—at the northern tip of the Delta in 1861. Though still technically a subordinate of the sultan, Isma'il's position became more and more like that of the ruler of an independent empire, as he gained authority even to conclude treaties.

Purportedly with the purpose of combating the slave trade, Isma'il rounded out his territory in the south. Military expeditions extended his rule to the lakes of equatorial Africa and to the littoral of the Horn of Africa. But an invasion of Abyssinia (Ethiopia) in the mid-1870s failed dismally in the face of powerful local resistance. And a revolt in 1881 led by the head of a Sufi order, Muhammad Ahmad (proclaimed by his followers as "the Mahdi" or "Guided One"), was threatening to drive the Khedevial forces out of the Sudan.

For the first time, a parliament of sorts, the Consultative Assembly of Delegates, came into being with the issuance of a Fundamental Law in 1866, a rudimentary constitution preceding the first one adopted for the Ottoman Empire by a decade. The indirectly elected body was made up mostly of village mayors (shaykhs, later called umdahs, whose local influence made elections largely a formality) and others of the rural notable class. A major goal was to associate them with the khedive's financial policies and also reflected a goal of keeping the top elite of Turks and Circassians in rein (that is, a divide-and-conquer strategy). It was meant to be a tame body, with no legislative functions, but it later began to assert itself.

With the continuing development of large estates in the hands of officials and other favorites of the regime, the viceregal family headed the landlord class. The regime confiscated private estates at will, acquiring nearly a million faddans by 1878.

Though still under a foreign ruling class, indigenous Egyptians were gaining a greater role. With the size of the bureaucracy increasing and the number of available Circassians shrinking, Egyptians became prominent in the lower rungs, such as chiefs of the subdistricts of provinces. Such Egyptians as the French-educated engineer Ali Pasha Mubarak, who held top positions in the fields of education and public works, were advancing to high bureaucratic positions. Prominent local families whose members held the post of village mayor acquired significant landholdings (though small compared with those of the Turkish and Circassian elite), and their sons advanced in the army. Sa'id allowed them to rise to the rank of colonel. Members of the elite often married Egyptian women. Arabic was gradually pushing Turkish out as the language of administration, but not of the army.

European penetration intensified as Egypt's strategic importance became increasingly compelling. By the 1870s, almost a hundred thousand Europeans, especially Italians and Greeks, and also Syrian Christians had settled in Egypt. Together with such other minorities as Copts, Armenians, and Jews, they would dominate financial and commercial affairs in Egypt for decades and fill high posts in the bureaucracy. European consuls increasingly interfered in Egyptian affairs. The Capitulations, a centuries-old arrangement whereby Europeans were in many respects outside the jurisdiction of Egyptian courts, continued to make them a privileged class (and put Egyptians at a severe disadvantage), although one of Isma'il's supposed achievements, which may instead have worked to the advantage of European interests, was the establishment of a system of Mixed Courts made up of both Egyptian and foreign judges. European bankers flocked to Egypt to provide loans to the government, and Europeans bought up bonds issued by the Egyptian government. Telegraph lines were being installed and roads improved. Railroads—the first in the Middle East—were completed during the reign of Sa'id connecting Cairo with Alexandria and later Suez. By the 1830s, steamships regularly connected Britain with Alexandria and Bombay with Suez as the importance of this overland link between the seas increased.

Proposals for an interoceanic canal bore fruit as Sa'id granted a concession to a Frenchman, Ferdinand de Lessups, in 1854. The Egyptian government had 44 percent of the shares in the new Universal Suez Maritime Corporation (Suez Canal Company or SCC for short), whereas the rest of the stocks were in the hands of French investors. Egyptian peasants who, under the terms of the concession, were provided to do the hard labor, suffered and died by the thousands but finally completed the Suez Canal, which opened in 1869. Extending 101 miles from Port Said in the north to the city of Suez in the south, the new waterway renewed Egypt's significance for European imperial ambitions.

Temporary financial opportunities buoyed Cairo's exuberance. There was increased demand for Egyptian grain during the Crimean War of the 1850s. And when the American Civil War temporarily cut off a major source of cotton for Europe, Egypt helped fill the vacuum. Revenues soared. But American cotton was coming back on the market by 1864, a major factor undermining the khedive's position. Increasingly he had to take out more loans just to pay principal and interest to British and French bondholders. Demonstrating the regime's desperation for short-term solutions, the Muqabala Law of 1871 provided that landholders paying six times what was due in taxes for one year subsequently would get 50 percent reductions. Out of desperation, the khedive sold the Egyptian shares of the SCC to the British government in 1875.

Bankruptcy resulted in subjection to domination by Europeans who were motivated by financial interests and a desire to gain control over this strategically important country. Following an initial attempt to play the British and French off against each other, Isma'il finally acquiesced in 1876 in the formation of a Public Debt Commission made up of representatives from Britain, France, Italy, and Austria to supervise the collection of revenues and pay his debt. This subsequently made way for an arrangement for Dual Control—by an Englishman and a Frenchman—of Egypt's debt. Other Anglo-French commissions ran the railroads and customs. With the collaboration of the malleable Armenian Prime Minister, Boghos Nubar Pasha, an Englishman and a Frenchman headed the ministries of finance and public works, respectively, leaving the khedive no longer effectively in control of the government. He even had to give up much of his landholdings. With the khedive no longer in a position to mete out rewards to those around him, more and more members of the ruling class now were eager to collaborate with the foreigners. But however much the Europeans squeezed, they could not extract enough to cover the debt.

URABI'S ABORTIVE REVOLUTION: "EGYPT FOR THE EGYPTIANS"

A new movement of protest against the Turkish and Circassian ruling class and growing foreign domination was emerging. One influence was the important religious scholar known as Jamal al-Din al-Afghani (that is, "the Afghan," although in fact he was an Iranian who used this name to hide his Shi'ite background), who came to teach at al-Azhar in 1871. He advocated new interpretations of Islam that would make it compatible with the modern world and allow Muslims to have greater control of their destinies, and he called for a combination of national and pan-Islamic solidarity to resist the growing European encroachment on Muslim lands, including Egypt. Mostly opposed by the elite class, the resistance to European domination was centered on the heretofore pliant Consultative Assembly—and generally the small indigenous landholders, the "mayor class," that made it up—as well as the middle-level army officers of peasant origin led by Colonel Ahmad Urabi, himself from a rural mayoral family, who bore the brunt of drastic cutbacks in the size of the military resulting from the European diktat.

With Isma`il's apparent encouragement, army officers demonstrated in 1879 against a plan for several hundred officers to be retired at half pay. The protesters insulted both Nubar Pasha and Sir Rivers Wilson. In turn, the khedive appointed a new cabinet—still entirely from the Turco-Circassian elite—headed by the supposedly constitutionalist Muhammad Sharif (a moderate Circassian who, like many others, later broke with the Urabists) in April and called for better terms for debt payment. He also supported a demand for an elective parliament and the principle of cabinet responsibility—key components of the kind of parliamentary democracy that slowly had been emerged in Europe. Complying with European demands, the sultan formally dismissed Isma`il in June to make way for the latter's son Tawfiq, a more willing collaborator with the Europeans, to succeed to the throne and appoint Mustafa Riyadh as prime minister. The Consultative Assembly was dissolved but protested against this by meeting in private homes. The British and French dual controllers were effectively in charge of the country, and the policies of the Riyadh government, particularly the Law of Liquidation adopted in 1880, angered even members of the Turco-Circassian elite.

Khedive Tawfiq's minister of war, Uthman Rifqi, increasingly antagonized the peasant officers. With a plan to dismiss them becoming known in 1881, Urabi and two other Egyptian officers associated with him protested. When they were arrested, their troops intervened to prevent the ensuing courts-martial, and the khedive appointed the poet Mahmud Sami Pasha al-Barudi, who, though a Circassian, was more acceptable to the rebels, as minister of war. When al-Barudi was replaced later that year, Urabi—whose stature as leader of the peasant opposition by now had skyrocketed—led a demonstration at Abdin Palace on September 9 with demands that included dismissal of the Riyad Pasha government. And so the Assembly was reconvened, with Sharif Pasha coming back as prime minister. Barudi became minister of war and Urabi deputy minister. With an Anglo-French Joint Note in January 1882 promising support for the khedive, the Consultative Assembly and the Urabists drew closer together, resulting in the triumph of the latter for the time being as Barudi, backed by the Assembly, headed a new government in which Urabi was elevated to minister of war, although most of the members still were Turco-Circassians. An increasingly influential Urabi was able to carry out a new policy of promoting peasant officers and raising their pay as well as dismissing many Turko-Circassians. The Assembly asserted its authority, with a Basic Law giving it legislative and budgetary powers, as well as a broader right to supervise the government.

The situation came to a head during 1882. An anti-Urabist plot by Circassian officers came to light. Troops were disorderly at times. There were rumors of plans to overthrow the khedive. And the British (who now had by far the greater economic stake) and the French were concerned that their financial interests in Egypt—and, especially in the British case, the security of the road to India—were in danger. Even British Prime Minister William Gladstone's personal investments were at stake. British officials encouraged the khedive to resist the Urabists, and in May London and Paris called for the end of the Barudi cabinet and for Urabi's exile. With Urabi accusing the khedive of collaborating with European plans to invade, the cabinet resigned, but Tawfiq was persuaded to reappoint him as Minister of War.

Buoyed by rising popularity, Urabi seemed about to control the country as the khedive fled to Alexandria to seek protection from European navies. The pent-up anger of ordinary Egyptians evoked increasing violence, apparently unplanned by anyone. The privileged class of European immigrants clashed with Muslim Egyptians in Alexandria in June. British warships appeared in the Alexandria harbor, as Urabi resisted demands to dismantle his coastal defenses. With the French at the last minute deciding not to participate in the operation, the British navy bombarded Alexandria, and Urabi declared war. He and the khedive pronounced each other a rebel and a traitor, respectively, as outbreaks of violence in the countryside accelerated. Egyptian forces, however, were no equal to the British army, and in the battle of Tal al-Kabir of December 1882, the latter easily prevailed, ending the Urabi Revolution and beginning a long British occupation. Tawfiq was restored to the Khedivate, whereas Urabi and other leaders of his movement were exiled.

UNDER BRITISH RULE

Though still technically an Ottoman land, Egypt had in all but a formal, legalistic sense become part of the British Empire. Backed by the occupying army, a series of British proconsuls bearing the misleading title Consul-General emerged as the real rulers, with the khedives as their rubber stamps. The epitome of racist European arrogance, Lord Cromer

(Sir Evelyn Baring) ruled the country with an iron hand from 1883 to 1907, to be succeeded by Sir Eldon Gorst (1907–1911) and then by Lord (formerly Sir Horatio) Kitchener. Malleable, collaborationist members of the old elite, starting with Nubar Pasha, served as Prime Minister. The various Egyptian ministries had to toe the line of British "advisors."

The British rulers carried out some important reforms. With an eye on collecting Isma'il's debt, they got the economy back on track, making major improvements in agriculture, especially in further developing irrigation. Muhammad Ali's Nile Barrage, now clogged with silt, was restored and improved, and a dam at Aswan (not to be confused with the later High Dam), was completed in 1903, allowing more land to be cultivated on a perennial basis. Within a decade after the occupation began, enhanced agricultural productivity, notably cotton raised for the world market, produced a budget surplus. Such old practices as the subjection of peasants to the whip and to conscripted labor were abolished. Also, there were significant improvements in health conditions.

For outsiders who had no nationalist opinion to express or who were not worried about Britain's authoritarian control, Egypt provided an attractive haven. Thus Syrian intellectuals, particularly Christians, who were unhappy under Ottoman rule flocked to Egypt and played an important role in the development of the country's press. As one case in point, today's leading newspaper, *al-Ahram* ("the Pyramids"), was founded by two Christian brothers from Lebanon, first in Alexandria in 1875 and then revived in Cairo following the British occupation.

On the other hand, the British did not favor improvements in education. Men such as Cromer detested educated "natives." It was not until he had left, in 1907, that the Egyptian University (today's Cairo University) came into existence through volunteer contributions. Even elementary and secondary education for the subject Egyptians was not in favor. Neither did the British want Egypt to industrialize.

The British aborted Egypt's beginnings of constitutional and representative government. The Assembly, which in any case likely would have lost out to the Urabist officers if there had been no occupation, was dissolved. A newly established Legislative Council was largely appointive and had only advisory functions. The Legislative Assembly of 1913, made up mainly of landlords, was a slight improvement. Elective provincial councils emerged only in 1909.

Events in the Sudan provided an important sideshow. The Mahdi's followers annihilated a British-commanded Egyptian force in 1883 as well as the rescue mission under General Charles Gordon sent to Khartoum. Egyptian soldiers commanded by Kitchener finally defeated the rebels in

1898, but in effect Egyptian rule there was over, as the "Anglo-Egyptian" Sudan emerged the following year—with the country now technically a condominium (that is, officially under joint rule), but with the British really in charge. For Egyptians, this would long remain a sore point, with a major aspiration of Egyptian nationalists during the early twentieth century being to restore the unity of the Nile Valley.

A sense of resignation pervaded Egypt during the early years of the occupation. Such a former supporter of the Urabists as Muhammad Abduh (an associate of Afghani) returned from exile to concentrate on reconciling Islam with modern science, insisting on the need for rethinking what scholars in earlier centuries had agreed upon. He pushed his modern ideas as the country's chief mufti (one who issues rulings on Islamic jurisprudence) and as a member of the supreme council of al-Azhar. Upon Abduh's death in 1905, Rashid Rida, of Syrian background, emerged as the leader of the Islamic modernist movement. Although Rida is sometimes considered to have veered in a more traditional direction than his mentor, he, too, articulated innovative ideas about such topics as the caliphate.

A small incident in 1906 in the village of Dinshawai provided a spark that caused the already seething resentment against the British to flare up. When some British officers engaged in pigeon hunting accidentally shot an Egyptian woman in this village, the enraged local people attacked and wounded two of them. Many villagers were arrested, and a special court meted out harsh sentences. Four men were promptly hanged. The potent stuff of legend surviving to this day, the Dinshawai incident provided an intense focus for those who had been oblivious to nationalist sentiment. The fact that it was a Coptic judge, Boutros Ghali Pasha (who as foreign minister had signed the Condominium agreement), reinforced the tendency of Egyptian Muslims to see the occupation in religious terms.

By the turn of the century, new movements emerged representing varying mixtures of loyalty to an Egyptian *watan* (homeland, usually defined as including the Sudan) and to the broader Islamic *ummah* (global community of all Muslims). A French-educated lawyer, Mustafa Kamil, headed a Patriotic Party *(al-Hizb al-Watani)* and delivered fiery speeches invoking nationalist and pan-Islamic themes and demanding an end to the British occupation. Following his death in 1908, the party came under the leadership of Muhammad Farid. Another group with even more pan-Islamic tendencies was the Party of Constitutional Reform, headed by Ali Yusuf, who started a nationalist newspaper, *al-Mu 'ayyad*, in 1889. Both Kamil and Yusuf seem to have been encouraged by Khedive Abbas Hilmi, who, unlike more collaborationist members of his family, tried to resist being a British puppet (by 1913 Lord Kitchener was determined to replace him). Representing a purely secular Egyptian nationalism and a gradualist move toward independence and individual rights was Ahmad Lutfi al-Sayyid's newspaper, *al-Jaridah* (literally, "The Newspaper"), and his Ummah Party (*Hizb al-Ummah*, whose name indicated an attempt to give purely secular content to a religious term), which drew support from big landlords.

Several incidents illustrate the Islamic content in the anticolonial movement. A dispute between Istanbul and Cairo over a small border area found popular sentiment among Egyptians supporting the sultan (now perceived in his role as caliph) against their own British-dominated country. The tendency of some Copts to be particularly willing to collaborate with the occupier—as exemplified by Boutros Ghali's agreement to extend the Suez Canal Company's concession indefinitely, leading to his assassination by a fervent opponent of British rule—threatened to cause tension between Egyptian Christians and Muslims.

From its beginnings in 1914, the First World War helped bring matters to a head by making the occupation more noxious than ever before. With the Ottoman Empire now allying itself with Germany, the British unilaterally—and illegally—declared Egypt a British protectorate (meaning that it was now officially part of the empire, though under its own local ruler). The recalcitrant Khedive Abbas Hilmi made way for a more docile Husayn Kamil (succeeded by his brother Ahmad Fu'ad following his death in 1917), whose title now became "sultan." Ottoman offensives directed at taking the Suez Canal were repelled, and there was little actual fighting on Egyptian territory. But the country became a veritable armed camp, a base from which the British invaded Syria. They ruthlessly requisitioned crops and animals from the peasants and took them away from their villages to form labor battalions on the various war fronts. There was much economic suffering because the British kept cotton prices low while the cost of living shot up. A tight lid was kept on dissent, with any gathering of as many as five people outlawed, as the bitterness against British rule permeated previously apathetic sectors of the population.

But there was reason to think that the end of the war might bring something better. The British referred to the possibility of ending the Capitulations. And President Woodrow Wilson's statement in 1918 favoring the principle of self-determination evoked hope.

A CENTURY OF CHANGE

For better or for worse, the period from 1798 to 1918 brought tremendous changes. The face of the country was transformed, as modern innovations were introduced (in some cases only a little after their appearance in the most developed countries), if mainly for the benefit of the privileged few. Such innovations as perennial irrigation completely changed the countryside, although that was for the benefit of the land-lords. The chaos of the late eighteenth century—and the beginnings of the nineteenth—made way for centralized control. The old pattern of village autonomy disappeared. This provided more security—though not for the peasants from the ruling class—but also more authoritarianism under the foreign Turco-Circassian elite and later under British proconsuls such as Cromer and Kitchener.

Egypt became part of a world market in which it, like the rest of what in later usage is called the Third World, played the role of producer of raw materials for the industrialized countries. Increasingly, that meant trading cotton for the manufactured goods of Britain. Muhammad Ali's attempt to industrialize Egypt failed, a development that clearly meshed with European wishes and, some say, was engineered by Great Britain's imposition of free trade. The ordinary peasants ceased to have rights to the soil they tilled. Arguably, rapacious tax farmers were often exploitative before, but it was in the nineteenth century that a few people, favored by low taxes, came to own the land outright. Improvements in agriculture vastly increased yields, although the cultivators now were producing not for their families but for export—eventually in large part to pay off the massive principal and interest on loans from European investors that the ruling class incurred. The growing numbers of urban workers were badly exploited, and there were only the beginnings of labor union activity. The renewed strategic importance of Egypt as a link between the oceans—connected by railroads and a canal—combined with the greed of European investors to bring it under de facto colonial rule.

Under a new foreign yoke, Egyptians gradually were demanding in-dependence. With the old Turco-Circassian ruling class shrinking, it tended to melt into the indigenous population. A second stratum of the landed class emerged from the local notability, and with the whole coun-try subjected to British rule, the old ethnic division was becoming less relevant, making way for a unified Egyptian nationalism that often not only demonstrated an Islamic component but also incorporated both Mus-lims and Copts.

The introduction of modern medicine enabled the population to ex-plode, particularly from the late nineteenth century. Although diseases such as bilharzia and trichinosis remained endemic, there were major ad-vances, notably in wiping out the bubonic plague. In part a legacy of the Black Death of the 1300s, the population did not exceed 3.5 million in 1800 but approached 10 million a century later. In 1918, it reached almost 13 million.

5

"Liberal" Egypt

As World War I ended, underlying anger over British rule surfaced to fuel what Egyptians would call the 1919 Revolution. On November 13, 1918, only two days after the armistice, a delegation headed by Sa'd Zaghlul, a prominent lawyer who recently had consulted with various other leading figures, sought an audience with the British High Commissioner, Sir Reginald Wingate. Zaghlul's purpose was to demand independence and to call for Egyptian participation in the forthcoming Paris Peace Conference. The British imagined that they could do as they liked with a quiescent Egypt and may have contemplated turning it into a crown colony. Egyptian participation in the Peace Conference was not on the agenda, and the inclusion of Syria at the Conference further rubbed salt in Egyptian wounds. Zaghlul also asked permission to head a delegation to London to present its demands. This was the beginning of the Wafd [delegation] Party, which would soon emerge as the organization representing the Egyptian people and sure to win any free election. Zaghlul would come to be dubbed "the father of the Egyptians."

But London refused to accept either Zaghlul's delegation or even an alternative group, as Wingate proposed, led by tame members of the British-backed Egyptian government led by Rushdi Pasha. Zaghlul's followers formed local committees and collected depositions authorizing the

Wafd to act as the nation's sole representative, the appropriateness of which now was so obvious that Rushdi did not dare accept a later proposal by Wingate that he head a delegation to London that did not include Zaghlul. Wafdist pamphlets permeated the country, and when Rushdi's government resigned, the sultan for a while did not dare appoint a new prime minister in the face of pressure from Zaghlul. The nationalist movement now constituted such a threat to their country's British rulers that in March 1919 they sent Zaghlul and three of his associates to exile in Malta.

THE 1919 REVOLUTION

Zaghlul's exile provided the match to set the country on fire. Massive demonstrations and strikes ensued in cities and villages throughout Egypt. Guerrilla attacks on British troops and on telephone lines and railroads evoked harsh suppression by military courts and threats to retaliate by destroying whole villages as the implementation of the marital law established during the war intensified. With even the most ardent collaborators, such as big landowners who sometimes faced attacks by peasants, cowed into silence, it seemed as though the country was speaking with one mind. Copts marched against the British no less than did the Muslim majority. And women joined in, too.

The British sent General Sir Edmund Allenby, the recent conqueror of Palestine and Syria, to replace Wingate and get the situation under control. To try to calm the situation down, Allenby released Zaghlul and his associates and even allowed them to proceed to Paris, only to face the devastating news that President Woodrow Wilson had reneged on his support for self-determination in this case by formally recognizing the British protectorate, as did the peace conference. Strikes and demonstrations continued in Egypt.

Another response of the British government was to send a commission headed by Lord Milner to study the causes of unrest and to make recommendations on how to preserve the protectorate. Aside from the collaborationist government, all Egyptians boycotted the Milner Mission, as militant offshoots of the nationalist movement accelerated their guerrilla campaign. So impressed was Milner with the Egyptian people's solidarity that his report went beyond the initial instructions and recognized the need to terminate the protectorate, that is, to allow Egypt to gain its formal independence. Leaving Paris disappointed, Zaghlul proceeded to London in June 1920 to talk with Milner after the latter's return home, but the gap between a nationalist movement and a British government still committed to something less than real independence for Egypt made the talks a futile endeavor, and the Egyptian collaborationists were too intimidated by public support for the Wafd to conclude an agreement with the British on their own. Now back in Egypt, Zaghlul opposed the delegation the government sent to London in June 1921, and in December the British exiled him again, first to Aden and then to the Seychelles, in the Indian Ocean.

The British decided that with even the collaborationists not daring to reach an agreement with them, the only solution was unilaterally to declare an end to the protectorate. Thus with a declaration issued by Allenby in February 1922, Egypt officially became an independent state but, in light of major rights reserved by Britain, remained a de facto part of the empire. The intention was to undercut the Wafd to work with collaborationist leaders such as Rushdi and his colleague Adli Pasha without necessitating the kind of agreement with them that they could not defend in the face of nationalist criticism.

Allenby's unilateral declaration of Egyptian sovereignty "absolutely reserved" four important matters for continuing British control. The four reserved points included: (1) the security of communications of the British Empire, (2) the defense of the country, (3) the protection of foreign interests and minorities, and (4) the Sudan, which Egyptian nationalists considered to be an integral part of their country, but which now officially would continue to be an Anglo-Egyptian condominium effectively ruled by Britain. Now claiming to head an independent country, Sultan Ahmad Fu'ad became King Fu'ad. The martial law that the country had endured under the British ended in 1923.

THE "LIBERAL" ORDER

Formal independence ushered in what many writers call Egypt's "liberal age." This is meaningful to the extent that the country had a largely liberal, that is, market, economy (if less so after 1930), in contrast to the socialism of a later era. It is also meaningful in the sense that the prevailing nationalism, at least in the beginning, was one that united everyone in the country without distinction of religion in a territorially based Egyptian nation. And there emerged a considerable amount of freedom to form political parties and other associations, to speak and write freely, and to contest elections. Under the new constitution drawn up by a commission appointed by the government (and in large part designed to restrain popular majorities expected to support the Wafd) and put into effect in 1923, there was an element of democracy, but always partially and sometimes completely eclipsed by a combination of factors that included a narrow franchise, continuing foreign rule, and power still wielded by kings and oligarchical cliques.

The 1923 constitution established a structure of government that in many ways paralleled that of European constitutional monarchies. There was an elected Chamber of Deputies, though chosen at first (and again for a while starting in 1925) indirectly in a two-stage process. The cabinet (headed by a prime minister) was responsible to it (i.e., requiring majority support in the chamber, as in other parliamentary systems). The electoral law of 1923 extended the right to vote to all adult males, although this sporadically was replaced by a more restrictive franchise that included a property-ownership requirement. The female half of the population did not obtain the suffrage during the "liberal" era, but a women's movement emerged under the leadership of Huda Sha'rawi, with some members shocking conservatives by publicly unveiling their faces.

Two other main forces recurrently belied the reality of democracy. First of all, British troops remained in Egypt and regularly interfered in the country's politics. Secondly, the king retained important authority—to dismiss parliament or the cabinet, to approve bills passed by parliament (only a two-thirds vote in parliament could override the king's objection), to appoint two-fifths of the members of the Senate (upper house), and the like, not to mention special rights in such matters as religious institutions and army commissions. In most European countries, such provisions of a constitution would have been exercised on the monarch's behalf by a cabinet responsible only to parliament. But King Fu'ad (until his death in 1936) and then his son King Faruq not only treated these as personal powers but also augmented them by disregarding the constitution altogether and sometimes abrogating it for extensive periods. There was a regular pattern of royal alliances with establishment religious leaders, including the rectors of al-Azhar.

The British tended generally to support the king against the Wafd. The latter long had overwhelming popular support, although its credibility eventually eroded. There were other authentic parties, but most of the groups given that label were mere ad hoc cliques organized on behalf of the monarch to subvert the democratic process.

The ups and downs of the Wafd reflect the struggle between democratic and authoritarian features of the Egyptian government during this period. Despite its dissatisfaction with bogus independence and a constitution drawn up by the collaborationist "king's men" and designed to thwart popular control, Zaghlul decided to contest the general elections held in January 1924. His party won a remarkable victory—obtaining 195 of the 214 seats in the Chamber—that showed the extent to which it was synonymous with Egypt. But a crisis emerged later that year when the British commander in chief and governor-general of the Sudan, Sir Lee Stack, was assassinated in Cairo. The Wafd bore no responsibility for this, but the British responded with harsh demands that Zaghlul could not accept, and they occupied the customs house in Alexandria. As a result, his government resigned in November, and one of the "king's men," Ahmad Ziwar Pasha, took his place, with parliament dissolved. The king's men were organized in the form of the narrowly based Unity *(Ittihad)* Party designed to reward opportunistic politicians. Despite massive governmental interference, new elections resulted in a Wafdist majority, but the response of the king—in what in effect was a "palace coup" against the constitution—was simply to dissolve parliament again. The king and his men hoped to be rid of the Wafdist challenge, but this time pressures from the British prevented the royalists from going as far as they wished, and elections in 1926 gave the Wafd a big majority again, although now Zaghlul did not dare to demand to form his own government in the face of continuing royal hostility and thus settled for participating in a cabinet dominated by small parties.

Zaghlul died in 1927, and his successor as head of the Wafd, Mustafa Nahhas Pasha eventually headed a new government in March 1928. But the king dismissed him three months later to rule autocratically without a parliament. He relented again in October of the next year by restoring the constitution and allowing elections, in which the Wafd again won the preponderance of seats.

The most blatant resort to authoritarian rule began in 1930. Another Wafdist government came into existence in January of that year but made way for still another palace coup in June, with a propalace cabinet headed by Isma'il Sidqi, who formed his own so-called People's Party. A new authoritarian constitution replaced that of 1923. For a while, even the new constitution was repealed in favor of absolute monarchy. The 1923 constitution was not restored until 1935. Again, there were relatively free elections in 1936, and Nahhas was able to form another government, which, however, made way for a royalist cabinet in December 1937, followed by dissolution of parliament and corrupt elections designed to keep the Wafd out of power, a goal that succeeded until a British *diktat* brought Nahhas back for a while as the head of a new government during World War II.

Even the Wafd failed to provide a model for democratic leadership. Zaghlul behaved in a blatantly authoritarian manner, running his party with an iron hand. He would not tolerate criticism and sometimes ardently applied restrictions on the press that he opposed when out of office.

Except among a small progressive faction of the party, there was little interest in social reform in a country made up mainly of impoverished, landless peasants whom the Wafdists and others directed to the polls with instructions on how to vote. Splinter political parties, such as the breakaway Sa'dists (named for Zaghlul) after 1937, were not fundamentally different. An earlier breakaway from the Wafd, the Liberal Constitutionalists, was even more clearly a landlord party. In any case, none of these parties posed a popular challenge to the Wafd. One constant was the equation of truly free elections with Wafdist landslides, but the party was allowed to head the government for a total of only seven years during the three-decade "liberal" period.

CONTINUING STRUGGLE FOR INDEPENDENCE

An overriding goal of Egyptian nationalists during the decades following formal independence was to end the British occupation and interference in the country's affairs. The Stack assassination brought a setback to national aspirations, as Ziwar Pasha's government acquiesced in all British demands—for heavy reparations and punishment of accused "terrorists" and withdrawal of Egyptian troops from the Sudan. In 1927, the British squashed calls for an end to certain British controls over the army, including the appointment of an Egyptian to replace the British commander and ending the membership of a Briton in the Army Council. Sporadic proposals by London for a treaty of alliance of the sort that increasingly defined British relations with other Arab countries came to naught in the face of Wafdist opposition to an arrangement that did not restore the Sudan to Egypt and that allowed British troops to remain in Cairo and Alexandria.

The mid-1930s witnessed a desire on both sides to compromise in the face of a growing Italian threat in the region. With a new Wafdist government headed by Nahhas installed, negotiations between the two sides resulted in the conclusion of an Anglo-Egyptian Treaty of Alliance in 1936 in which the British agreed to defend Egypt from aggression. The treaty limited the future British military presence—once Egypt constructed certain roads and barracks—mainly to the Suez Canal area, with the number of land forces limited to 10 thousand except in wartime, when the limit would not apply and when Egyptian communications facilities would be at Britain's disposal. The British naval base in Alexandria would be terminated after eight years. The treaty also allowed Egyptian troops to return to the Sudan and Egyptians to immigrate there, basically restoring the situation that existed before the Stack assassination. The British envoy would henceforth be an ambassador rather than a high commissioner, and there would be no more British personnel in the Egyptian army and police, aside from a British military mission to advise Egyptian forces. Of unanticipated significance in relation to the later army involvement in politics, Britain would no longer restrict the size of the Egyptian armed forces. The treaty ended Britain's protection of foreigners and minorities, and the British agreed to support an end to the capitulations, which was achieved with the conclusion of a separate agreement at Montreaux the following year. Also, a British commitment to support Egypt's membership in the League of Nations led to its admission in 1937. In effect, Egypt was still in many ways an informal part of the British Empire, and the Wafd's acceptance of the treaty helped to undermine its legitimacy with some nationalists, but this limited occupation in the guise of an alliance had at least moved Egypt a step closer to real independence.

POVERTY AND INDUSTRIALIZATION

Economic conditions deteriorated in important ways. With the population increasing from about 13 million in 1918 to about 21 million in 1952, there was little improvement in overall productivity. Unlike during previous decades, the amount of land under cultivation remained about the same, although there was some increase in perennial irrigation, but prices for cotton and other agricultural products that Egypt exported underwent decline. According to one estimate, per capita income suffered about a 25 percent drop between 1913 and 1948.

Unequal distribution of wealth meant that although a few enjoyed luxurious lives, the vast majority suffered dire poverty. With most people still living in the countryside and depending on agriculture for their livelihood, nearly half the peasant families were landless, and millions of others owned minuscule plots that could not provide even minimal subsistence. By contrast, the top 1 percent of landowners held nearly three-quarters of the land. The same group of big landowners dominated political life, providing a substantial majority of members of the Egyptian cabinet during the "liberal" period.

Millions of villagers migrated to cities during this period. Cairo grew from less than 800,000 in 1917 to more than two million by the late 1940s, with most of its new inhabitants living in miserable slums. Mainly after the end of the Capitulations in 1937, Egypt experienced some important industrialization. Bank Misr (the Bank of Egypt), founded by Tal'at Harb in 1920, took the lead in this endeavor, providing capital for several types of factories, notably for manufacturing textiles. Egypt pushed further ahead in industrialization than most of the Middle East, but by 1952 this represented only about one-fifth of the country's gross national product (GNP). And now the industrialists increasingly were Egyptians, although the foreigners who had so long virtually monopolized business activity still played a disproportionate role in that area of life, particularly at the higher levels. With workers suffering from incredibly low pay and bad working conditions, union activity appeared, resulting in several strikes during the late 1940s. Small communist factions emerged, mainly among the foreign minorities and Jews.

ISLAMIC UPSURGE

By the late 1930s, signs of Islamic resurgence were clear. The liberal, secular nature of the 1919 Revolution and the 1923 Constitution notwithstanding, Islamic ways of thinking about politics and society were deeply entrenched. Some have said that even in 1919, when Muslims and Copts struggled together for Egyptian independence and the middle classes identified with the secular concept of an Egyptian nation, the Muslim masses tended to think in terms of defending the lands of Islam from rule by disbelievers. And some recent commentators see a contradiction between the 1923 Constitution's proclamation of the Egyptian nation as the source of all law and the vague declaration in the same document that Islam was the state religion as well as brouhaha in the parliament in 1924 when the Turkish government abolished the office of caliph, the holder of which, according to Islamic doctrine, was the formal head of a worldwide political community, rather than a strictly religious figure. The alliance of the palace and the religious establishment at al-Azhar was a constant factor of Egyptian politics during this time. The right to appoint religious leaders generally remained, as before, in the hands of the king. And both King Fu'ad—who responded to the Turkish action by calling an international Muslim Congress to meet in Cairo in 1925 to deal with the question of the caliphate—and his successor, King Faruq, recurrently aspired to gain the office of caliph for themselves or at least wrapped themselves in this issue to solidify their own support. Parliament made only a few minor changes in the application of Islamic law in such matters as marriage and inheritance.

A secular tendency dominated writings published in the 1920s. Following the abolition of the Ottoman caliphate, a prominent religious scholar, Ali Abd al-Raziq, wrote a book that disputed the traditional connection between religion and state in Islam, arguing that the union of the two in earlier times was not an inherent part of the faith. But although his views won respect in intellectual circles, such ideas met violent rejection, with al-Raziq penalized by having his diploma as a religious authority revoked. And when another Egyptian writer, Taha Hussein, published a book arguing that what had been considered pre-Islamic poetry actually was a product of a later age, he evoked a great furor, for this undermined an important tool backing the traditional interpretation of the Qur'an.

Leading writers shifted from a Western, liberal orientation to increased emphasis on Islam by the late 1920s and 1930s. Even those who had been in the forefront of the modern, Westernizing trend dealt more and more with religious topics to defend Islamic ideas from Western criticism and to assert the superiority of their civilization.

Starting in 1928, the reaction against secularism begat a new movement in the form of the Society of the Muslim Brothers. The founder was Hasan al-Banna, a devout, magnetic young schoolteacher in Ismailia. During the following century, the Muslim Brothers would stand in the forefront of those in Egypt and the Islamic world generally who called for re-Islamization—for reversing secularization and restoring the Shari'ah, substituting the Islamic identity for nationalism insofar as the two were in conflict, and resisting Western domination. Led mainly by those with modern education rather than by religious scholars (ulama) and organized hierarchically, with al-Banna at the apex as General Guide, the Muslim Brothers hardly represented a throwback to traditional Islam.

In many ways, the Muslim Brothers represented a synthesis of modernity and Islam. They called for rethinking older concepts and played down such prominent ideas as that of restoring the caliphate, but nevertheless fervently demanded the creation of a truly Islamic society. The society grew to be several hundred thousand strong during this period—two million in 1948, according to one estimate—and appeared in the forefront of militant opposition to British rule and to the Zionist threat to the Muslim Palestinians. Its secret apparatus recurrently assassinated Egyptian leaders accused of selling out their country—and the overall Islamic homeland—to foreign interests. Among its many activities in the realm of supporting the well-being of poor Egyptians, it provided soup kitchens for the unemployed and electrification for some villages as well as establishing industries that provided employment and material necessities. It called for social justice, and some of its members would later write about the socialist nature of Islam.

Other radical movements emerged that combined Islamic ideas with Arab and Egyptian nationalism and demonstrated fascist influence. Such was Ahmad Hussein's Young Egypt (Misr al-Fatat), founded in 1933 and later named the Egyptian Socialist Party. Mobilizing a youth militia of

Green Shirts, Young Egypt called for ending foreign domination and creating an Egyptian empire that would lead the Islamic world and the East in general.

PAN-ARAB INVOLVEMENT

Liberal Egyptian nationalists tended to see their movement as totally distinct from Arab nationalism. Zaghlul told the Paris Peace Conference that his country's problem was "not an Arab problem" at all and belittled Arab unity as adding "one zero to another zero." Such people as the writer Lutfi al-Sayyid, who has been credited with providing the most solid ideological basis for Egyptian nationalism, claimed his country had preserved a "Pharaonic core" that not only distinguished it from the Arabs but also would allow it to be confident that Western influences would not undermine its Egyptian character. And unlike the Arab nationalism of Syria and Palestine that insisted on the oneness of Muslim and Christian Arabs, Muslim Egyptian involvement in the eastern Arab world long tended to reflect Islamic more than secular Arab ties.

Although Arab identity did not displace Egyptian nationalism, it was a reality that did not have to wait for a later period to appear. Egypt's territorial distinctiveness notwithstanding, its linguistic, religious, and cultural commonalities with the other Arabs could not indefinitely prevent Arabism from eclipsing the notion of a purely Pharaonic identity that was so fashionable in the 1920s. Together with the opportunism of Egyptian political leaders looking for a role in a larger arena, this led to increasing involvement in Arab Asia, particularly after the conclusion of the 1936 Anglo-Egyptian Treaty.

Several specific situations accelerated such involvement. First, the question of Palestine became more and more a concern for many Egyptians but also provided Egyptian politicians a way of competing in the Arab world. Secondly, Egyptian leaders sought to counterbalance potential rivals for leadership in the eastern Arab world. From the 1920s on, members of the Hashimite family—British client rulers—sat on the thrones of Transjordan and Iraq. Amir Abdullah ruled the former and his brother, King Faysal, the latter. They came from the Hijaz (western Arabia), where their father was the ruler until the Sa'udi family of Najd (central Arabia) invaded it in the mid-1920s, resulting in the present Kingdom of Saudi Arabia. The Sa'udis and the Hashimites long carried on a blood feud because the former threatened to return to the Hijaz. The Hashimites aspired to put someone from their family on the throne of Syria, too, where Faysal had been king for a while before being driven out by the French. The struggle for Syria long remained a central feature of inter-Arab politics. The struggle involved all of geographic Syria, including Lebanon and Palestine. As for the latter, Amir Abdullah professed solidarity with the Arab Palestinians but ardently hoped for an alliance with the Zionists that would facilitate his objective of annexing at least part of Palestine, and Israeli historians now have documented the fact that he secretly was in cahoots with them all along. In this situation, Egypt established an informal alliance with Saudi Arabia to thwart Hashimite dominance in the area.

WORLD WAR II

The outbreak of World War II in September 1939 brought home Egypt's continuing subordination to Great Britain. Although Egypt remained technically neutral almost until the end of the war in 1945 (finally declaring war on Germany only to be invited to the San Francisco Conference that adopted the United Nations Charter), the British military presence accelerated, as allowed by the 1936 treaty. In the fall of 1942, one of the war's great battles occurred at El Alamein, on Egyptian territory west of Alexandria, but without Egyptian participation in the conflict. Many nationalists saw Germany as a possible liberator from British imperialism, and King Faruq wrote a sympathetic letter to Hitler, perhaps as insurance in case the latter emerged victorious. The British could not depend on the series of non-Wafdist governments in office during the early years of the war, even though they complied with demands to sever diplomatic relations with the Axis powers.

This situation induced Britain to bring Nahhas back as the head of a Wafd government in a way that further belied Egyptian independence. The Wafd angered the British at the beginning of the war by asking for a commitment to replace the 1936 treaty with one more favorable to Egypt. Yet not only was this the only major force that had not shown pro-German sympathies, but its popularity still was such that only it could provide the kind of legitimacy needed during wartime. With the German threat growing and following futile British requests to the king to call on Nahhas to form a new government, British tanks appeared outside the palace, and Ambassador Sir Miles Lampton tramped up the stairs to call for the king's abdication but then agreed to his plea for "another chance." The crude way the British brought it to power in this humiliating "February 4 Incident" exposed the king's servility. And it eroded the Wafd's credibility as a nationalist force. So did a dispute between Nahhas and a member of his cabinet, Makram Ubayd, whose expulsion of the party later in the year and formation of a new party, the Independent Wafdist Bloc, was followed by publication of a *Black Book* exposing his former party's financial scandals.

Although subsequent elections brought another impressive Wafdist victory, the king dismissed the Nahhas government in 1944 as the turn of the tide of war made it less imperative for the British to keep the party in office. Knowing that the elections held the following year were being rigged, the Wafd boycotted them, leaving the government to the "king's men" during the latter half of the 1940s.

The wartime period also led to further developments in Egypt's inter-Arab role. With British Foreign Minister Anthony Eden giving his support for Arab unity in 1942 a series of plans emanated from Transjordan and Iraq for unification of the Fertile Crescent under Hashimite leadership. It was largely to thwart such schemes that Nahhas called a conference of Arab countries that met in Alexandria in 1944 and then another conference the following year, which established a regional organization called the League of Arab States (or Arab League). The name had an appeal to believers in Arab solidarity, but the League's Charter actually perpetuated the principle of separate sovereign Arab states. Considering the fractiousness of inter-Arab politics, the league hardly moved the region toward unity. But with its headquarters established in Cairo and with a prominent Egyptian politician, Azzam Pasha, named Secretary General, the organization henceforth enhanced Egypt's role as the center of the Arab world.

CONFLICT OVER PALESTINE

The question of Palestine pulled Egypt into Arab affairs. With a population of about 750,000 that was overwhelmingly Arab and with only a small Jewish minority (less than 60,000) that was mostly a result of immigration from Europe inspired by the recently organized Zionist movement, which hoped to create a Jewish state there, Palestine at the end of World War I was fully a part of the Arab world. But in the Balfour Declaration of 1917 the British government stated its support for a Jewish "national home" there. And when as part of the peace settlement the League of Nations assigned Palestine as a mandate to Britain, it incorporated the provisions of the Balfour Declaration into the mandate document. Although contradictory commitments in the Balfour Declaration and the growing conflict in Palestine slowed this down, the British decades allowed the Zionist movement to organize massive Jewish settlements in Palestine to the extent that the ratio of Jews and Arabs came to be one to two. For the Arab Palestinians and the Arab world generally the specter of losing Palestine and the displacement of its Arab population emerged as their most passionate concern.

Paralleling the overall weakness of their Arab identity at the time and also reflecting the centrality of the struggle for their own country's independence from Britain, Egyptians tended at first to show less interest in the Palestine question than did other Arabs. Some Egyptian political leaders even expressed sympathy for moderate Zionist goals, although not for turning Palestine into a Jewish state. But concern grew as Palestine's Arab character seemed increasingly threatened, particularly after the outbreak of a Palestinian Arab Revolt against the British and Zionists in 1936, but even then the Egyptian response often tended to be moderate. Recognizing the Palestine issue as a popular cause, King Faruq used it to bolster his position vis-à-vis the Wafd and in inter-Arab affairs. Demonstrations against the Balfour Declaration provided a staple for recurrent student political activity. And groups such as the Muslim Brothers and Young Egypt ardently promoted solidarity with the Arab Palestinians.

The UN General Assembly's adoption of a proposal to partition Palestine into Jewish and Arab states (with an internationalized Jerusalem) in November 1947 brought the issue to a head and led to military involvement by Egypt and other Arab states. Pointing to the disproportionate part of Palestine assigned to the Jewish minority, the Arab states proclaimed their opposition to the plan. In fact, King Abdullah of Transjordan reached an agreement with the Zionists according to which he would accept a Jewish state while they and he would divide up the areas the partition plan left to the Arab Palestinians. Considering its longtime policy of containing Hashimite expansion, the Egyptian government was determined to prevent Abdullah from realizing this ambition, and this motive meshed with popular pressures in Egypt to stand up against the Zionists.

Popular anger in Egypt grew as civil war raged in Palestine after November 1947. The Jewish state that took shape even before it was officially declared the following May 15 was expanding into areas the General Assembly had designated for the Arab Palestinians, and the Arab population was being uprooted. Various groups—notably the Muslim Brothers, but also Young Egypt and even the Wafd—organized volunteers to fight in Palestine and blamed the regime for standing aside. Calls were out for soldiers to desert and join their fellow Arabs in the struggle, and some army officers provided training on the side.

Under Prime Minister Nuqrashi Pasha, a Sa'dist appointed by the king in 1945, the Egyptian government was sucked into the fire in Palestine even as it eagerly demonstrated its receptivity to compromise solutions. In addition to popular pressure to support the Arab Palestinians, power politics helped pull Egypt into Palestine to thwart King Abdullah, who, along with his Hashimite kinsmen in Baghdad, was dead set on intervening. All of this flew in the face of the fact that the Egyptian army, with defective weapons resulting from governmental deals with cronies, was woefully unprepared and heavily outnumbered by the Jewish forces, who had the beginnings of their own arms industry as well as weapons now coming from Czechoslovakia. Not until May 11, 1948, did Nuqrashi inform a secret meeting of the Egyptian Senate of the likelihood of military intervention. The movement of Egyptian and other Arab troops came less than four days later as the British finished their withdrawal and the new state of Israel officially declared its existence.

Successes for Egyptian troops did not last long. They moved northward toward Tel Aviv—mostly within areas the partition resolution had designated for the Arab state—and also into east-central Palestine (part of the area designated for the Arab Palestinians but soon to constitute the "West Bank" of Jordan). By the early part of 1949, the Israelis had occupied about 78 percent of Palestine, including much of what had been designated for the "Arab state," and three-quarters of a million Arab Palestinians found themselves uprooted from their homes. Egyptian forces held only the narrow "Gaza Strip," which they continued to administer during the following years, but without annexing it. Israeli forces even penetrated into Sinai during the early part of 1949, and only British threats forced them to withdraw. In February, Egypt became the first of a series of Arab states to enter into armistice agreements that froze in place the Israeli military conquests.

The realization of the nature of the Arab disaster (nakbah, as the defeat came to be known) provided a powerful shock to Egyptian domestic politics. Martial law, declared at the beginning of the war, remained in effect. Several foreign-owned institutions suffered from bombings, as did the local Jewish minority, starting its eventual departure from the country. An attempt by the government to liquidate the Muslim Brothers at the end of 1948 led to Nuqrashi's assassination by a member of that organization. Al-Banna in turn was assassinated in February of the next year, apparently by agents of the king, and Hasan al-Hudaybi succeeded as General Guide. The defeat in Palestine helped bring to a head a revolutionary situation created by the deeper socioeconomic and political malaise, as did the continuing crisis in Anglo-Egyptian relations.

SUEZ AND THE SUDAN

As World War II ended, demands for more authentic independence accelerated. With British troops still present in Cairo until 1947 and not in a hurry to withdraw to the Canal Zone as agreed in 1936, Nahhas renewed the call in July 1945 for an end to the British occupation and for the "unity of the Nile Valley." This remained the basic demand of various Egyptian governments during the following decade as they faced strident anti-British demands and sometimes attacks on British troops and as the Muslim Brothers and other opposition groups—and student demonstrators—agitated for an end to British imperialism. Negotiations initiated by the Sidqi government during 1946 resulted in a draft treaty that would have renewed the alliance with Britain, which agreed to evacuate Egypt by the end of 1949 with the right to return during wartime. But in the face of strong nationalist sentiment, the agreement foundered over the question of the Sudan, where opinion now was divided over the issue of independence or union with Egypt. An Egyptian appeal to the Security Council in 1947 brought no results.

Egypt had a relatively fair general election in January 1950 (its last such so far). Pointing to its decline from its former position as the undisputed voice of the nation, the Wafd won only 40 percent of the popular vote this time. But it won a big majority of the seats, and the last Wafdist government, the seventh and last headed by Nahhas, came to power. It lasted two years as the country underwent growing turmoil.

The Wafdist government entered into a new round of negotiations with the British. A proposal by Britain, France, the United States, and Turkey in 1951 that the Suez Base be turned into a multilateral one, with the formation of a Middle East Command, evoked a strident objection by Egypt, and the talks ended soon afterward. Instead, the Egyptian parliament voted to unilaterally abrogate the 1936 treaty and proclaim Faruq King of Egypt and the Sudan.

British troops in the Canal Zone were facing attacks by guerrillas organized by various Egyptian factions, particularly the Muslim Brothers, sometimes with the covert backing of the Egyptian government. In January 1952 British forces attacked the Egyptian auxiliary police force in Ismailia that were accused of supporting the guerrillas, killing about 50. This provided the spark that on January 26 ("Black Saturday") brought an explosion among the already highly combustible populace of Cairo

and demonstrated that the country was on the verge of a popular revolution. It is not entirely clear whether the reaction was spontaneous or
whether some elements of the Muslim Brothers started it. But before the
army could get the situation under control, the "burning of Cairo" occurred as mobs targeted hotels, bars, cinemas, and other symbols of luxury
and privilege.

The Nahhas government was dismissed on January 27 and martial law
declared. A series of shaky cabinets appointed by the king appeared fleet-
ingly during the following six months—under Ali Mahir until March 1,
then under Nagib Hilali, under Hussein Sirri from July 2, and finally under Hilali again. The old order was crumbling, and a little-known group
of young army officers waited to replace it.

6

Nasir's Revolutionary Era

During the early hours of July 23, 1952, a military faction calling itself the "Free Officers" carried out a coup d'état that ushered in a new era for Egypt and the Middle East. The Free Officers consisted of perhaps 300 members, nominally led by General Muhammad Nagib but in reality by 34-year-old Lieutenant Colonel Gamal Abd al-Nasir. Quickly and almost bloodlessly taking the reins, they made way for what ultimately would with some justification be known as the Egyptian Revolution as they carried out radical social changes, a process begun the following September with the promulgation of the Middle East's first land reform program. And the new regime eventually brought Egypt into the center of the Arab nationalist movement to an unprecedented degree.

Although deeper changes came slowly, the Free Officers immediately swept the old governmental system away. The country came under the rule of a newly constituted 14-member Revolutionary Command Council (RCC), made up of the leaders of the Free Officer movement, as demonstrations were banned. The institutions of the 1923 constitution were no more, and new arrangements that eventually emerged put power in the hands of a populist authoritarian president, who would recurrently win reelection unopposed with near unanimity. On July 26, the new rulers effectively disposed of the monarchy, as King Faruq was escorted to a yacht in Alexandria, given a 21-gun salute, and sent on his way to the Italian Riviera. The country technically remained a monarchy until almost a year later, with Faruq succeeded by his infant son, Fu'ad II, under a regency council made up of leading Free Officers. Egypt formally became a republic in June 1953, with Nagib its first president. Although the Free Officers at first installed Ali Mahir, a holdover from the old regime, as prime minister, he did not last long.

WHO WERE THE FREE OFFICERS?

The Free Officers came from the middle ranks of the army, ranging from captain to colonel. They were relatively young, that is, in their thirties. The apparent exception was the nominal head of the RCC, General Nagib, a much-respected man known for his capable performance during the Palestine War. He soon replaced Mahir as prime minister and became president once the country was declared a republic. Although Nagib soon gained popularity and momentarily eclipsed his comrades, the youthful rebels picked him almost at the last minute as a sort of figurehead who could help legitimize their coup.

The real leader of the movement from the beginning was Nasir. He was a bright and magnetic man—and one who within a few years would entrance large audiences, although at first he was shy about speaking to crowds. The way he avoided self-aggrandizement, as in continuing to live in the same house as before (though much enlarged), by not using his office to accumulate personal wealth (he had only LE620 in his personal bank account when he died), and by not favoring his own relatives as associates and successors, set him apart from most Middle Eastern leaders. He proudly pointed to the fact that his driver's son gained admission to Cairo University while his daughter Muna's examination was one point too low for her to get in. Also, observers noted the relatively gentle style of his authoritarianism that could boast of how it had shed so little blood and created so few exiles while carrying out a revolution, although political prisoners, torture, and use of secret police would recurrently characterize his regime, too. And he was a clever manipulator of people, once allegedly boasting in his later years that he had read Machiavelli's *The Prince* 17 times. (Of future significance, his copy of the book was a gift from his colleague, Anwar al-Sadat, who already had read it.) Nasir had served with honor in Palestine by holding out while surrounded by the enemy. In his booklet, *The Philosophy of the Revolution* (said actually to have come from the pen of his close friend, the journalist Muhammad Hasanayn Haykal), he related that during this time his thoughts were on Egypt, which he saw as the site of the real battle. He was much involved in nationalist activities as a youth and seems, like so many of his generation, to have been associated temporarily with more than one radical political movement. The goal of liberating his country from foreign domination and from corrupt local rulers may have motivated him to become an army officer. The dignity of Egypt and the Arabs generally always remained an obsession for him, as did his preference for the ordinary people and his resentment of those who had looked down on them.

Like others who were not part of the upper classes, Nasir failed to get admitted into the Military Academy on his first try. He resorted to studying law for a short time. But the enlargement of the officer's corps following the conclusion of the Anglo-Egyptian Treaty of 1936 (as graduation from secondary school replaced property qualifications as a prerequisite to admission to the Military Academy) gave him and others of similar social origin the opportunity he had sought, although those from upper-class backgrounds still could be expected to keep them out of the higher military ranks.

In all this, Nasir was typical of the leadership of the Free Officers, most of whom entered the newly enlarged Military Academy at about the same time and graduated in the late 1930s. Most came from similar modest class backgrounds, but none from really poor families. Some emerged from families with modest land holdings of 100 acres or so, evoking recent comparisons with the conservative Russian *kulaks* ("rich peasants") who resisted collectivization of agriculture under Stalin. This purports to explain the moderate nature of the Egyptian Revolution's policies. In only a few cases, the Free Officers, such as Abd al-Hakim Amir, came from relatively large landowning families.

These revolutionaries had no fixed ideology. Some of them, notably Sadat, had been associated with the Muslim Brothers, others with Young Egypt, the Wafd, or the Sa'dists. A few, notably Khalid Muhi al-Din, had Marxist tendencies but generally would remain on the sidelines. Most were not affiliated with any political party. They could agree to little more than a set of six principles stressing opposition to imperialism, feudalism, and monopoly capitalism and calling for social justice, a strengthened army, and the restoration of parliamentary rule. The actual policies of the new government would only slowly emerge.

THE STRUGGLE FOR POWER

The Free Officers had no fixed ideas about what type of political system to establish. There was a widespread idea that it was too early to restore democracy, and American diplomats in Cairo—who embraced the Free Officers and Nasir in particular for a while—were as keen as anybody about the need for a "transitional dictatorship." Although there is some controversy about Nasir's original position on this matter, at least in later years he spoke about the tendency of landlords, as was so well known during the previous "liberal" age, to make democracy a sham by herding illiterate peasants to the polls. He also spoke of the danger that competitive political parties would be infiltrated by foreign powers and predicted that Western-style democracy would not be feasible for another generation.

Nasir gradually consolidated his power in the face of several challenges. At first, the RCC ordered the old political parties to reform themselves and then, when the results were disappointing, abolished them. The Liberation Rally, the first of a series of regime-sponsored political movements, took their place. The constitution was suspended at the beginning of 1953 in favor of a three-year transition period.

A struggle between Nasir and Nagib emerged. By mid-1953 the latter held the offices of president, prime minister, and chairmanship of the RCC, and his popularity tempted him to assert himself. He demanded a veto over RCC decisions. Calling not only for real power but also for a quick return to constitutional government, Nagib resigned in protest from the positions he held in February 1954, with Nasir taking over as prime minister and head of the RCC, but Nagib was restored to the presidency again in response to popular demonstrations and as the cavalry, commanded by Khalid Muhi al-Din, mutinied. Then the RCC cleverly announced that it was restoring the constitution and political parties, an action that seemed to be taking the country back to the old regime. Nagib took back the positions of prime minister and chairmanship of the RCC for a short time. This evoked widespread protests led by the Liberation Rally that soon returned Nasir as prime minister. Having lost in the struggle for power and accused of working with the Muslim Brethren, Nagib was relieved of the presidency before the end of the year and put under house arrest.

Nasir also clashed with the Muslim Brethren. The Free Officers had amicable relations with them at first. The ban on political parties did not cover them, as they were officially a religious association. But as the most powerful mass organization in the country, they wanted a veto over decisions of the RCC, which was not forthcoming. The Brothers condemned the regime's agreement with Britain in 1954, and a member of the movement's "secret apparatus" barely failed in an attempt to assassinate Nasir as he was delivering a speech in Alexandria in October 1954. A crackdown on them ensued, including the imprisonment of thousands as well as six executions. Throughout the Nasir period the Muslim Brothers would be anathema to the regime, although some moderate former members of the organization remained in the government.

NEGOTIATIONS WITH THE BRITISH

Negotiations with the British were successful in resolving the two major issues. Before the end of 1952 the new regime dropped Egypt's previous insistence on the unity of the Nile Valley, and an Anglo-Egyptian agreement concluded the following February provided that both countries would withdraw troops from the Sudan, which then would determine its own future. Although the prounity forces won Sudan's first parliamentary elections, the country eventually opted for independence, which it obtained in 1956.

The more difficult Suez base question also proved susceptible to compromise. An agreement reached in 1954 provided for withdrawal of British forces by June 1956 with the right to return in case of an outside attack on Turkey or a member of the Arab League during the next seven years (with ununiformed British technicians maintaining the base). Thus Egypt's demands and Britain's concerns about a possible war with the Soviet Union were reconciled, with the provision regarding Turkey indirectly linking Egypt to NATO.

THE ROAD TO SUEZ

The new regime's moderation vis-à-vis the Sudan and Suez reflected its overall foreign policy. While rejecting anything that smacked of continuing colonialism, it showed signs of being basically pro-Western. Domestically, Nasir was anti-Communist, and Moscow at first saw him as the head of a pro-American—even fascist—regime. Ties with the United States were notably amicable during the early years. Nasir's policies evoked much praise from the American ambassador, Jefferson Caffery, whose good offices proved instrumental in resolving the Anglo-Egyptian disputes. And Nasir had close ties with CIA operatives such as Kermit Roosevelt, but there was no prospect that the rising Egyptian leader would be a puppet of anyone. And the new regime rejected the idea of membership in any Western alliance, at least until its disputes with Britain were resolved.

Although the armistice concluded with Israel in 1949 had not made way for an end to the formal state of war, Nasir played the conflict down to concentrate on domestic reform and on ending the British occupation. Israel's armistice line with Egypt generally was quiet, although an occasional Palestinian refugee in the Gaza Strip evaded detection by the Egyptian authorities and slipped across the frontier to carry out a small attack. And in 1954 several Israeli agents, including some local Jews, were caught plotting to firebomb various American and British sites in Cairo and Alexandria, apparently in an attempt to prevent the Suez Base agreement from being implemented and also to thwart the emergence of an Egyptian alliance with the United States as well as—according to allegations against hawks in his government made by Israeli Prime Minister Moshe Sharrett—to provoke a war that would allow Israel to expand its territory. Few outsiders at the time believed this, but the facts came out seven years later as blame for the "security failure" emerged as a heated issue in Israeli politics. When two Israelis were hanged for their role in the incident. Nasir considered the possibility of commuting their sentences but found it politically difficult to do so since members of the Muslim Brotherhood had recently been hanged.

In February 1955 the Israeli army carried out an attack on the Gaza Strip that left 58 Egyptians killed. The Gaza raid was just the first of a series of such attacks that occurred sporadically during the following year, and this had a major repercussion on Cairo's foreign policy. One response was to organize Palestinian guerrillas (*fida 'iyin*, "self sacrificers") to attack Israel. And the demonstration of his army's inadequacy threatened to create dissatisfaction within its ranks, inducing Cairo to seek modern weapons.

A second development that came early in 1955 was the formation of the Baghdad Pact. The culmination of Western efforts to organize a Middle Eastern counterpart to NATO, this was an alliance of Iraq—under its British client Hashimite monarchy led by Prime Minister Nuri al-Saʿid—with Britain, soon to be joined by Turkey, Iran, and Pakistan and with the United States cooperating in various ways but never becoming a member. For Egypt, this seemed to be a quasi-colonial arrangement. It maintained that Iraq's alliance with non-Arab countries stood in the way of implementing a purely Arab alliance such as the previously concluded Arab Collective Security Pact. Egypt and Iraq had long been rivals for leadership in the Arab world, and Cairo saw the Baghdad Pact as a scheme to build up a subservient Iraq. A bitter propaganda war ensued, with Cairo Radio's Voice of the Arabs regularly assailing the Iraqi regime and undermining plans to bring other Arab states, particularly Jordan, into the Baghdad Pact. Nasir's stand against the unpopular Iraqi leaders boosted his nationalist standing in the Arab world and made him an important symbol of the growing move in Asia and Africa to adopt a policy of "neutralism" (or nonalignment, to use the term that later emerged), that is, a refusal to join alliances with either side in the East–West cold war (while accepting aid from both camps).

Nasir's participation in the Bandung Conference of Afro-Asian countries in April 1955 provided further impetus to his neutralist inclination. His recognition alongside Nehru of India and Sukarno of Indonesia as a major Afro-Asian leader enhanced his prestige in Egypt and throughout the Arab world and attracted him further to a neutralist position.

Facing accelerated Israeli raids and uneasiness in his own army, Nasir turned to the United States for arms. With many Americans saying, "You're either for or against us," Washington showed no eagerness to provide arms to a neutralist country, particularly one at odds with pro-Western Arab regimes, and so the negotiations foundered, supposedly over terms of payment. So Cairo reluctantly turned to Moscow, resulting in the announcement of an arms deal in September 1955 (at first said to be with Czechoslovakia but actually with the USSR). Nasir's heroic image in the Arab world shot up further as he seemed to have ended the Western arms monopoly. From Washington's vantage point, Moscow had leap-frogged the Baghdad Pact to begin penetrating the Arab world.

Its initial panic over the arms deal notwithstanding, Washington briefly adopted a positive approach to counterbalancing Soviet influence. Along with Britain and the World Bank, it offered to finance the first stage of a huge project that Nasir had dreamed of, that is, the construction of a High Dam at Aswan that promised to enable Egypt to irrigate additional land and produce large amounts of hydroelectricity. With Washington insisting on overseeing the Egyptian budget in ways that smacked of colonial control, Cairo delayed its acceptance of the offer. And when the Egyptian ambassador met with Secretary of State Dulles in July 1956 to accept the terms, he was stunned to hear that the United States had changed its mind. Dulles further insulted the Nasir regime by claiming that its commitment to paying for Soviet arms undermined its ability to take on the Aswan Dam project. In reality, Dulles was responding to concerns of the Israel lobby and of American cotton growers who feared increased competition. But American resentment against various manifestations of Egypt's neutralism—notably recognition of the Communist government in Beijing in May, at a time when for many Americans dealings with "Red China" put countries beyond the pale of acceptance—provides the real key to the decision to renege. For Nasir, the brutal way the United States pulled the rug out from under him seemed to threaten his survival, and a dramatic response seemed in order.

THE SUEZ CRISIS

Nasir awed not only his own people but also the whole world as he delivered a long speech in Alexandria July 26, 1956, on the fourth anniversary of King Faruq's departure. His image as a daring anticolonial hero ascended to the stars, as did his reputation as a "new Hitler" in some Western circles. As he recounted the story of exploitation his country suffered during the previous century, including the horrors of forced labor used for digging the Suez Canal, Egyptian forces waited for him to pronounce the name "Ferdinand de Lessups," whereupon they entered the offices of the Suez Canal Company as the president announced to the ecstatic crowd that it was being nationalized at that moment, with the shareholders to be paid the full value of their stocks on the Paris Bourse (stock exchange). Not only was Egypt finally ending this remnant of colonialism, but also the profits from the canal would finance the High Dam, making Dulles's help unnecessary.

So began one of the major international crises of the twentieth century, the outcome of which determined whether the Egyptian regime would survive. The British and French governments were enraged by the news of nationalization and began to prepare for war. With his judgment undermined by illness, British Prime Minister Anthony Eden became wildly obsessed with the idea that this was a replay of the Munich crisis of 1938, although opinion was divided on the matter, with one member of his cabinet resigning and with the Labour Party opposing his belligerent policy. Aside from anger over the Canal, the French government wanted to destroy Nasir, as they imagined him as the source of the ongoing anticolonial revolt in Algeria. This had already driven them into an informal alliance with Israel, which now saw the Suez crisis as an opportunity to join in a tripartite attack on Egypt before it had time to make effective use of its new Soviet weapons.

The crisis intensified throughout the summer and fall. Two conferences met in London to deal with the issue, resulting in the creation of a Suez Canal Users' Association, which however, was to no avail as the United States failed to back its allies' militant policies, particularly their idea of "shooting their way through the Canal." Aside from their disappointment with Washington (and Nasir's strong backing from Moscow and the Third World), London and Paris were frustrated by the way nationalization had been conducted in accordance with international law. They insisted that the "seizure" of the Canal was in violation of Egypt's obligation under the Constantinople Convention of 1888 to keep it open, although this confused two separate issues. And their argument that Egyptians simply were incapable of running such a waterway was dashed when the new Canal authority operated it with amazing efficiency, despite the withdrawal of most foreign pilots. And when British and French vessels refused to pay transit fees, the Egyptians let them pass through anyway, further undermining any claim to a *casus bellum*. In October Egypt accepted "six principles" proposed by UN Secretary General Dag Hammarskjold.

But representatives of Britain, France, and Israel were determined to go to war. They agreed on a plan for Israel to invade the Sinai and the Gaza Strip, following which the other two countries would feign impartiality and threaten the belligerents with an occupation of the Suez Canal unless they withdrew 10 miles from the waterway to safeguard it from hostilities. In other words, Israel could continue its invasion while Egypt would have to withdraw from both sides of the Canal. The ultimatum was meant to be so unreasonable that Egypt could not accept it, thus allowing the invasion to proceed.

Everything went according to plan at first as Israel struck on October 29, 1956. The Egyptians were no match for them, and in any case most of their forces had been withdrawn to protect the Canal from the expected Anglo-French invasion. Within days, most of Sinai was in Israeli hands, with hundreds of Egyptian prisoners of war massacred and buried in a mass grave. When the invasion started, Britain and France issued their bogus ultimatum, which the Egyptians rejected, and began bombing strategic sites.

British and French troops landed at Port Said and began to move southward in the face of considerable popular resistance. To hinder the invasion, the Egyptian military sank ships in the Canal, thus closing it, if only temporarily. And before the invaders could finish their takeover of the waterway, international pressures forced them to stop. With Britain and France vetoing actions against them in the Security Council, the General Assembly met to condemn them with near unanimity. The USSR hinted unrealistically at the possibility of launching attacks on London and Paris. More to the point, the United States joined in the condemnation. President Eisenhower adamantly rejected the idea that any country should be allowed to attack another one and then demand concessions in return for withdrawal. Dulles in particular seems to have been enraged over the way the three powers had schemed behind his back. He also was angry over the timing of the attack, as it threw a monkey wrench into an Anglo-American scheme to carry out a pro-Western coup in Damascus. More broadly, he believed that such open aggression would play into the hands of the USSR. With Britain and France finding that they were bringing financial disaster on themselves as they faced severe oil shortages and a loss in their monetary reserves, they had no choice but to comply with UN demands for a cease-fire and withdrawal to get the United States to extend the aid they desperately needed. The establishment of a UN Emergency Force (UNEF), made up of contingents from small countries, facilitated their withdrawal, which was complete before the end of the year.

Ben Gurion resisted demands for Israel to withdraw and called for the annexation of the Gaza Strip and part of Sinai. Washington adamantly rejected this and threatened economic sanctions, although it supported Israel's right of passage through the Gulf of Aqaba. With the UNEF taking up positions on the Egyptian side of the frontier, the Israelis were gone by March 1957. Also, a UNEF presence at Sharm al-Shaykh, at the entrance to the Gulf of Aqaba, inhibited Egypt from closing it to Israeli shipping during the following decade.

NASIR AS A PAN-ARAB HERO

Nasir had turned military defeat into a remarkable political victory. Unlike in the recent past, an Egyptian leader was able to survive an attack not just by one traditional European great power but by two, in addition to Israel. Although this was due to international pressures on the aggressors, for many Arabs it seemed that Nasir was their "new Saladin" who would lead them to unity and victory over Western domination. More than ever before, Nasir was the hero of the Arab masses who opposed their own corrupt, pro-Western regimes. Inter-Arab relations took on the character of a more clear-cut polarization of nonalignment and revolution on one side and pro-Western forces, mostly monarchies, on the other side (one exception for now being the anachronistic ruler of Yemen, who sought to appease popular forces by befriending Nasir's Egypt). Saudi Arabia in particular set aside its old feud with the Hashimites to join them in opposing popular Nasirist forces.

Egyptian relations with the United States deteriorated following the Suez crisis. Washington proclaimed the Eisenhower Doctrine, which provided for economic and military aid and the possibility of sending troops to Middle Eastern countries threatened by "international communism." Supporters of nationalism and nonalignment saw this as, in fact, being directed against them. Events in Syria in particular aggravated American tensions with Egypt, as CIA plots—in which Iraq, Saudi Arabia, and other pro-American regimes became involved—continued against the parliamentary regime in Damascus in which nationalists, particularly the Ba'th Party, were increasingly influential and as the Communist Party there was active. King Husayn of Jordan confronted nationalist forces that controlled the parliament after free elections in 1956. Such was the growing intensity of the tension between "progressive" and "reactionary" regimes that King Sa'ud of Saudi Arabia offered a prominent Syrian politician a million dollars to assassinate Nasir, and although Sa'ud's brother Faysal—thought at the time to be more favorable to Nasir—soon took over effective leadership in his country (and later became king himself), the feud between revolutionary Egypt and the Sa'udi monarchy continued. The summer of 1958 saw a revolt in Lebanon against a pro-Western president, Camille Chamoun, the only Arab leader who had publicly endorsed the Eisenhower Doctrine and who, having rigged parliamentary elections the previous year, was ready to push through a constitutional amendment allowing him to seek another term. In the face of exaggerated reports of arms shipments to the rebels, U.S. marines landed in Beirut in July 1958.

During 1967, Syrian leaders were calling for union with Egypt. Despite his increasing pan-Arab rhetoric, Nasir was hesitant about such a hasty arrangement. But he eventually agreed on condition that this would mean full unification and that all Syrian political parties would be abolished, and so came into existence the United Arab Republic (UAR) in February 1956. That Syria would in effect ask to be annexed by another state stands as a remarkable testament to Nasir's stature as a charismatic leader. But the immediate motives of the Syrians related to their insecurity in the face of local communist influence and, even more, fear of "reactionary" forces backed by Washington and Baghdad. Some of the Syrians, particularly Ba'thists, also hoped to play a key role in the enlarged state.

Egypt now constituted the Southern Region of the UAR. At least superficially, the Arab identity had prevailed over loyalty to specific countries, which Arab nationalists dismissed as regionalism. With Nasir's stature as the "ra'is" (chief or president) throughout the Arab world at its height, the pan-Arab nationalism that he represented to so many people, particularly among the young generation, seemed on the ascendancy. Most Egyptians remained essentially Egyptian at least as much as Arab nationalists, and Nasir in particular was not carried away by such grandiose ambitions. But many imagined that one Western-backed unpopular regime after another was going to tumble to make way for one Arab state led by Nasir reaching from the Atlantic Ocean to the Persian Gulf. Events such as those in Lebanon in 1958 seemed to be part of this popular pan-Arab momentum.

But the momentum soon slowed down. The overthrow of the Hashimite monarchy in Iraq in July 1958 seemed at first to constitute another huge victory for Nasir, but in fact its leader, General Abd al-Karim Qasim, soon clashed with Iraqi Nasirites, who were eager to join the UAR, making way for a renewed feud between Cairo and Baghdad. Many observers now became aware that revolution against Western-backed monarchies did not guarantee the implementation of Arab unity.

The biggest blow to Nasir came in Syria. His initial reservations about a hasty union soon proved true as conservatives there resented his increasingly socialist policies and as Ba'thist leaders failed to gain the important roles they had expected. When rightist army officers carried out a coup there in September 1961 and declared Syria's secession from the UAR, Nasir refused to send troops to restore the union. He preserved Arab unity as an ideal by retaining the name "UAR" although this now was simply Egypt. When other coups—heavily Ba'thist in each case—took place in both Syria and Iraq during 1963, the new leaders of those countries attempted to wrap themselves in Nasir's mantle by calling for a renewed UAR, but he put them off, and a new tripartite unity scheme came to naught.

THE DEEPENING REVOLUTION

Nasir was adopting more radical policies on both the domestic and the inter-Arab levels during the early 1960s. One response to the Syrian secession in 1961 was to blame himself for having cooperated with reactionaries there. He rejected what he called his old policy of unity of ranks in favor of a new emphasis on unity of goals, that is, one of working with fellow progressives in the Arab world.

Only moderate reforms came in the immediate wake of the 1952 coup. The most dramatic was the Land Reform Law of September 1952, which limited ownership to 200 faddans (and an additional hundred faddans for other family members), with compensation in the form of 30-year bonds at 3 percent interest (later modified to be less favorable to the former owners). The law provided that landless peasants would receive plots of three to five faddans on favorable terms. Nasir and his colleagues leaned from the beginning toward measures favoring the poor, and the enactment of various laws and regulations—and policies intended to improve health conditions and to promote education—followed. On the other hand, the government initially embraced policies favoring foreign investment. But it also gradually took control of more of the economy, nationalizing property of British and French nationals during the 1956 invasion and that of Belgians when their country invaded the newly independent Congo in 1960. Also in 1960, it nationalized Bank Misr as well as the National Bank of Egypt. The regime had adopted economic planning, and private ownership made implementation difficult.

Domestic radicalization accelerated even before the end of the unity experiment, which it helped to spark by antagonizing the Syrian business class. In July 1961, Nasir announced the adoption of "Arab Socialism." A series of decrees nationalized most big businesses, whereas the government took over 51 percent of the ownership of other enterprises. The property of reactionaries was sequestered in the wake of the Syrian secession. Other policies, including a highly progressive income tax (including a 90 percent rate for income over LE10,000), were designed to create a more egalitarian society. Also, there was a deepening of land reform, with the maximum ownership now set at 100 faddans (and reduced to 50 faddans, with an equal amount for other members of the same family, in 1969). Small enterprises continued under private ownership, as well as urban real estate (though in the latter case with rigid governmental controls on rent). Aside from the agricultural sector (itself controlled by government-run cooperatives), Egypt became one of the most socialistic countries outside the Communist world.

Proponents of Arab Socialism made a case for the distinctiveness of their ideology. They stressed its differences with communism, including the role it allowed for private property that was not exploitative, its rejection of the class struggle (although echoes of that theme sometimes appeared), and its respect for religion. Nasir argued that all religions advocated socialism, and he pointed to various Islamic doctrines that had a socialist flavor. The government even promoted a book by a Syrian Muslim Brother, Mustafa al-Siba`i, titled *The Socialism of Islam*.

In many ways, the effects of Arab Socialism were not as radical as the rhetoric implied. The limits on land ownership for individuals did not prevent extended families from continuing to control large acreages. And there were not enough small plots for distribution to most peasants, who remained sharecroppers or day laborers. Much money from socialist enterprises trickled into the hands of private contractors. A "new class" of technocrats emerged. Minimum wage laws existed mainly on paper, and the highly progressive income tax was flouted so regularly that it often came to be considered a joke.

Some of the inadequacy of the social revolution emerged in 1966 when members of the still-rich landowning class in an Upper Egyptian village murdered an official of the Arab Socialist Union (ASU), that is, the country's single political party. To many people this demonstrated that exploitation and "feudalism" continued. The government appointed a Committee for the Eradication of Feudalism to deal with the situation, but skeptics pointed out that it was headed by Amir, himself of landlord background. Leftists in the ASU and government pushed a further radical agenda, and Nasir seemed to share some of their feelings, but it is hard to say whether he would have succeeded, even if the upcoming war and his own subsequent death had not intervened.

As for the wider Arab arena, Nasir's first opportunity to support a "progressive" Arab regime came with the overthrow of the monarchy in September 1962 and declaration of a republic. With the Saudis supporting the imam's counterrevolution by subsidizing tribes loyal to him, Egypt sent troops to back the new regime. The job turned out to be much harder than expected, and Nasir found himself sending more and more troops, who numbered 70,000 by 1967. Nasir once called this his "Vietnam." Also, this intensified his conflict with the Saudis, with whom several border clashes occurred. Egyptian support for forces struggling for South Yemeni independence also put it at odds with Great Britain.

RELATIONS WITH THE SUPERPOWERS

Cairo's clashes with pro-Western monarchies and ties with Moscow persistently undermined relations with Washington, and Israel's supporters in the United States lobbied against amicable ties with Egypt. But Washington realized that Nasir was anti-Communist, and some people saw his reformist policies in a positive light. Relations with the United States improved during the last two years of the Eisenhower administration, particularly as Nasir backed anti-Communist groups in Iraq and clashed with Qasim, who for a while depended on Communists to counter pan-Arabists. This inspired anti-Communist polemics in the Egyptian press and even some angry exchanges between Nasir and Soviet Premier Nikita Khrushchev. Especially after the Kennedy administration came to office in 1961, the idea that Nasir represented the kind of anti-Communist progressive stance that would promote long-term stability had its day. Egypt became a major recipient of American economic assistance, with American agricultural products paid for in local currency of little international value emerging as a mainstay of the Egyptian food supply. And Washington gave diplomatic recognition to the Egyptian-backed revolutionary government in Yemen.

But as the Yemen War threatened to spill over into Saudi Arabia, it helped to undermine United States–Egyptian ties. And after Lyndon Johnson became president, the downturn in relations accelerated. Johnson was ardently pro-Israel, and he seemed to detest radical Third World leaders in general, who to him were said to represent the Mexicans against whom his Texan forebears had fought. And one of Nasir's close associates later told how he found some of the new American president's personal behavior crude and boorish. By 1966, attacks on Nasir in American political circles had brought an end to food aid.

Relations with the Soviet Union strengthened from the mid-1950s on except during the short-lived clash over Iraq. In 1958, the Soviets took on the task of building the High Dam, and by 1970 this monumental attempt to harness the Nile was complete. Soviet help enabled Egypt to develop such important industrial projects as the steel-producing complex at Helwan. Total economic aid from the Communist world in general amounted to over $1.4 billion during 1954–1965. The Egyptian armed forces came to depend almost entirely on Soviet military aid that totaled $1.5 billion in the decade starting in 1955.

ISLAMIC UNDERCURRENTS

The Nasir regime pursued a moderate policy of secularism. Policies were always justified as being consistent with Islam. Religion continued to be taught in the schools, with each child instructed in his or her own faith. Secular law codes had already replaced the *shari'ah* in most areas of life; such matters as marriage and divorce continued to be governed by religious law, with a few changes. There was no hostility to religion like that in Turkey under Kemal Atatürk, although the government definitely tried to keep Islamic institutions under its control. More than ever before, top religious authorities, such as the rector of al-Azhar University, came to be dependent on the government and served as its "yes men." For example, when the government abolished the traditional religious courts in 1956 and turned over the implementation of religious law to the regular judiciary, the response of the religious authorities was positive. The same was true when the government enlarged al-Azhar University by adding the sorts of faculties (law, agriculture, and the like) that existed in other institutions of higher education. The Arab national identity promoted during this period, emphasized the unity of Muslim and Christian Arabs.

The Muslim Brothers continued to suffer from suppression. Many languished in prison after the plot to assassinate Nasir in 1954. One such prisoner, Sayyid Qutb, developed an especially militant brand of Islamic revolutionism. Qutb maintained that the rulers of the Islamic world as well as the population at large had reverted from Islam to something like the paganism of pre-Islamic Arabia, that is, what Muslims call the period of the *Jahiliyyah* (literally, ignorance) and that it was left for the small group of true Muslims to form an association (*jama'ah*) to wage an armed struggle (*jihad*) against this state of affairs. When word of another impending plot came to the attention of the authorities (and after Nasir discovered

Qutb's tracts following the latter's release from prison), there was another crackdown. Many Brothers were imprisoned again or else took refuge in Saudi Arabia. Qutb's life ended at the gallows in 1965, but contrary to the conventional wisdom that such movements were dying out as the world modernized and secularized, his message lived on. He became a main inspiration for the radical Islamist trend that eventually would make an explosive impact in Egypt and indeed throughout the world, filling the vacuum left in the latter part of the twentieth century by the demise of secular revolutionary movements.

SEARCH FOR A POLITICAL SYSTEM

Nasir became a charismatic figure whose heroic image bolstered his rule, but ultimate success required viable institutions. And his achievements in that regard were limited. A political organization called the Liberation Rally, formed in January 1953, served to organize pro-Nasir demonstrators in the face of challenges from Nagib and the Muslim Brothers during the three-year transitional period. In 1956, the country got a provisional constitution that provided for a popularly elected president and National Assembly to replace the RCC. Nasir was elected president unopposed in typical authoritarian fashion by 99.8 percent of the voters. The constitution also provided for a National Assembly, elections to which the tripartite attack delayed until the following year, and the nominees underwent careful screening to ensure that they were loyal to the regime. A National Union replaced the Liberation Rally as the country's only political organization. The union with Syria in 1958 required that all this be modified, as Nasir now became president of the UAR, and the National Assembly and the National Union were enlarged. With the end of the union in 1961, these institutions underwent modification again. The following year, a 1,700-member National Congress of Popular Powers, made up of representatives of various associations, engaged in some meaningful debate and adopted a National Charter, intended as a statement of the revolution's official ideology. The National Union now made way for a new political organization, the Arab Socialist Union (ASU). A newly elected 350-member National Assembly—half of whose members had to be workers and peasants, although these class categories were defined so broadly as not to have much meaning—adopted a new, still-provisional constitution in 1964.

These institutions never gained much real life. The National Assembly was basically a rubber stamp, although debate did emerge occasionally on some issues. Unlike in authentic single-party regimes, the ASU never emerged as the real center of power. It was large and unwieldy, notwithstanding the eventual creation of a vanguard group in it. Reflecting the diversity of opinion within the regime, the National Charter was vague and failed to create a clear ideology comparable to that of other single-party regimes (e.g., the Soviet Union). The foundations of Nasir's regime remained fundamentally charismatic and personal, resting on the president as an individual and his personal ties to various individuals as well as being dependent on the armed forces. Various networks of cronies or centers of power formed among the inner and outer circles of influential people.

Among the former members of the RCC, only Major Abd al-Hakim Amir remained in the military. Promoted to the rank of field marshall and overall commander, Amir acquired the armed forces as essentially an independent fief. Officers lionized him, and this was bolstered by the favors he could get for them. Far from being an absolute ruler, Nasir was dependent on Amir to keep the army loyal, fearing a military coup if he failed to keep him and his supporters happy. Amir grew corrupt, in contrast to the puritanical Nasir. And the officers' corp evolved into a privileged class not in keeping with military effectiveness. Nasir's close friendship with Amir turned into thinly veiled distrust. Following both the defeat in 1956 and the Syrian secession Nasir allegedly wanted to dismiss Amir but found himself inhibited by the field marshall's supporters in the army. According to one interpretation, the purpose of the ASU was to counterbalance Amir's powerful circle. Only after 1967 did outsiders come widely to understand these basic dynamics of the regime.

ECONOMIC DEVELOPMENT

The Nasir regime exerted great effort to develop Egypt. This included the creation of schools and health centers throughout the country. A major increase in the literacy rate occurred, although in the end about half the population remained illiterate. Many peasant children still did not attend school despite the law that required them to do so. Expansion of universities, now tuition free, provided opportunities for students from less-privileged classes (although those who could not afford private tutoring suffered from a severe disadvantage) but also left most graduates with little future other than guaranteed positions in a bureaucracy that involved little real work and very low pay. The High Dam promised to increase the amount of cultivatable land, but the continuing rapid growth of the population from about 20 million in 1952 to 33.3 million in 1970, some governmental efforts to push birth control notwithstanding, made this an uphill battle.

Industrialization was a high priority. A series of five-year plans made important strides in this direction, and—protected by strict restrictions on imports—the great variety of locally manufactured goods grew, although the quality typically was inferior. Industry grew from 21 percent of the GNP in 1952 to 38 percent by 1970. But the regime's plans to double the GNP during the 1960s proved unrealistic. The growth rate was fairly high for a while but slowed down in the mid-1960s. After June 1967, it plummeted below zero.

THE "SETBACK" OF JUNE 1967

The Egyptian-Israeli frontier remained quiet following the Israeli withdrawal and the establishment of the UNEF in 1957. Although Nasir's heroic stature in the Arab world rested in part on the vision of him as the leader of Arab unity and eventually liberator of Palestine, he was realistic about both issues. He repeatedly told those who were impatient over the loss of most of Palestine in 1948 that the Arabs were not ready to defeat Israel. And yet in June 1967 the situation got out of hand at a time when much of the Egyptian army was tied down in Yemen and when the United States, under President Johnson, was not ready to repeat Eisenhower's condemnation of an Israeli invasion.

The immediate background to the 1967 war was extremely complicated. Tension between Israel and Syria intensified after a militant regime that backed Palestinian guerrillas came to power in Damascus in 1966. Wary of this regime, Cairo entered into a security treaty with it in the hopes of controlling it. But with Israeli attacks on both Syria and Jordan increasing and with Israelis making threats to occupy Damascus (and Soviet reports, which later turned out to have been greatly exaggerated, of Israeli troops massing near the border), there was increasing pressure on Nasir to do something. In order to deflate his heroic image, King Hussein of Jordan ridiculed Nasir for "hiding behind the skirts" of the UNEF. And indeed the presence of these peacekeepers on the frontier undermined and discredited Nasir's ability to deter an Israeli attack. On May 16, he asked for the withdrawal of some of the units from the frontier. When UN Secretary General U Thant said it was a matter of full withdrawal or nothing, Nasir gave the go-ahead for the former alternative.

The sequence of events leading to war now accelerated. With the UNEF no longer at Sharm al-Shaykh, the excuse for not closing it to Israeli shipping, as before the 1956 attack, was gone, and so it was announced that Israeli vessels could no longer pass through these straits. Actually, the announced closure was never tested, and there were signs that Cairo was ready to reach an agreement. Vice President Zakariyyah Muhi al-Din was scheduled to visit Washington on June 7, and Nasir committed himself not to carry out a preemptive attack, although he declared that if Israel attacked Egypt his response would be to destroy it. He thought he had Washington's commitment not to tolerate a war started by Israel.

On the morning of June 5 the Israeli air force launched a devastating attack that virtually destroyed its Egyptian counterpart on the ground. Israeli forces moved overland into the Gaza Strip and Sinai, quickly reaching the banks of the now-blocked Suez Canal. Before a cease-fire went into effect six days after the war began, Israel occupied not only the Gaza Strip and Sinai but also the West Bank of Jordan (including East Jerusalem) and southwestern Syria (the Golan Heights). Thousands of Egyptian soldiers died or were taken prisoner, many of them massacred by the Israelis after surrendering or else turned loose in the hot sand to make their way home barefoot. This was a terrible disaster for Nasir and for the Arab world—in Nasir's more optimistic spin, a "setback" *(naksa)* that had now followed the disaster *(nakba)* of 1948.

NASIR'S LAST YEARS

Amazingly to some, the regime survived after the public found out that media reports of great victories were totally false. After Nasir appeared on television to announce his resignation, the country erupted in an amazing fashion. Millions of weeping people—largely spontaneously but partly trucked in by the ASU—took to the streets in protest. It seemed that personal affection for their leader combined with a feeling that the enemy must not have the pleasure of overthrowing him. With Nasir to be replaced by Vice President Zakariyyah Muhi al-Din—reputedly representing "pro-American" tendencies—the resignation seemed all the more to represent capitulation to Washington. Banners proclaimed "No Zakariyyah, No Dollar." It is unclear whether Nasir really meant to resign or was engaged in a Machiavellian ploy. In any case he agreed to stay on, but his increasingly severe diabetes and heart condition combined with both the psychological blow of June 1967 and his zeal for working long hours to cut his life short.

The defeat brought major changes in the regime. Nasir now defied Amir's followers in the army and dismissed him from his position. Later accused of plotting a coup, Amir was put under house arrest, where he committed suicide in September (or, according to some accusations, was murdered). Hundreds of others, including army officers, were dismissed, and some got prison sentences.

Massive demonstrations, mainly of students and workers, erupted the following year. Dominated by leftists, the students protested against the light sentences given to army officers found responsible for the defeat. They also demanded broader reforms. Endorsing some of their demands, Nasir replaced many people in high-level positions, some by university professors, and issued the so-called March 30 Declaration that provided for the renewal of the ASU through elections at all levels. But this attempt to conciliate the protesters brought little change.

Egyptian foreign policies adjusted to the new reality. The feud with "reactionary" Arab regimes now came to an end to allow Cairo to concentrate on ending the fruits of the recent Israeli victory as Nasir met with other Arab leaders at Khartoum in November 1967. Egypt became the recipient of vital financial aid from the oil-producing Arab monarchies and ended its involvement in Yemen. It also accepted Security Council Resolution 242, passed in November 1967 and providing for peace and for Israeli withdrawal from territories occupied in the recent war. The Khartoum Conference declaration on this matter also affirmed the need for a peace settlement, though with some other phrases added as protection against more radical voices. Nasir had ceased to constitute a threat to "reactionary" rulers, and the idea of a pan-Arab state emerging under his leadership seemed more unreal than ever, although the overthrow of the Libyan monarchy by Colonel Mu'ammar al-Qadhafi in 1969 produced a zealous disciple for him and new talk about union, with a coup led by Ja'far al-Numayri in Sudan the same year adding another name to a trio of reputedly progressive and nationalist leaders.

The "Six-Day War" did not end. Small-scale clashes continued along the Suez Canal, with the population of the cities along that waterway evacuated. In March 1969, Nasir declared a War of Attrition involving regular artillery barrages. The Israelis built what they considered to be the impenetrable Bar-Lev Line on the eastern bank of the Canal. They sometimes carried out daring raids deep inside Egypt, recurrently bombing the Cairo area during the early part of 1970.

The defeat pulled Egypt into the Soviet sphere as never before. The Soviets provided arms on a massive level that soon more than replaced the losses of 1967. For the first time, they acquired naval facilities in Egyptian ports. In February 1970, Nasir flew to Moscow, obtaining advanced Soviet missiles that finally stopped Israel's deep-penetration raids. The Soviets also provided thousands of military advisors. Accusations that

Egypt was becoming a Soviet satellite were understandable, if off the mark.

Other currents were moving in the opposite direction. The rapprochement with Arab monarchies provided an obvious example of this. Also, some of the more left-leaning (or pro-Soviet) figures got demoted—a remarkable case being that of former Prime Minister Ali Sabri, who in what some observers saw as a plot by more rightist elements, was forced out of his position as Secretary General of the ASU when he got caught smuggling goods into the country, although this did not prevent him from vying for power in the future. And in July 1970 Nasir's acceptance of United States Secretary of State William Rogers's proposal for a three-month cease-fire in the war with Israel seemed to point to his understanding that the road to ending the Israeli occupation passed through Washington. All of this, however, would be left for others, notably the reputedly rightist Sadat, whom he had installed as vice president the previous December (although perhaps not with the idea that Sadat would succeed him except as a temporary stopgap), as Nasir's arduous attempt in September 1970 to mediate the growing conflict between the PLO and the Jordanian monarchy ended with a fatal heart attack.

7

Sadat and Counterrevolution

Nasir's death left a gaping void that few imagined anyone could fill. For nearly two decades, he seemed almost synonymous with Egypt. Now there was an overwhelming feeling of loss. Admittedly, he was authoritarian, sometimes harshly repressing those who threatened his regime. But he was the first real Egyptian to rule Egypt since the days of the Pharaohs. He had both defied Western imperialism and taken up the cause of the disadvantaged at home, although success in reversing the 1967 disaster appeared unattainable, and his revolution was far from complete. His funeral drew more mourners than that of any other human being before him, as millions took to the streets weeping.

Vice President Anwar al-Sadat, who fainted at the funeral, seemed a particularly unlikely candidate to fill Nasir's shoes. But it was convenient for those who thought they were more serious contenders for leadership to allow him to take office as provisional president and soon afterward to be nominated by the Higher Executive Committee of the Arab Socialist Union (ASU) (with subsequent unanimous approval by the National Assembly) for a regular six-year term. Needless to say, he won the election, if only by 90 percent of the voters rather than the usual 99.9 percent. Sadat was one of the original Free Officers but was the butt of many jokes. It was his voice on the radio that first announced the news of the 1952 Revolution when it occurred, although he had taken his family to a triple-feature movie when the actual event started and almost missed the action. His survival within the circle centering on Nasir (but kept out of any serious positions of power) seemed to result from his "yes-man" qualities. His reputed hotheadedness, epitomized by his arrest in 1942 over attempting to make contact with the Germans, made it hard for him to be taken seriously. But Sadat's subsequent actions were to demonstrate that his many detractors were off the mark, as he proceeded during the following years to awe the world with dramatic acts that seemed in almost every way to reverse Nasir's policies.

SADAT'S "CORRECTIVE MOVEMENT"

Sadat soon began to adopt policies that enraged those who saw themselves as more authentic heirs of Nasir. Some of them even sought advice from their late leader by resorting to a spirit medium. Not only were Sadat's actions a violation of his published agreement that there would be collective rule during his presidency, but he soon demonstrated a tendency suddenly to announce surprising decisions without consulting anybody, as in renewing the cease-fire and in accepting the idea of an interim, stage-by-stage Israeli withdrawal. One issue that intensified the conflict was Sadat's agreement in April 1971 to form a Federation of Arab Republics that was to include Egypt, Libya, and Syria (Sudan originally was expected to join but dropped out because of the civil war in the south). It was not Arab unity per se—and the new arrangement eventually came apart—that caused the division but rather Sadat's critics' belief that he was using this as a scheme to overhaul the country's governmental system.

Chief among Sadat's critics was a center of power headed by Vice President Ali Sabri, reputedly the favorite of the Soviets. The group also included Interior Minister Sha'rawi Gum'a, whose image was marred by his past role in oppressing the regime's critics, and Minister of Presidential Affairs Sami Sharif, in control of the security apparatus. Minister of War Muhammad Fawzi was on their side, too.

Sadat played his hand skillfully in undermining these people. He alleged that Nasir himself had complained against a "gang" that was in control. He played on the personal animosities of some of them to one another. He got the support of many on both the right and the left who were angry over the repressiveness associated with his opponents. Notably among his backers was Chief-of-Staff General Muhammad Sadiq, whose resentment of Soviet advisers had widespread echoes in the armed forces. After ending his May Day speech in 1971 with a dramatic attack on "centers of power," Sadat suddenly withdrew all of Sabri's responsibilities. Gum'a was fired after an Interior Ministry official brought Sadat a collection of taped conversations that allegedly revealed the existence of a coup plot. A large group in the anti-Sadat camp attempted to make the president's position untenable by resigning en masse, but he responded by arresting more than 90 top leaders, several of whom soon received long prison or death sentences that in fact later were commuted. Culminating what he called his May 15 Correction, Sadat revealed that his opponents had bugged his office and broken into the late president's safe to read his personal notes. Symbolizing an apparent break with oppressive practices, Sadat publicly conducted a bonfire of telephone conversation transcripts and secret files from the Interior Ministry. Before the end of the year, the country had a permanent constitution, approved by 99.8 percent of the voters (a not-so-subtle indication that democracy still had not arrived).

THE CROSSING

As Sadat was prevailing over his rivals in the government, the "no war, no peace" with Israel continued to hang over him. Following renewals of the original 90-day cease-fire, he declared that 1971 would be "the year of decision." When the year ended without any movement either toward peace or toward renewing hostilities, he explained that the diplomatic "fog" brought on by the war between India and Pakistan had got in the way, only to evoke ridicule from those who made it seem that he was talking literally about atmospheric conditions. As more time passed, the whole idea that the Egyptian army would ever dare attack the Israelis seemed more and more to be a joke.

Sadat repeatedly called for a peaceful settlement, starting with a statement made to an American emissary at Nasir's funeral. In February 1971 he proposed the possibility of an interim settlement in which the Israelis would withdraw from the east bank of the Suez Canal and Egypt would reopen the waterway. In the same month, Sadat eagerly agreed to a proposal by United Nations mediator Gunnar Jarring for an Egyptian–Israeli peace agreement based on Security Council Resolution 242 but Israel's strident rejection of the suggestion brought an end to Jarring's effort. Washington still failed to take either Sadat's staying power or his sincerity seriously.

Then, to the amazement of the world, the great "Crossing" of the Canal took place on October 6, 1973. Sadat and Syrian President Hafiz al-Asad—

whose forces simultaneously attacked the Israeli-occupied Golan Heights—had carefully planned the offensive and kept it secret. Egyptians had already slipped across the waterway to seal off the pipes the enemy had constructed to pour flaming napalm into the Canal. The Israelis failed to see what was happening until only hours before Egyptian forces began massively at 2:10 P.M. to fire artillery across the Canal. Egyptian soldiers then began to cross to the eastern side. High-pressure water hoses washed away the walls of sand the Israelis had built, and the Bar-Lev line crumbled as hastily constructed pontoon bridges allowed further troops and armor to cross to Sinai. After taking a strip about three to five miles wide along the eastern bank, the Egyptians paused to consolidate their gains. Some argue that this cautious policy was a big mistake and that the liberators lost an opportunity to take the strategic passes of central Sinai, something they failed to accomplish when they finally attempted to do so on October 14, after the Israelis had gained their composure and as massive supplies of American weapons and equipment were airlifted, sometimes directly to the battlefield.

By the time Sadat announced this unbelievable achievement to his parliament, a major setback was occurring. Finding a gap in the lines between Egypt's Second Army in the north and the Third Army in the south, Israeli General Ariel Sharon was able to slip a few tanks through and, without being detected, cross the Canal "to Africa." Sharon augmented his force west of the Canal and posed a deadly threat to Egyptian communications as he moved southward. Security Council Resolution 338 ordered a cease-fire for October 22, which was supposed to be followed by negotiations to settle the conflict on the basis of Resolution 242, but Sharon's force kept pushing southward anyway until it had virtually cut the Egyptian Third Army off from the west side of the Canal. The Soviets' suggestion that if the United States would not enter into a joint force, as requested by Sadat to implement the cease-fire, they would send troops on their own led U.S. Secretary of State Henry Kissinger to announce a worldwide nuclear alert.

Although Egypt had suffered defeat again, its astonishing initial success enabled it to perpetuate a myth of victory. Acclaimed as "the Hero of the Crossing," Sadat had attained the stature of a great leader. And considering that his aim was not to completely defeat Israel but rather to jump-start a movement out of the "no war, no peace" situation, Egypt's military debacle in 1973 seemed like a political victory, especially as the unity of the Arab world in supporting the war was unsurpassed and as Arab oil producers announced a cutback in production and a boycott of certain countries, particularly the United States.

SHIFTING ALIGNMENT

It seems that from the beginning Sadat was intent on moving into Washington's orbit. Having visited the United States in 1966, he was much impressed with what he saw, although there is no evidence to back up allegations that he was in the pay of the CIA. He calculated in the post-1967 period that Washington was the key to getting Egypt out of its nightmarish situation. From the beginning of his presidency, he sent messages through such intermediaries as Kamal Adham, an old friend and key member of Saudi King Faysal's circle. It is notable that, far from the bitter ideological conflict of the 1960s, Egypt now was moving beyond Nasir's post-1967 détente with the Arab monarchies to establish close ties with them and also with the shah of Iran, with whom Nasir had severed diplomatic relations in 1960 but whom Sadat particularly admired. He also, along with Colonel Qadhafi of Libya, helped to thwart a communist coup in the Sudan in 1971. But the consensus in Washington was that Sadat could not be taken seriously and that he would not last.

Dependence on Soviet assistance created unease in Egypt. The victory of Sadat over the Sabri group in May 1971 pointed to an eventual end of the Soviet–Egyptian relationship, although most contemporary observers failed to see this. When Soviet President Nikolai Podgorny soon afterward appeared in Cairo, Sadat agreed to a 15-year friendship treaty, which, if taken at face value, meant that Egypt had finally become a formal ally of the Soviets, but in reality this was an attempt to paper over widening cracks.

By 1972, Soviet military personnel numbered 20,000. They sometimes went beyond the role of advisers, for in at least one case a Soviet pilot clashed with an Israeli aircraft. Many Egyptians resented the Soviet presence. In April 1972, Sadat received a petition whose signatures included some of the original members of the Free Officers calling for an end to such "extravagant dependence" and the reestablishment of true nonalignment.

In July 1972, Sadat startled the world by ordering the Soviets to withdraw almost all their military personnel within 10 days. The Soviets continued to provide additional military equipment in an attempt to preserve their relationship with Cairo, and in fact they engaged in a major airlift of arms during the October War.

The 1973 war brought Egyptian ties with the two superpowers to a head in ironic ways. Despite new Soviet military aid and diplomatic support during the war and the qualitative increase in American aid to Israel that occurred at this time, the hope that Washington would pressure Israel into a diplomatic settlement seemed to dictate a turn in that direction. Sadat in particular would repeatedly declare that "America has 99 percent of the cards."

Starting a process pushed by Kissinger, Egyptian officers met with their Israeli counterparts at Kilometer 101, on the Cairo-to-Suez road, at the end of the 1973 war. The negotiations failed to achieve any Israeli pull-back, even from those areas on the western side of the Canal occupied in violation of the October 22 cease-fire, but an agreement to allow a relief corridor through Israeli lines to the Third Army did ensue on October 28.

An international peace conference convened in Geneva in December 1973, with Egypt, Israel, and Jordan attending and the United States and the Soviet Union jointly presiding. But this was merely ceremonial and ended after one session, as the United States wanted to keep the Soviets out of the negotiations and to follow a step-by-step approach, a position that Sadat eagerly embraced. To his critics in the Arab world, this seemed to be designed to play Arab countries against each other and to proceed with incremental steps that would put the Israelis in the end in a position to resist demands for full withdrawal.

Many Egyptians and other Arabs saw Sadat as so eager to please the Americans that he squandered the advantages he gained in the October War. He seemed to them to be so flattered by praise from Kissinger, who visited Cairo shortly after the cease-fire, and by the adulation he began to receive in the United States generally that he was ready to trust Washington to work out a just settlement even as he gave away his diplomatic cards. In June 1974, shortly before being forced out of office, President Richard Nixon received an exaggerated heroic welcome in Cairo, while increasingly the Egyptian president was speaking harshly about the So-viets and also—in a renewed assertion of a separate Egyptian identity—about the other Arab countries.

Kissinger began a series of "shuttles" between Egypt and Israel that would get the former out of the Arab–Israeli conflict. The first Egyptian–Israeli disengagement agreement came on January 17, 1974. Belying Sa-dat's previous commitment not to give up the fight without full Israeli withdrawal, this provided for an Israeli pullback from the western side of the Canal and from a strip in Sinai about 15 miles wide along the waterway's whole length without any concrete commitment for further withdrawal. The agreement also required Egypt to pull back most of its troops and weapons from Sinai. And by proceeding in June 1975 to reopen the Canal as well as to start rebuilding the cities alongside it, Sadat seemed to be undermining his future military options. Despite vows that the Arab oil weapon would continue to be used until Arab goals were fully achieved, Sadat persuaded King Faysal to end the boycott following the disengagement agreement.

This agreement threatened Cairo's relations with Damascus. The Syrians had no choice but to go ahead and conclude a disengagement agreement for the Golan Heights, but when Sadat concluded a second disengagement agreement with Israel (Sinai II) in September 1975, an angry response resounded from most of the Arab world, especially Syria. The Arab unity shown in the October War had vanished, strengthening the Israeli position further. Aid that Sadat provided for right-wing Maronite militias in response to Arab criticism may have helped to tear Lebanon apart and further inflame Arab politics generally.

In accordance with Sinai II, Israel withdrew from another strip. This included the Abu Rudays oil fields, which Israel had exploited, and all or most of the passes, putting Egypt in control of about a tenth of Sinai but with its military presence severely restricted. On the side, the United States made assurances to Israel, including an agreement to provide further sophisticated weapons and not to deal with the PLO unless it made important concessions. Sadat secretly agreed not to come to Syria's aid even if Israel attacked it.

TO JERUSALEM AND CAMP DAVID

New factors converged in 1977 to produce dramatic developments. Food riots (see later in this chapter) left Sadat desperate. He needed peace so as to be able to concentrate on the economic crisis. Also, that was the year of the "earthquake" election in Israel that brought the militant Menachim Begin and his Likud Party to power. Considering that the Likud was devoted, first of all, to absorbing the whole of pre-1948 Palestine, including the West Bank and the Gaza Strip, into Israel, it turned out that it would be ready to give up Sinai under certain conditions to facilitate this objective, although few at first perceived this.

The new administration of U.S. President Jimmy Carter favored a shift from Kissinger's step-by-step methods to working on a comprehensive settlement of the Arab–Israeli conflict. Thus a joint U.S.–Soviet communiqué in October 1977 called for reconvening the Geneva Conference, as Moscow and the Arabs long had preferred. But by now Sadat had decided that the comprehensive approach would get in the way of his goal of recovering Sinai, and he did not want Moscow involved.

On November 9, 1977, without consulting anyone in advance, the Egyptian president provided the world with another example of his "electric shock" technique. He announced in the People's Assembly (as the country's representative body now was called) that he was so intent on peace that he would be willing to go to the Knesset (Israel's parliament) to present his case, a proposal that was so extraordinary that it took a while for anyone to realize that Sadat was serious.

After receiving an invitation, Sadat flew to Israel November 20 and gave a flowery speech to the Knesset. He eloquently stated the Arab case but pleaded for peace and overdid himself with exaggerated affection toward Israeli leaders. From this point on, he came to be idolized in the West, and at least for a while the vast majority of Egyptians seemed to hope that he had embarked on a road to peace and prosperity. But even after the trip to Jerusalem peace was hard to come by, as ensuing Egyptian–Israeli negotiations demonstrated. Israel was ready to withdraw from Sinai as part of a peace settlement, but Sadat could not blatantly desert the broader Arab cause to get this. When Begin met Sadat in Ismailia in December, he offered mere autonomy for the Palestinians of the West Bank and Gaza Strip—not for these territories as such—under continuing Israeli rule.

With the momentum for peace in danger, Carter invited Sadat and Begin to a meeting at his retreat in Camp David, Maryland. The tripartite summit of September 5–17, 1977, resulted in an agreement—which would earn them the Nobel Peace Prize later that year—on the framework for an Egyptian–Israeli peace treaty that would fully end the occupation of Sinai but with strict limits on Egyptian military forces located there. Begin and Sadat also accepted a framework for a broader settlement of the Arab–Israeli conflict involving projected negotiations to establish Palestinian autonomy for five years (bypassing the PLO), with the final status of these territories to be the subject of further talks. Hurdles remained, as Begin made clear that Israel intended to keep the occupied Palestinian territories and as Sadat, who was coming under heavy criticism in the Arab world for moving toward a separate peace—called for a link between any Egyptian–Israeli treaty and the resolution of the Palestine issue. But following a trip by Carter to Jerusalem and Cairo in March 1979, Begin and Sadat finally signed a peace treaty that went into effect the following month. It provided that Israel would fully withdraw from Egyptian territory by April 1982. In accordance with the treaty, the two countries established normal relations in January 1980, at a time when Israel still occupied a third of the Sinai.

The treaty did not provide the link that Sadat had called for. To the Arab world this appeared as a separate peace that would so diminish the coalition confronting Israel that any inducement to settle the Palestine question except on its own terms would be gone. With neither the Palestinians nor the Jordanian regime willing to work within the new framework, Egyptian–Israeli talks on Palestinian autonomy proceeded for a while, but Cairo broke the discussions off in 1980 after the Knesset passed a resolution reaffirming the eternal nature of an undivided Jerusalem as the Israeli capital.

The Egyptian alliance with the United States blossomed. From now on, Egypt would receive about $2 billion a year in American aid, making it second only to Israel. The United States would get base facilities in Egypt, and joint United States–Egyptian air force maneuvers would occur. With the Iranian revolution of 1979 overthrowing the shah's regime, Sadat's Egypt seemed to inherit his mantle as a top U.S. client state. Sadat gave refuge to the dying shah and became an enemy of Iran's revolutionary regime, as well as a supporter of the Islamic guerrilla resistance in Afghanistan after the USSR occupied that country in 1979. The relationship with the Soviet Union deteriorated, with Sadat abrogating the Friendship Treaty in 1976. He suspended payment on Egypt's debt to the USSR the following year and expelled the Soviet ambassador in September 1981.

The rest of the Arab world was horrified by Sadat's separate peace. A meeting in Tripoli, Libya, in December 1977 established a Steadfastness Front of Syria, the PLO, Algeria, and South Yemen aimed at freezing relations with Egypt. The Iraqi delegate walked out of the meeting to protest its failure to take an even stronger stand. Sadat severed diplomatic relations with all of them. Following the Camp David agreements, popular anger in the Arab world was so intense that even conservative regimes dared not express displeasure. An Arab League meeting in Baghdad in November 1978 called for severing diplomatic relations with Egypt, suspending it from the Arab League, and moving the organization's headquarters to another country if Sadat went ahead with the separate peace with Israel. When the treaty was concluded, a meeting of Arab foreign ministers called for cutting off all economic relations with Egypt as well. Almost all the Arab states implemented these sanctions. With Egypt's membership in the Arab League—and other organizations too, including the Organization of the Islamic Conference (OIC)—suspended, the Arab League moved its headquarters from Cairo to Tunis. Egypt's isolation from the Arab world seemed nearly complete, as Sadat lashed out with epithets such as "dwarfs" and "madmen" toward other leaders. Insofar as his peace with Israel would remain popular at home, it seemed that Egyptians were rejecting their Arab identity altogether.

EGYPTIANS IN THE ARAB WORLD

One facet of Egyptian ties with the Arab world that the Arab sanctions left intact was the continuing presence of Egyptians throughout the region. If Arab oil producers had wanted to punish Egypt severely, expelling Egyptian workers would have been the way to do so, but they would have punished themselves as well, for their economies could not function without people from such poor Arab countries, Egypt in particular. In any case, the sanctions were supposed to be against Sadat's regime, not the Egyptian people.

For millennia, Egyptians had been known for rarely migrating out of the Nile Valley. But the boom in Arab oil-producing countries in the Persian Gulf region (and, on a smaller scale, Libya) created a demand for professional people and manual laborers. The pay for such work was incredibly high by Egyptian standards, and by the late 1970s more than three million Egyptians had migrated to these countries. There was even a scheme for large numbers of Egyptian peasants to develop Iraq's great agricultural potential.

All of this had a tremendous social and economic impact. Remittances from Egyptians working abroad became a major source of family income. And consumer goods that few had dreamed of now became more and more common, with refrigerators and television sets appearing in many peasants' and ordinary city dwellers' homes. Yet some perceptive observers believed that detrimental consequences outweighed the advantages of this, as families were separated and as some failed to maintain professional skills when lured by high pay for unskilled work in countries such as Saudi Arabia. At first, the intermingling of populations seemed to promise a renewed sense of Arab unity, but the reality proved the opposite, as outside Arabs in the oil-rich countries—totally dependent on their local sponsors to keep their visas—faced various kinds of discrimination (one writer called it *apartheid*, whereas others called it a new form of slavery).

ISLAMIC RESURGENCE

During the preceding century, the trend in the Islamic world had seemed to be in the direction of secularism. Onlookers tended to relegate religion, particularly its political manifestations, to the category of the traditional, which ultimately had to give way for the modern. Of course, religion had remained central to the lives of Muslims and Copts, but the usual view was that secular ideologies such as socialism were in the ascendancy. The temporary appearance of the Muslim Brothers as a bogeyman for Nasir in the mid-1960s seemed to many hardly to represent an overall trend.

But change was in the air after the 1967 War. Little plastic hangers proclaiming "God is Greater" increasingly appeared. Of a more sensational nature, hundreds of thousands of Muslims and Copts in the months following the 1967 defeat testified that the Virgin Mary (emphasized in the Qur'an as well as in Christian scriptures) appeared over churches in Cairo. The 1967 defeat and Nasir's subsequent death also meant that those who had been inspired by his secular nationalism had to turn to other protest movements. The way Nasir's defeat strengthened Saudi Arabia, the foundations of which were a conservative brand of Islam, in the inter-Arab arena also provided another basis for the new trend.

This was only one early manifestation of what subsequent decades showed to be a worldwide Islamic revival. The effects of the broader movement helped to fuel developments in Egypt, which, however, also impacted on the rest of the world. Sadat represented the right wing of the Free Officers and had once had ties with the Muslim Brothers. Even for Nasir, it was important for newspapers to show photos of him praying, and during the 1956 invasion he delivered the sermon at al-Azhar Mosque. But Sadat carried this further, sporting the little growth on his forehead caused by praying so much and loving to be described as "the pious president." Stressing a long-unused first name, he began to call himself *Muhammad* Anwar Sadat. His new constitution formally recognized Islamic law as the main source of legislation. On the other hand, Sadat's support for new legislation—the so-called "Jihan's law," allegedly under the influence of his wife Jihan—that went against the grain of Islamic law on matters of marriage and divorce antagonized Islamists and conservative Muslims.

For Egyptians, the war of October 1973 was "the Ramadan War," from the name of the Muslim month when Sadat launched it. It was during Ramadan that the Prophet Muhammad's first revelation came from the Angel Gabriel. It is the month of fasting. This also was the month the Prophet attacked his Meccan oppressors in the Battle of Badr (624 A.D.), and indeed the 1973 offensive was officially known as Operation Badr. Replacing the uninspiring secular slogans of 1967, *Allahu Akbar* (God is Greater) served as the battle cry in the Ramadan War. There were stories that, as in the tradition of the original Badr, angels joined in the fight in 1973. And the Prophet Muhammad appeared smiling among the troops, at least in dreams that were reported. According to Muhammad Haykal, there was so much concern that this was getting out of hand that the government tried to mute it by announcing that a Coptic general's infantry brigade had crossed the Canal first.

People showed renewed devotion to Islam. Beginning with a trickle of young women adopting Islamic rules for dress that their grandmothers had discarded, the return of the "veil" (that is, the *hijab,* or covering, that hides the hair but not the face) increasingly became the norm by the end of the 1970s. The number of mosques, increasingly ones independent of the state, was soaring. Several militant preachers, notably the blind Shaykh Abd al-Hamid Kishk, began to gain prominence as cassettes of their sermons, some of which condemned Sadat, were widely distributed.

The religious revival affected the Copts too. The election of the activist, inspirational Pope Shenouda III in 1971 provided a boost to this. Fueled by rumors of attempts to convert Muslims to Christianity and by bureaucratic procedures making it difficult to get permission to build new churches, clashes between militants on each side and such incidents as the burning of a church in 1972 began to mar long-peaceful Coptic–Muslim relations.

Political liberalization dictated that those Muslim Brothers imprisoned by Nasir be released. Though still technically banned, the movement began to operate in the open under Hasan al-Hudaybi, who was succeeded by Umar Tilmisani following his death in 1973. By 1976, the Muslim Brother magazine *The Call* (*al-Da'wah*) appeared on newsstands. But the mainline Muslim Brothers, basically reformers willing to work for gradual Islamization, were not to have the field by themselves as a more revolutionary, extremist trend influenced by the ideas of Sayyid Qutb and drawing on the fourteenth-century Islamic theologian Ibn Taymiyyah, some of whose writings were used to justify revolution against nominally Muslim rulers who replaced the *Shari'ah* with secular law, came on the scene.

During the early 1970s the opposition to Sadat came from Nasirites and Marxists, as university students in particular opposed his rightist course. Aside from repression by the police, a major response of the Sadat regime was to use militant Islamic associations (groups that eventually merged to form the Islamic Group, *al-Jama'ah al-Islamiyyah*) that, having started on a small scale during the later Nasir years, now increasingly proliferated on the campuses. These groups at first were diverse, and their names varied. Some of Sadat's leading intimates, particularly the wealthy Islamist businessman Uthman Ahmad Uthman, are said to have encouraged him to rely on them. With the regime's encouragement, the militant groups clashed with leftists and increasingly gained ascendancy on university campuses. By the late 1970s the Islamists were unbeatable in student elections. Their momentum by now was so great that this continued to be the case even after the government, seeing that they were getting out of hand, stopped its support.

With growing disillusionment over the Camp David agreement, the Islamic Group was becoming more radical and spawned even more extreme organizations. The first major event bringing this to the attention of the public was an attack by a splinter organization, Muhammad's Youth Group, headed by a Jordanian, Salih Sirriyyah, on the Military Academy in 1974 designed to acquire arms and initiate a general unpairing. The second such manifestation of violence was the kidnaping—and eventual murder—of the minister of Waqfs (Islamic endowments) in 1977 by a little group calling itself the Society of Muslims but which the government called *Takfir wa al-Hijrah* (Denunciation [of others as unbelievers] and Withdrawal). Headed by Shukri Ahmad Mustafa, this organization concluded that the whole society had become so degenerate and un-Islamic and that it now was left for a tiny band of true Muslims to withdraw and live in isolation. Growing out of the Sariyyah group was one that would have more lasting influence, *al-Jihad* ("Striving," in this case, violently for a holy cause). Among the major figures in Jihad was a young electrician, Abd al-Salam Farag, who wrote a manifesto titled *The Neglected Duty.* Although such groups were at odds with the establishment ulama, Jihad was able to recruit Shaykh Umar Abd al-Rahman, an Islamic scholar at the Asyut branch campus of al-Azhar.

LIBERALIZATION AND REPRESSION

Sadat moved Egypt in a liberal direction in at least two senses, starting with a shift away from the state-run, socialist economy. In 1971, he ended the Committee for the Elimination of Feudalism, and he returned some property that had been under sequestration, while further desequestration occurred in 1974 and 1981. But only after the Crossing of the Suez Canal did Sadat launch an "economic Crossing" as well—the policy that he called the *infitah* (economic open door; literally, opening). His October Working Paper (named for the month of the Crossing) of April 1974 announced a new receptiveness to private, including foreign, investment, and this was followed up by Law Number 43 in June of the same year providing new rules on taxation, labor, and other matters favorable to foreign investors. This left much of the socialist legacy, including state-owned enterprises, intact, but further legislation the following year allowed individuals to acquire more land than the reforms under Nasir permitted and removed other protection for poor peasants.

Aside from Sadat's longtime capitalist inclination and desire to please the United States, the logic of the *infitah* was that it provided a promising solution to Egypt's dire economic condition. Egypt had a surplus both of unskilled labor and of educated people. In combination with Western technology and investment by Persian Gulf countries that at the time were overflowing with petrodollars as a result of a sharp increase in oil prices, it seemed that the potential for an economic transformation was present. The peace that was believed to be in the making was supposed to expedite this.

The new policy produced disappointment except for the few who benefitted from it. Various factors ranging from bureaucratic hurdles to the danger of continuing conflict prevented substantial foreign investment in productive enterprise. Money was invested that provided expensive housing for foreigners but drove rent up for poor Egyptians. Some students of modern Egypt conclude that, having survived the Nasir period and being augmented by newly rising elements, the prerevolutionary rich class or landed bourgeoisie had returned to a position of ascendancy. While the condition of the ordinary people deteriorated, Egypt emerged as a land of fat cats. The extent of corruption and the number of millionaires grew exponentially. The president who presided over all this moved into Abadin Palace, and the number of his other residences multiplied as he awed the rich and stylish of the West with his fancy clothes and as his wife Jihan emerged as a darling of the Western world, with an interview with her published in such a publication as *Playgirl*, which disgusted ordinary Egyptians who got wind of it. Using his connections, Sadat's brother quickly transformed himself from a poor taxicab driver into a multimillionaire. By the beginning of 1975 (and on a bigger scale two years later), demonstrating workers were chanting, "O Hero of the Crossing, where is our breakfast?"

Secondly, although authoritarianism never made way for democracy, as Sadat claimed, there was a shift—at least for a while—toward a more liberal political system. The October Paper's commitment to a more diverse ASU led to the creation two years later of separate platforms (*minbars*; literally, pulpits) within that organization. Thus Sadat allowed his key crony (and brother-in-law), Mahmud Abu Wafia, to form a center (government) platform, whereas a rightist grouping—the Liberals—emerged under the leadership of former Wafdist Mustafa Kamil Murad, as well as a leftist faction headed by the Marxist Free Officer Khalid Muhi al-Din. Competing in parliamentary elections in 1980, the government faction got 280 seats, leaving 48 for independents, 12 for the rightists, and 4 for the left.

Later that year, Sadat agreed to let the platforms become political parties. The government group at first called itself the Egyptian Arab Socialist Party but later changed its name to National Democratic Party (NDP), opposed by Muhi al-Din's Progressive National Unionist Party (PNUP or *Tagammu*, Progressive, made up of Marxists and Nasirites), and Murad's

Liberal Party (LP or *Ahrar*). But with the PNUP's criticism of his foreign and domestic policies bringing down Sadat's ire, it refused to follow through with pressure from him the next year officially to disband and thus was forced to discontinue political activity. As a replacement for the PNUP, Sadat promoted the emergence of a center-left Socialist Labor Party, headed by a former leader of the prerevolutionary Young Egypt, Ibrahim Shukri. Also in 1978, Sadat agreed to let surviving Wafdists, headed by Fu'ad Sirag al-Din, form a New Wafd Party (NWP), with several independents and former members of other parties in the People's Assembly joining it. Representing outright rejection of the July 1952 Revolution and calling for accelerated liberalization, the NWP soon found itself beyond Sadat's pale. The party disbanded after he banned participation by people who had previously corrupted political life (i.e., prerevolutionary politicians), although some of its leaders remained in the People's Assembly.

The new multiparty system thus allowed limited opposition among parties that the government chose to permit. That meant the exclusion of some groups, notably the Muslim Brothers (as the rules forbade a religiously based party). No Nasirite party could get acceptance either, for to do so would imply that Sadat had renounced the 1952 Revolution. It was well known that the NDP would not be allowed to receive anything less than a landslide in any foreseeable parliamentary election or to diverge from Sadat's policies. Various kinds of patronage and vote rigging guaranteed that. And there was no prospect of competition for the presidency, where real power resided. But this limited political competition served as a safety valve to release pressure for further change. And even those who recognized the absurdity of Sadat's boast that Egypt had become "an island of democracy" could argue that a slow process of democratization had begun.

The regime underwent a serious shock in January 1977 that threatened its survival as Sadat autocratically extended his previous policy of economic liberalization in response to outside pressures. Among the aspects of Nasir's legacy that remained intact were subsidies that put the price of basic foods within reach of the poor (e.g., a large flat loaf of bread for a piaster, that is, about two cents) at the cost of LE553 million in one year. The United States and the Western-dominated World Bank and International Monetary Fund (IMF) were pushing for the removal of subsidies, said to undermine economic efficiency (with bread so cheap, some people fed it to animals). After long resisting pressure, an unexpected bombshell came on January 17, 1977, in the form of an announcement of cuts in subsidies and of other price increases that would cost the public LE500 million a year.

When workers' delegations in both Alexandria and Cairo set out the next morning to present protests to the authorities, clashes began to erupt. It did not take long for millions of people throughout the country to turn into a frenzied mob calling for "Nasir," attacking symbols of luxury and hurling slogans against Sadat and his wife and the "thieves of the *infitah*." With hundreds dying and wounded as the army tried futilely to suppress them, the government was able to abort this popular revolution only by canceling the price increases, followed by unsubstantiated charges by Sadat of a communist conspiracy. To be precise, the government recklessly charged that four illegal communist organizations had engaged in the plot, and there were insinuations about PNUP involvement.

Sadat behaved in an increasingly blatant authoritarian manner, earning the description "one-man ruler." As economic problems intensified and criticism of his policies toward Israel grew, he repeatedly resorted to referenda that produced "yes" votes from, typically, 99.96 percent of the voters, as in the case of the one that approved imprisonment for life with hard labor for anyone involved in a hostile organization or in antigovernment demonstrations. Not only did he emasculate the NWP and the PNUP, but he also adopted new institutional devices to bolster his position, including the creation of a partly appointive upper house, the Maglis al-Shura (Consultative Council), and he had the constitution changed to remove the original two-term limit for the president. He took on the office of prime minister himself. In 1980, the parliament enacted an ambiguous Law of Shame providing that anyone who undermined the dignity of the state could face being deprived of such rights as running for office or leaving the country. Criticism from the Lawyers' Syndicate brought pressure from Sadat to change its leadership, followed in June 1981 by a takeover of the syndicate's headquarters by government-organized dissidents. Israeli attacks on Arab countries at a time when Sadat could not afford to say anything that might prevent withdrawal from Sinai from being completed put him on edge. He began to fear that he would share the fate of his friend, the shah of Iran. The idea even circulated that Washington had conspired against the shah and might do the same against Sadat.

"I HAVE KILLED PHARAOH"

As he played to Western audiences and became increasingly out of touch with his own people, Sadat struck harshly in ways that some say pointed to insanity. The climax came in September 1981, when he ordered the arrest of 1,536 prominent people who ranged from Islamists of all varieties to Coptic bishops. Even Pope Shenouda III, who had been wildly accused of plotting to establish a breakaway Coptic state and who had criticized the peace with Israel, was arrested and confined in a monastery in the desert, while the government withdrew its recognition of his occupancy of the office. The list of those incarcerated included leading members of all opposition parties, legal or otherwise, but some militant Islamists got overlooked, including a 24-year-old lieutenant, Jihad activist Khalid al-Islambuli, whose brother was among Sadat's recent victims. Learning that he would be a participant in the annual parade on October 6 celebrating the Crossing, he saw a unique opportunity to spark a general uprising by killing the president, an act that Shaykh Abd al-Rahman issued a ruling purporting to legalize. When the vehicle carrying Islambuli and his fellow assassins arrived in front of the presidential reviewing stand, they rushed toward it in what some observers apparently thought was part of the military show until bullets began to fly. Sadat and five others lay dead. Islambuli proclaimed proudly, "I have killed Pharaoh."

8

The Mubarak Era

Among those with Sadat when he was killed was Vice President Husni Mubarak, a former general in the air force and a commander in the October War. Mubarak survived, with relatively minor wounds, from the assassination ordeal and took the helm as acting president. Soon afterward, a plebiscite occurred in which the voters officially made him president for a six-year term. He was a colorless figure who had no experience in political life before Sadat picked him as vice president in 1975, and there was little reason to expect Mubarak to survive for long. But by the time another plebiscite approved him for a fourth term in 1999—as always with near unanimity without opposition—he had surpassed all other rulers since independence in terms of the sheer number of years in office.

This seems all the more remarkable in light of the Egyptian people's reaction to the death of the one whose shoes Mubarak filled without shifting direction. Although there was mourning in Israel and in the United States, where the televised funeral was like what one would expect if an American president was killed, there were few signs of grief in Egypt. One might explain this, in part, as resulting from a fear of being caught in further violence, but in such sharp contrast to what happened when Nasir died, the streets were almost deserted in Cairo as dignitaries from all over the world congregated at Sadat's funeral.

The assassination failed to spark a revolution. Only in Asyut, in Upper Egypt, did the Islamic militants attempt a revolt, resulting in more than 70 deaths before the army restored order. But the next two decades would see a sporadic low-intensity war between the government and militant groups, perpetuating a cycle of repression and terrorism.

CONTINUITY IN LOW KEY

Mubarak continued the basic approaches that he inherited from his predecessor, but with a different style. He substituted soberness for Sadat's flamboyance. He was not the kind of person to try to shock the world with sudden announcements. It was not his style to make abrupt changes in policy or to make decisions without consulting others. Instead of Sadat's recurrent gambles, Mubarak demonstrated caution. And there were none of the rough edges that Sadat showed in vilifying his opponents or conducting massive clampdowns. He did not proclaim his policies so dramatically, nor did he advertise his piety so blatantly (not repeating, for example, his predecessor's constant reminder that his first name was Muhammad). Indeed, he started his administration by releasing many of the people that Sadat had arrested and actually meeting with them, giving the impression that he was a different kind of ruler. Some of these people expressed optimism about the change that was taking place. A few corrupt people, including Sadat's brother, were jailed.

In his early years as president, Mubarak depended heavily on his minister of defense, Field Marshal Abd al-Halim Abu Ghazala. There were suggestions that Abu Ghazala—sometimes thought of as Mubarak's "Amir"—was the favorite of the Americans and that he might eventually take over the leadership. It may have been for that reason that Mubarak eventually replaced him.

ECONOMIC LIBERALIZATION

The economic liberalization that started with Sadat's open-door policy sputtered along for a long time but accelerated during the late 1990s. The fear of evoking another mass uprising like that of January 1977 long continued to make it impolitic for Mubarak to proceed with drastic cuts in subsidies. Because the capitalist developed countries that dominated the IMF and World Bank shared the goal of preserving political stability, these institutions muted their expectations for reform. The IMF and the Paris Club of international creditors recurrently reached agreements with Cairo that provided financial relief without the normal stringent demands relating to subsidies, and Egypt was admitted to the World Trade Organization, signifying its integration into a liberal global economic system, in 1995. Gradually, though, Mubarak was able to slip changes in that brought increases in the cost of living, as by decreasing the size of bread loaves, rather than adding to the price per loaf. A law enacted in 1992 removed rent controls for agricultural land (effective by 1997), a big blow to poor peasants. After 1996, the process proceeded faster, particularly under the government of Prime Minister Atif Ubayd, which came to office in 1999 with a strong commitment to liberal economic policies. The artificially high exchange rates for the Egyptian pound of the Nasir era had been modified over the years, and the transition to floating rates determined by the market finally went into effect in 2003. The value of the Egyptian pound consequently plummeted (soon valued at little more than $0.14). Expected to provide a boon for exports, this deeply cut into the purchasing power of ordinary people.

The regime's goal of privatizing state-owned enterprises also proceeded slowly. By the mid-1990s, few companies had been sold to private entrepreneurs. The process proceeded more seriously from 1996 on, but by 2000, about 60 percent of the businesses designated for privatization still were state run.

Although magnifying the gap between rich and poor and reducing the consumption levels of the latter in absolute terms, the more liberal economic policies produced economic growth that proceeded fairly fast for a while. The growth rate (that is, increase in the GDP) ranged at around 5 percent or more in the late 1990s—admittedly leaving an 18 percent unemployment rate and failing to provide jobs for many thousands of university graduates each year—but subsequently dropped to about half of that. Although the economy had suffered from such developments as falling oil prices in the 1980s (which not only reduced the country's modest oil income but, more important, also cut down on remittances from expatriate Egyptians) and then by the return of large numbers of people from Iraq and Kuwait at the beginning of the 1990s. Egypt's role in the 1991 war to restore Kuwait's independence brought it an unprecedented windfall, that is, the cancellation of about half of its $50 billion foreign debt (with $14 billion forgiven immediately by the United States and the Gulf monarchies and with a later additional cut of $10 billion by the Paris Club as well as rescheduling and reducing the interest on the rest).

Economic woes continued to beset the country. After recovering from the losses following a massacre of foreign tourists in 1997, Egypt's income from tourism plummeted in the wake of al-Qa'ida's attack on New York in September 2001 and increased insurance rates brought on by the war in Iraq in 2003 cut into Suez Canal traffic and tolls. Remittances were down again, too. Meeting in Sharm al-Shaykh, a group of 37 donor countries and international financial institutions agreed to provide $10.3 billion in grants and loans over a three-year period. But a World Bank report issued in 2003 pointed to a recent serious deterioration in the standard of living of ordinary people and projected that the percentage of Egyptians in poverty would increase, a reversal of the trend in the late 1990s.

POLITICAL LIBERALIZATION?

Mubarak began his rule by avoiding some of his predecessor's dictatorial tendencies and by seeming to promote a more meaningful degree of democratization. He allowed the opposition parties that Sadat had thwarted to resume their activities. He also restored government recognition to Pope Shenoudah III. But by 1987 he was specifying that democracy had to come "in doses" and within "limits." In all fairness, although Mubarak's regime was definitely an authoritarian one, this was provoked by real disorder (even if arguably provoking more of such), and its repressive nature neither constituted an innovation for Egypt nor proved as egregious as that in some other countries.

The number of legal political parties continued to increase as the government saw fit or sometimes as courts decided. The main opposition parties now included the New Wafd Party (NWP), the Labor Party (formerly called the Socialist Labor Party) legalized again after being banned by Sadat and now taking an Islamist stance but then again suspended in 2000, the Liberal (Ahrar) Party, the Progressive National Unionist Party (PNUP), and a Nasirite Party. A minor Islamist organization, the Ummah Party, also received approval.

The exclusion of the Muslim Brothers continued. Even a clearly moderate, liberal Islamist Wasit [Center] Party was rejected by the government on the ground that it was a front for other Islamists. There was reason to believe that the Muslim Brothers constituted the real opposition and likely would win any free election. The ban on their participation as a political party thus constituted a profound testimony to the absence of real democracy, as did the government's accelerated attempt from the mid-nineties on to suppress members of the group, even when they were not engaged in violence. However, some individuals associated with the Muslim Brothers ran as independents in most of the parliamentary elections from 1984 on and sometimes participated in electoral alliances with other parties. Such coalitions helped their members evade the rule then in force that slates with less than 8 percent of the overall vote could not get seats.

A few members of the Muslim Brethren recurrently got elected, although they often faced arrests, particularly before elections for parliament and for trade union and professional syndicate councils. The predominance of the Muslim Brothers in most of these latter associations was so great that the government—arguing that low turnout produced results that were not representative of their overall membership—resorted to nullifying election results and imposing its own leadership.

Parliamentary elections guaranteed the NDP huge majorities. It received almost 73 percent of the vote in the 1984 general elections, the first ones held during the Mubarak period, whereas the NWP, the only opposition party to win enough votes (15.1 percent) to gain representation, got 59 seats. The size of the majority did not radically vary from this in elections held in 1987 (after the president preempted a judicial decision that the failure to allow independent candidates invalidated previous elections by holding a referendum dissolving the existing body), 1990, 1995, and 2000. This last occasion was the first time that elections, as a result of a court decision that previous balloting had been unconstitutional, were conducted under judicial supervision. Only 353 members of the NDP slate won, but 35 of the 72 victorious independents actually were affiliated with it. This compares with 17 Muslim Brothers (elected as independents), 7 for the NWP, 6 for the PUP, 3 for the Nasirites, and 1 for the LSP.

The overwhelming victories of the governing party, an organization dominated by the old upper class and by others from the military and bureaucracy who had gained wealth and connections, requires some explanation. In part, this was a result of the way it was able to wield patronage—that is, to dole out rewards to those who supported it and get them and their families and their networks of friends to the polls. Perceptive scholars portrayed the NDP as essentially a patronage network. The low voting rate for the general population (nobody believes official statistics showing the contrary), partly resulting from an assumption that the exercise was a sham, facilitated this. But massive electoral fraud and efforts to prevent opponents of the government from voting constituted a major part of the story. Thus, although judicial supervision of the polling stations in 2000 ate into the government's opportunities for fraud, large numbers of Muslim Brothers were arrested, in accordance with the emergency law, just before the balloting, and those who had previously been convicted were barred from running. Even those opposition parties that participated in elections and whose members sometimes sit in the People's Assembly were being co-opted, that is, given rewards—a share of the patronage—for legitimizing the existing political system. Thus, although the paucity of democratic procedures was obvious to anyone who looked closely, the electoral process allowed the regime to present itself to the outside world as one that was democratizing, however slowly.

And with the president confident of the support of his party as well as constitutionally authorized to issue many legislative decrees, real power remained centered in his hands. Before each six-year term expired, the NDP-dominated People's Assembly recurrently nominated Mubarak for reelection, followed by a referendum. There was never an opposition candidate. The "yes" vote ranged from 98.5 percent in 1981 to 93.8 percent in 1999, hardly more credible than the famous over-99-percent approval his predecessors had boasted of. Aside from this authoritarian kind of election, it was illegal to publicly criticize the president or his family (and members of the government and foreign heads of state), although this often was not enforced. With particular reference to the widespread belief that Mubarak was planning for his son Gamal Mubarak—who was given a key position in the ruling party in 2002—eventually to succeed him, someone dubbed the system a "presidential monarchy." Mubarak's failure to appoint a vice president added to the suspicion that his son eventually would replace him.

The range of tolerated expression was greater than before, but there were important limits, too. Radio and television were government controlled, as were the main newspapers. But opposition parties had the right to present their views in their own publications, which, however, at times were suspended for going beyond the bounds the regime permitted. Articles sometimes were censored. It was difficult for new publications to get licenses. Books and pamphlets sporadically were confiscated. Journalists sometimes were detained for writing on such topics as government corruption. Defending Islamists in court occasionally brought prison sentences for lawyers. A new law in 2000 allowed the government to dissolve nongovernmental organizations without resort to the judiciary.

A central reality of the Mubarak years was the Emergency Law put in force at the beginning of his rule and renewed by the People's Assembly every three years with only a few opposition members opposing it. It was a crime for more than five people to meet without a permit. Publications deemed a danger to national security could be banned. The law could deprive people of essentially any civil rights. In accordance with legal authorization to detain people without charges for a month (renewable indefinitely), the police regularly held thousands in custody, sometimes just for stating their opinions, for demonstrating against Israel's actions in the occupied territories or against the American war on Iraq in 2003, or even for writing a book critical of U.S. policies.

Special military courts had authority to detain people without charge.

In what seemed to constitute nothing more than a cosmetic reform, the High State Security Court was abolished in 2003 and its previous decisions made subject to appeal, but another tribunal, the Emergency State Security Court still could try important cases, with no appeals allowed (except to the president requesting a pardon). Also, in 2003, the regular courts got new authority to detain people without charge for six months. Human rights advocates suggested that the emergency measures now were so ingrained in the civil code that the government would not even need to renew the emergency law again. The conclusion stated in the Egyptian Organization for Human Rights' 2001 report that "The law ultimately suspends democratic rights that are inconvenient for the government" remained true.

Human rights organizations regularly documented gross violations, including a "systematic pattern of torture." The thousands of people detained without charges—including members of the Muslim Brotherhood not involved in violence—suffered torture severe enough that dozens died as a result. Demonstrators sometimes were violently assaulted by the police. There were reports of actual or threatened rapes of female detainees or members of detainees' families. Human Rights Watch documented a pattern of taking fugitives' family members, including women and children, as hostages and subjecting them to torture and rape. Several dissidents simply disappeared. Such methods purported to combat violent extremism but may also have helped create more of it.

BURGEONING ISLAMIST MOVEMENTS

Islamist movements grew into an even more pervasive force than ever during the Mubarak period. Elections held within the professional syndicates, such as those of lawyers and doctors, produced councils dominated by supporters of the Muslim Brothers, evoking government intervention and sometimes the imposition of unelected members. Islamists gained increasing influence in the universities, resulting in a new law providing that deans would be appointed by the government. Also, from 1994 on, mayors of villages were appointed by the central government rather than being elected, as before. Some knowledgeable Egyptians believed that in free elections the Muslim Brothers still would not win an actual majority, but others sensed that the result would be much like that in Algeria, where the Islamist FIS was winning a landslide in the 1992 general elections in that country and was prevented from doing so only by a military coup that Western powers embraced with renewed aid.

The Muslim Brothers made up a network that in some ways seemed to outdo an enfeebled (if dangerously repressive) state that had little legitimacy as an institution serving Egyptian society. They provided inexpensive clinics and other welfare services, demonstrating a kind of dedication, honesty, and efficiency lacking elsewhere. The earthquake that devastated parts of Cairo in 1992 provided a notable case of the Muslim Brethren's ability to extend immediate relief at a time when the government bureaucracy found itself paralyzed by rigid rules. Some physicians working for the organization were arrested for providing such emergency services and thus increasing the Islamists' popularity.

Fringe Islamist movements violently confronted the regime. Some members eventually merged with similar revolutionary organizations in other countries to create a worldwide force that attacked the United States. Mubarak survived an attempt by Egyptian militants to assassinate him during a visit to Ethiopia in 1995. Small groups such as the Survivors of the Fire [of Hell, a reference to Mubarak's prisons and torture chambers] in the late 1980s and The Promise in 2002 engaged in assassinations and became the object of government repression. Others were accused of belonging to the Islamic Liberation Organization, which had carried out attacks during Sadat's rule. The biggest militant organizations remained al-Jihad and particularly the Islamic Group. The latter, which had evolved from the Islamic groups Sadat initially supported as allies against the left, carried out brutal attacks, killing Farag Fudah, a professor known for unorthodox views. Nagib Mahfuz, winner of the Nobel Prize for Literature seven years earlier, whose writings some considered blasphemous, survived a stabbing by members of the same group.

Another brutal tactic adopted by some militants during the 1990s was to murder tourists. The goal was to punish the regime and hopefully bring it down by undermining tourism, which provided a vital source of foreign exchange. This reached its climax with the killing of 62 German tourists (and four Egyptians) at the famous Temple of Queen Hatshepsut in Luxor in 1997. This nearly destroyed tourism for a while, costing the country billions of dollars. It also horrified the Egyptian people in general.

The Luxor massacre accelerated repression to the extent that leaders of the Islamic Group unilaterally declared a cease-fire in 1999. In 2002, the government organized a meeting—in prison—of imprisoned militants with hundreds of other members of the Islamic Group to tell the latter that peace had been concluded. Now it seems that they had already agreed on a cease-fire at the time of the Luxor massacre but were unable to get word to the unit that carried it out. Hundreds of militants who renounced violence were released from prison in subsequent years, although other Islamists continued to face arrest.

With most of the militants rejecting violent activities in the late 1990s, others fled to Afghanistan, where the Taliban regime was giving sanctuary to Usama bin Ladin and al-Qa'ida and where hundreds of Egyptian militants had fought alongside him against the Soviets in the 1980s. Dr. Ayman al-Zawahiri, the physician who had come to many people's attention earlier as he appeared in court in a cage with others accused in Sadat's assassination and who was a veteran of the war against the Soviets in Afghanistan, formally united his faction of Jihad with al-Qa'ida and emerged as the top lieutenant of bin Ladin to pursue a direct global terrorist campaign against the United States, which the militants saw as the patron of the Egyptian, Saudi, and other Arab regimes as well as of Israel, rather than continuing the fight at home. Already following the attempt to blow up the World Trade Center in 1993, several Egyptians affiliated with militant Egyptian Islamist organizations, notably Shaykh Umar Abd al-Rahman, were imprisoned in the United States. In September 2001, it was the young Egyptian al-Qa'ida operative Muhammad Atta who led the first kamikaze attack on the World Trade Center that allegedly in large part represented planning by Zawahiri.

The Mubarak regime reacted to the Islamist challenge not only by repressing the militants and, by 1994, increasingly the moderate Islamists as well but also in many ways by joining the movement to Islamicize Egyptian society. Those Islamists who railed against the regime were matched by television preachers that tried to provide religious legitimacy for it. Some leading Islamic scholars allied with the government made statements equating secularists with apostates. The judiciary became more Islamicized, as indicated by the sensational case of one university professor, Nasr Hamid Abu Zayd, whose marriage a court dissolved in 1995 on the ground that his heretical views made him a disbeliever and thus unqualified to have a Muslim wife, and there were unsuccessful attempts to punish the outspoken feminist Nawal al-Sa'dawi in the same way. Dramatic arrests of homosexuals in 2002 indicated that the regime was anxious to protect its religious credentials. Even actions designed to supervise religious activity, such as increasing attempts to bring private mosques under control and to determine the content of sermons (it was announced in 2003 that one sermon, approved by the government, now would be heard in all mosques), reflect something at odds with authentic secularism. The contest seemed more and more to be between populist and establishment Islam rather than between Islam and secularism.

The simultaneous resurgence of Coptic Christianity and Islam in Egypt endangered the relationship between the two religious communities. Sporadic clashes occurred between Copts and militant Islamists. In 2000 a dispute between two people escalated into a sectarian riot in the Upper Egyptian town of Kushah in which 20 Copts were killed. It was left to the Court of Cassation, responding to a request from the public prosecutor, to call for a retrial following light sentences and acquittals of the accused Muslims by the lower court. And in 2001 Copts in Cairo rioted after a Cairo tabloid (later closed down and condemned by the parliament and its editor sentenced to three years in prison for "insulting a heavenly religion") published an inflammatory photo of a Coptic monk (later reported to have previously been excommunicated) engaged in lewd behavior. Although the Muslim Brothers sometimes issued reassuring statements, Copts were apprehensive about the possibility that the Islamist opposition would come to power.

AN EXPLOSIVE SITUATION

The socioeconomic situation provided a tinderbox that one spark could ignite. A case in point occurred in 1987, when a rumor spread that the terms of service for the 300,000 conscripts in the Central Security Forces, whose monthly pay amounted to $4 dollars a month and who were subjected to beatings by their officers, would be extended. The conscripts reacted by spontaneously engaging in an orgy of rioting, looting, and killing. Such symbols of luxury as hotels and nightclubs provided a main target for these miserable young men. It took three days for the army to suppress them, and then only because the sheer destructiveness of the rioters discouraged others from joining in a broader revolt.

RETURN TO THE ARAB FOLD

Egypt's exclusion from the Arab world gradually receded. It helped for Sadat to be gone, as his successor was not personally associated with the Egyptian–Israeli peace to the same degree. And Mubarak avoided harsh rhetoric against other Arab countries. Some of Sadat's critics among Arab rulers had long had secret ties with Israel, and their official reaction to the Egyptian–Israeli peace treaty served mainly to appease their people. A punishment such as severing diplomatic relations was largely symbolic and did not always prevent amicable, though less-publicized, relationships from continuing. Even for governments that sincerely opposed Egypt's policies, the need for its backing in various conflicts soon manifested itself, as in conflicts between the two Yemens and between Algeria and Morocco. The Soviet invasion in Afghanistan tended to make the Egyptian–Israeli peace a less pressing concern for various Arab capitals.

Despite its facilitation by Sadat's peace treaty with Israel, the Israeli invasion of Lebanon in 1982 also eased Arab hostility to Egypt, as this brought a "freeze" in its rapprochement with Israel and created a situation in which the PLO desperately needed what help Egypt's "moderation" could bring. With the PLO in conflict with the Syrian-backed Amal militia in Lebanon in 1983, Egyptian support was forthcoming, leading to a visit by PLO Chairman Yasir Arafat to Cairo. By 1983, Mubarak was asserting, with some truth, that the Arabs had restored ties with his government except in a formal sense, and by the next year Jordan and Morocco renewed diplomatic relations with Egypt.

The Iranian Revolution's threat of contagion provided the strongest incentive for Arab regimes to normalize their relationship with Cairo. The opposite seemed true at first, as the Islamic nature of the revolution served as a warning to Arab elites that they had better take their loyalty to Muslim causes, such as that over Palestine, seriously. But feeling threatened by the popular appeal of the revolution to its Shi'ite majority, Iraq invaded Iran in 1980, expecting to overthrow the revolutionary regime. Instead, the Iranians fought back fiercely, and within two years there was reason to think that Iranian forces would overthrow the Iraqi regime and further threaten the status quo. Even though Sadat called Iraqi President Saddam Husayn the aggressor, he strongly supported his fight against Ayatullah Khumayni, providing about $3 billion in weapons and allowing Egyptian officers to participate in the war. With Iraq taking the lead in pushing for his "rehabilitation," almost all Arab states restored diplomatic relations with Egypt by the late 1980s. Egypt's membership in various Arab and Islamic organizations gradually resumed. In 1987, a meeting of Arab foreign ministers ended its suspension from the Arab League, whose seat returned to Cairo.

THE COLD PEACE

Sadat's peace with Israel stayed in place under his successor. Aside from a continuing dispute over Taba, a tiny piece of land on the border (resolved, through arbitration, in Egypt's favor in 1989), the Israelis completed their promised withdrawal from Egyptian territory in April 1982. Despite violent protests from settlers, they even evacuated the settlements they had established there. But it soon became apparent that this was a "cold peace," as Egyptians could not be indifferent to Israel's continuing occupation of Palestinian and Syrian territory and moves to absorb these areas, including building settlements and, in December 1981, formally annexing the Golan Heights. And barely had the withdrawal from Sinai occurred when the Israelis launched a major invasion of Lebanon on June 6, 1982. Egyptian critics of their regime's policies saw this as proof that their country's withdrawal from the conflict had put Israel in a position to attack other Arabs with impunity.

This and later crises would threaten to build up opposition to the government at home. Egypt was in no position to take any military action or even to break off diplomatic relations with its old foe, for to do so likely would result in the reoccupation of Sinai and loss of American aid. But various actions demonstrating the government's displeasure ensued, notably withdrawing the Egyptian ambassador from Israel and declaring a "freeze" on ties after massacres of Palestinians carried out by Israeli-backed Lebanese militias in the Shatilah and Sabra refugee camps in Beirut in September 1982, but nothing that undid Sadat's peace treaty. It was not until four years later that a new Egyptian ambassador was appointed or that Mubarak met with an Israeli prime minister. Again, the Egyptian ambassador to Israel was withdrawn again for a while following the massacre of 40 Palestinians in Hebron in 1994. Egypt also announced a freeze in contacts with Israel in 1999 in response to the Likud government's intransigent policies. In contrast to Sadat's exaggerated friendship with his former enemies, it was not until the occasion of the funeral of assassinated Prime Minister Yitzhak Rabin in 1996 that Mubarak visited Israel.

Most of all, the peace remained "cold" on a popular level. It was much easier for the government to conclude a treaty with Israel than for the Egyptian people to like the Israelis. With few exceptions, Egyptians refused to visit Israel, and professional associations in particular rejected any dealings with their Israeli counterparts.

Cairo consistently worked to bring about a comprehensive Arab–Israeli peace that would remove it from its awkward and dangerous position of being out of step with the Arab world. Examples of its mediatory role include a 10-point plan Mubarak presented in 1989 in an attempt to get Palestinian–Israeli talks started. Egypt participated in the Madrid Conference on the Arab–Israeli dispute in 1991, played an important role in various follow-up meetings, and eagerly supported the Oslo agreement two years later.

Aside from the issue of the "peace process," other matters sometimes threatened Egyptian–Israeli relations. With the Nuclear Non-Proliferation treaty up for renewal on a permanent basis in 1995, Egypt thought this was an issue on which it could confront Israel within the limits of the peace treaty. For a while, it demanded Israel's accession to the treaty as a condition of renewal by Arab countries, but it backed down under intense American pressure. Another development the same year that created much revulsion in Egypt and potentially made it difficult for the government to continue its diplomatic ties with Israel was the revelation by an Israeli soldier in the 1956 and 1957 wars of the existence of mass graves of massacred Egyptian prisoners in Sinai. But again the Mubarak regime's interest in keeping the peace overrode the popular anger.

Anger among the Egyptian populace intensified as the twenty-first century began with the breakdown of the Oslo "peace process," the start of a new, more violent Palestinian uprising that developed into suicide bombings by Palestinian Islamists, and brutal repression by the Israelis. Massive Egyptian student demonstrations during 2002–2003 called for breaking ties with Israel and boycotting Israeli and American products as well as for launching a *jihad*. Young Egyptians who slipped across the frontier to attack Israelis came to be hailed as martyrs. State control no longer sufficed to prevent the press and television from harsh denunciations of the Israelis. Even the normally quiescent official religious authorities appointed by the government could not be kept from praising Palestinian suicide bombers. In order to appease the public, the government announced the severance of all communications with Israel except, or so it was explained, for diplomatic efforts to assist the Palestinians. The Egyptian ambassador to Israel was withdrawn again in October 2000, not to return during the subsequent three years.

A PILLAR OF UNITED STATES POLICY

Mubarak continued to solidify his government's alignment with the United States. Admittedly, he normalized relations with the Soviet Union, restoring formal diplomatic ties in 1983. And Egypt continued to participate in the Nonaligned Conference along with other Third World countries ranging from Castro's Cuba to de facto allies and clients of the United States such as Saudi Arabia. But no one could confuse this with the nonalignment of Nasir's era. The approximately $2 billion in American aid each year—the largest amount for any Third World country—testified to the importance Washington gave to maintaining the relationship, the most obvious aspect of which was preserving the Egyptian-Israeli peace. Mubarak sometimes criticized U.S. policies on the Palestine question and on such issues as the harsh sanctions that punished the Iraqi people for so long, but this benefitted both him and his American patrons alike by legitimizing him at home and in the Arab world. He clearly had committed himself to the American-led world, and he could be counted on to cooperate in practice on important matters.

A notable example of such cooperation followed the Iraqi invasion of

Kuwait in 1990. Mubarak was particularly angry over the invasion because this was in violation of a clear promise to him from President Saddam Husayn but more broadly because of the dangers to the stability of the whole region. At first, he tried to use diplomatic means within the Arab world to get Iraq to withdraw but succumbed to U.S. pressure to drop this approach. When the United States saw fit to send troops to the Gulf region, Mubarak joined in by dispatching a 35,000-strong Egyptian force that participated in the war in 1991. More important than the actual military contribution was the fact that Egyptian (and Syrian) involvement made the predominantly American war against Iraq more palatable in the Arab world. Such was the significance of this for Washington that it earned Cairo a drastic reduction in its international indebtedness, as mentioned elsewhere. However, a plan announced soon after the end of hostilities for Egyptian and Syrian forces to stay in the Gulf region to continue to provide security to Arab monarchies soon fell through.

Mubarak eagerly joined the United States in its "war on terrorism" in 2001. More to the point, he felt that the United States was joining a struggle that he had been pursuing all along. He considered his own harsh methods of dealing with terrorists vindicated when the Americans seemed to be following in his footsteps in the period following September 2001. Press reports indicated that the Mubarak regime's lack of inhibition about such methods as tearing out fingernails served an important purpose for the United States, which in some cases transferred suspects to Egypt to obtain information from them.

Mubarak's critics saw him as the head of an American satellite regime that Washington helped to keep in power through its aid program and other means. They argued that Washington's support for democratization in other parts of the world did not extend to its Arab allies, including Egypt, whose peace with Israel and close alliance with the United States could be sustained only by an autocratic government. The regime's repressiveness almost never evoked serious criticism from Washington (aside from candid human rights reports annually issued by the State Department). A rare exception involved the conviction of sociologist Sa'd al-Din Ibrahim by a state security court in 2002 on trumped-up charges that the prodemocracy organization he headed had mismanaged funds from the European Union and produced a video documenting electoral fraud, thus allegedly bringing "shame" on Egypt. Because Ibrahim had dual American and Egyptian citizenship, this created an embarrassment for the United States–Egyptian relationship, resulting in the U.S. Congress cutting out a small additional aid program that had been planned but leaving the annual $2 billion package untouched. Perhaps the awkwardness of this situation that threatened to erode support in the United States for its Egyptian client regime contributed in part to the eventual decision of the Court of Cassation to free Professor Ibrahim. But few gave credibility to a highly publicized call by President George W. Bush in November 2003 for democratization in the Arab world in which he singled out Egypt.

Mubarak's role as a client of the United States as it was pursuing policies that caused fury among the Egyptian people threatened to undermine his ability to keep control. Although he pleaded with Washington in 2002–2003 that an invasion of Iraq would bring fearful consequences, he had no choice but to cooperate with the United States when the war occurred. Security forces battled with massive protests—larger than anything since 1977—against the invasion in March 2003, amid chants from demonstrators denouncing Mubarak and his son Gamal. Egyptian critics of the regime claimed that the extension of the state of emergency that year was designed mainly to contain opposition to its patron's war on Iraq. Indeed, peaceful protesters became the main victims of emergency detentions under the law. Several people were arrested and tortured for harsh criticisms of American policies toward Iraq, for "spreading false information," that is, communicating with human rights organizations, for accessing human rights materials from the Internet, or—as in the case of a young engineer, Ashraf Ibrahim, who had published an article in the London *Economist* on corruption in Egypt and who owned copies of books by Lenin and Chomsky—for forming an illegal leftist organization. Critics saw the continuation of authoritarian rule as an inherent part of the U.S.–Egyptian alliance at a time when U.S. policies were so unpopular. The American aid program pursued a program of "democracy promotion," though not seriously in the case of Egypt, and in fact Washington gave priority to keeping an authoritarian regime in power.

TORN BETWEEN REALITY AND IDENTITY

Basic to the Egyptian situation was the pull between its Arab and Islamic identity and the country's difficult reality. Admittedly, the issue of pan-Arabism was dead for now in the old sense of proposals for merging Arab countries. But the broader identity, though now more Islamic than Arab, remained strong at a popular level and continued to demand that the country devote itself to causes that were dear to the Arab and Islamic world, notably in the conflict with Israel but also in opposing what more and more saw as American imperialism in the area.

The reality was one of impotence. The regime could not risk losing

American aid by making more than symbolic and ineffective verbal stands to pay obeisance to popular feelings. And as Mubarak told Egyptians who wanted to do something about the repression of the Palestinians at the beginning of the 2000s, Egypt lacked the ability to finance a war with Israel. American aid helped keep the Mubarak regime in power, which in turn provided a major pillar for the United States position in the area, but at the same time the American occupation of Iraq and support for Israel angered much of the Egyptian public and threatened, along with more basic sociopolitical factors, to undermine the regime.

Epilogue

At the opening of the third millennium A.D., Egypt seemed, as at the end of the New Kingdom, again to be a "broken reed." Following ages of subordination to alien empires, it enjoyed another glorious role during the Middle Ages as a main center of Islamic civilization, which ceased to be alien once Egypt adopted the conquerors' religion, culture, and identity, although Turks and other foreign Muslims kept Egyptians out of the ruling class. As a century and a half of Western domination (interrupted by abortive resurgence under Muhammad Ali and Isma'il in the 1800s) was ending, authentic Egyptians came to power in the 1950s and the country asserted its independence and made a valiant effort to lead the rebirth of a pan-Arab nation and to play an important role in the overall assertion of the Third World against colonialism and underdevelopment. But recurrent setbacks left it behind to face increasingly adverse circumstances.

The future appears dismal. As the population continues to grow, how can Egypt support itself and provide jobs for growing numbers? Even now, it imports 60 percent of its food. Despite significant successes in reducing the birthrate, the fact that 40 percent of the people are less than 15 years of age—with their reproductive lives awaiting them—means that the number of Egyptians will continue to shoot up. One projection puts it at 100 million by 2020. Current plans to divert water from Lake Nasir to the Western Desert promise to enlarge the cultivated area only slightly.

No road to broader economic development seems open. A return to the populist socialist policies of the Nasir period is hardly on anyone's agenda, and in any case pressures from Washington and international lending agencies exclude such. Even a revolution led by radical Islamists would not pursue this course, at least not fully, although it might be inclined to strike a balance between global capitalism and populist policies.

The process of economic liberalization will continue, if fitfully. But the prospects of luring major international investments remain dim in the face of unchangeable bureaucratic hurdles and of a mediocre authoritarian regime whose future stability is questionable. Also, the threat that conflicts within the region will spread makes the country less inviting. As pointed out in a recent United Nations Development Programme (UNDP) report, such dismal trends characterize the whole Arab region, and it is difficult to see how they can be reversed.

Even if neoliberal strategies succeed in bringing economic development, they will widen the already dangerous gap between the country's haves and have-nots that has returned since the end of the Nasir era. Indeed, a recent study by the UNDP lists Egypt as a country in crisis in that the vast differences in the standard of living of Cairo and much of the countryside, particularly Upper Egypt, create the danger of major social, economic, and political unrest. The study pointed to a real per capita gross national product (GNP) in rural areas that is 45 percent less than that of the capital city. The rural adult literacy rate was not even half that of Cairo and life expectancy was six years lower.

One imperative—though not a panacea by itself—is democratization, but the obstacles to this seem compelling in the absence of solutions to socioeconomic problems. And the existing regime is not likely willingly to allow its opposition—which more and more seems to mean Islamists, particularly the Muslim Brothers—a chance to come to power. Without democratization, the regime will grow more stagnant than ever, and only electoral mechanisms allowing varying groups to alternate in power can prevent what is left of the legitimacy of the existing political order from vanishing.

There can be no democracy without the inclusion of the Muslim Brothers in the country's politics. We may or may not accept their claim that "Islam is the solution," although their cultural authenticity and their growing role in popular organizations may put them in a position to contribute to the solution. For the real opposition to be prevented from running its own slate of parliamentary candidates—and its own candidate for president—in free elections means an entrenched authoritarian system by definition. To many, this poses a conundrum, for they maintain that the Muslim Brothers and Islamist groups generally oppose democracy and would impose their own authoritarian rule once they were voted into power. The Muslim Brothers did criticize "Western democracy" in the past, and it is not clear whether by that they meant democracy in principle or what they saw as deficiencies in the process. Even if they embrace the democratic process today, as they say they do, circumstances after they came to power might induce them to resort to authoritarian methods of rule, as has been true of many political movements. The end result of this scenario might be a change from one authoritarian system to another, but such a possibility should not be used as an excuse to preserve the present system.

Even a political party lacking a commitment to the democratic process at the beginning may adapt once it obtains representation and needs to involve itself in parliamentary politics. And it is not clear that the Muslim Brothers would receive an overwhelming majority in free elections.

The international connection provides an important key to this. The American backing for the present regime (talk about "democracy promotion" notwithstanding) likely will keep it emboldened to hold on to power and not to open up in a meaningful way. Public opinion in Egypt is out of tune with American policies in the Middle East. A poll taken in 2003 shows that 94 percent of Egyptians have an unfavorable view of the United States, the country that backs their regime and other authoritarian regimes in the Arab world and provides military, economic, and diplomatic support to Israel that allows the continuing subjection of the Palestinians. True democratization under such circumstances would constitute a danger for Washington.

Only a removal of grievances would allow a democratizing Egypt as a country (as opposed to just a regime) to have an authentic alliance with America. If the Palestine issue in particular could be resolved in a way that the Arab and Muslim worlds, as well as the Palestinians themselves, consider to involve substantial justice, democratization would no longer constitute a threat to Washington's policies and consequently could occur more easily. The argument about whether the Islamists would destroy democracy if it came to power through a democratic process might become moot, for the Islamist movement, which shrank when Nasir offered another outlet for populism, has ballooned primarily as a protest against an authoritarian government that is seen as an American satellite or client regime and against broader grievances of other Arabs and Muslims. Thus, with a combination of democratization and a just peace, the Islamist movement likely would lose much of its electoral appeal. But optimism that these factors will fall into place seems unwarranted, leaving open the prospect of eventual violence and possibly chaos.

Notable People in the History of Egypt

Abduh, Shaykh Muhammad (1849–1905). Born in a village in the Delta and a graduate of al-Azhar, he was interested in philosophy and Sufism. An ardent follower of Jamal al-Din al-Afghani during his stay in Egypt during the 1870s and a supporter of Ahmad Urabi's revolt, he was deported following the British occupation of 1882. He and Afghani edited a journal, *The Indissoluble Bond,* in Paris. He returned to Egypt in 1889 to occupy several high judicial positions, including the post of Chief Mufti, and became a member of the Legislative Council. He concentrated on carrying out legal reform and modernizing al-Azhar rather than opposing the occupation. His stress on the need to reconcile revelation with reason put him in the forefront of the Islamic modernist movement.

Banna, Hasan al- (1906–1949). The founder of the most important modern Islamist movement, this son of a watchmaker was born in a village in the Delta. He studied in Qur'anic schools and Dar al-Ulum (a teacher-training institution) before becoming a schoolteacher. His piety led him to preach in public places at an early age. Living in Ismailiyya in 1928, he founded the Society of the Muslim Brothers, dedicated to the establishment of a more authentically Islamic society governed by the *shari`ah* as well as to resisting Western colonialism. His organization was committed to the Palestine cause and engaged in guerrilla actions there before the Egyptian army intervened in 1948. It is not clear what his relationship was to the organization's secret Special Section that engaged in violent activities such as the assassination of Prime Minister Nuqrashi Pasha in 1948, which led in turn to his own murder in 1949, apparently by the king's agents.

Baybars I (ca. 1223–1277). A Turk born in the Kipchak region west of the Caspian Sea and enslaved at an early age, he became one of the Ayyubid Sultan al-Salih's mamluks and distinguished himself in 1249 in the struggle against the Sixth Crusade and then commanded the mamluk forces that defeated the Mongols in 1260. He succeeded Qutuz (whose assassination he led) as sultan in 1260. Sometimes considered the real founder of the Mamluk Empire, he led military campaigns that expanded its control as far as Anatolia and the Sudan. Almost unrivaled in subsequent centuries as a legendary hero, he was noted for astute diplomacy and administration.

Boutros Ghali, Boutros (1922–). A member of a prominent Coptic family (grandson of Prime Minister Boutros Ghali) and married to an Egyptian Jewish woman whose father was born in Palestine, he was a prominent professor of international relations at Cairo University. He became Minister of State for Foreign Affairs in November 1977, in which office he played a major role in Sadat's diplomacy leading to the Egyptian–Israeli peace treaty. In 1991, he was elected Secretary General of the United Nations, but the United States vetoed his reelection in 1996, allegedly because of his release of a report showing that the Israeli bombing of a refugee compound in Lebanon in 1996 was intentional.

Faruq [Farouk], King (1920–1965). Son of King Fu'ad I who succeeded at age 17 to the Egyptian throne in 1936 (with a regent in control until his 18th birthday). He sometimes aspired to become caliph (head of the Islamic world). Widely admired at first, he later earned the reputation of a dissolute man and was considered an embarrassment by many people. Also, there was a widespread feeling of shame over the way he capitulated to British demands in 1942, begging to be allowed to keep his throne. He was blamed for sending the army to Palestine unprepared in 1948. From 1952 on, he lived in exile in Europe.

Hakim, Caliph al- (ca. 985–1021). The only son of Fatimid Caliph Aziz and a Christian mother who wielded great influence, he succeeded to the throne at age 11 in 996, although others, including a Slavic eunuch he later had killed, exercised real power for a few years. Apparently insane, this blue-eyed and allegedly odd-looking ruler turned out to be utterly strange. He got the nickname "lizard" from the way he slipped around spying on his subjects at night riding a gray donkey. He conducted affairs of state at night and ordered shops to open only after sunset. He banned raisins, honey, mulukiyyah (a popular green vegetable), and chess. He ordered that all dogs be killed. He switched from the usual policy of religious toleration to one of persecuting Christians. Many churches were demolished on his orders (carried out by high-level Christian officials). Then he resumed toleration of Christians and began to oppress Muslims, denying the validity of basic Islamic doctrines. He proclaimed himself divine, a doctrine central to the Druze religion. Facing increasing revolts, he rode a donkey into the hills outside Cairo and vanished.

Harb Pasha, Muhammad Tal'at (1867–1941). A lawyer born in Cairo, he was devoted to Egypt's independence and industrialization. Under his leadership in 1920, a group of landowners and merchants whose wealth came mainly from the sale of cotton established Bank Misr ("the Bank of Egypt"), to be controlled solely by Egyptians and to finance industrialization projects. For nearly two decades, he was the director of this bank, which established various business enterprises.

Husayn [Hussein], Taha (1898–1973). Born into a family of modest means in an Upper Egyptian village and blinded at age two, he came to be accepted as the Dean of Arabic Literature in his time. He studied in a traditional Qur'anic school and at al-Azhar (he told about these experiences in his book, *The Days*) before enrolling at the new national University, where he was the first student to receive a doctorate. Then he was sent to France, where he received a Ph.D. in literature and classics from the Sorbonne and married a French woman, who also was his close advisor. A proponent of liberalism and the scientific method, he became highly controversial by publishing a book in 1926 proclaiming the heretical thesis that "pre-Islamic" poetry actually was the product of a later time, resulting in his being fired as professor of Classical Arabic literature at the Egyptian University. He became Minister of Education in 1950, and his advocacy of free education is said to have influenced Nasir's policies. Aside from his scholarly studies, he wrote many novels portraying the condition of downtrodden Egyptians.

Isma'il Pasha, Khedive (1830–1895). Son of Ibrahim Pasha and grandson of Muhammad Ali Pasha, he ruled Egypt from 1863–1879, gaining the title Khedive ("Lord") in 1867. His expensive attempt to make Egypt a modern country resulted in a massive foreign debt after cotton prices dropped. Foreign intervention and eventual occupation followed. The Ottoman sultan replaced him with his son Tawfiq in 1879, and he was exiled to Istanbul.

Jabarti, Abd al-Rahman al- (1753–ca. 1825). Born into a pious family of Ethiopian origin, he studied at al-Azhar, where he then taught astronomy, later becoming a member of the Council set up by General Bonaparte. Then, starting as an apprentice to a Syrian historian, he became the most important historian of Egypt during the period starting in the late eighteenth century. His work, much of it widely translated, not only chronicles the years he covers but also provides biographical information. His unfavorable treatment of Muhammad Ali prevented his writings from being published in Egypt until 1878.

Kamil, Mustafa (1874–1908). Born in Cairo, he attended government schools and studied law in the French Law School in Cairo, and then in France. Long associated with Khedive Abbas Hilmi, who resisted British domination, he sought French support for the Egyptian nationalist cause. His ideas mixed local nationalism with pan-Islamic ideas, and he looked to the Ottomans as supporters. Working closely with another nationalist leader, Muhammad Farid, he founded the newspaper *al-Liwa* (the Standard) in 1900. He published a book, *The Rising Sun,* to celebrate the victory of a non-European country, Japan, over Russia in 1905. He organized the Patriotic Party *(al-Hizb al-Watani)* in 1907.

Lutfi al-Sayyid, Ahmad (1872–1963). The son of an Upper Egyptian village *umdah* (mayor) who attended Qur'anic schools and the modern School of Law, he propounded a systematic liberal theory of popular sovereignty and of Egyptian nationalism without any pan-Islamic (or pan-Arab) element. He approved Westernization on the ground that Egypt's "pharaonic core" was too strong to be threatened. He held important positions in journalism (notably as editor of the newspaper *al-Jaridah* from 1907 to 1914), education (as the rector of Cairo University), and government (as a minister in several cabinets). He founded the Umma Party in 1907 as an alternative to Mustafa Kamil's more pan-Islamic Patriotic Party.

Mahfuz, Nagib [Naguib] (1911–). Born in a middle-class family in one of Cairo's old quarters, he is the best-known Arab fiction writer. His international reputation was climaxed by receiving the Nobel Prize for Literature in 1988. The author of 32 novels and 13 volumes of short stories since 1939, he portrays the ills of society in a realistic way and demonstrates a commitment to social justice. Perhaps the best known of his works is "The Cairo Trilogy" (first published in 1956–1957 and later translated into English as *Palace Walk, Palace of Desire,* and *Sugar Street*), a unique portrayal of early twentieth-century urban Egyptian society.

Makram, Shaykh Umar (ca. 1755–1822). Born in Asyut in Upper Egypt and a graduate of al-Azhar, he was the Naqib al-Ashraf (head of the group of putative descendants of the Prophet Muhammad), in Cairo at the time of Bonaparte's occupation and leader of the popular resistance. His support for Muhammad Ali against the Ottoman governor in 1804 helped to bring the latter to power. But his opposition to the new ruler's policies resulted in exile to the Delta town of Tanta five years later, where he died.

Muhammad Ali Pasha (1769–1849). Long touted as the "father of modern Egypt," he was born in Kavalla, in Macedonia, of disputed ethnic origin, although he probably was a Turk. He was a tobacco merchant for a while but then was recruited as second in command of an Albanian unit the sultan sent to Egypt to fight against Bonaparte's forces in 1801. He eventually prevailed in the struggle for power there, and the sultan made him governor of the province. He made himself the ruler of an essentially independent state that expanded far beyond Egypt, threatening to topple the sultan himself—as a consequence of his establishment of a modern army and general modernization of the country. Only intervention by European powers in 1838 forced him to relinquish this goal and accept hereditary rule for his family in Egypt and Sudan. The dynasty he founded lasted until 1953.

Mubarak, (Muhammad) Husni (1928–). Born in a Delta village and son of a minor official, he graduated from the Military Academy in 1949 and the Air Academy in 1953. He went to the Soviet Union for further flight training. He became Air Chief of Staff in 1969, and Sadat made him the commander of the Air Force. To him has been credited much of the post-1967 improvements in the military as well as the successes in the 1973 war. He became vice president in 1975 and succeeded to the presidency following Sadat's assassination in 1981. Although his style is different from Sadat's, he has continued his predecessor's authoritarian rule and move toward capitalism while maintaining the alliance with the United States and the peace treaty with Israel.

Mubarak Pasha, Ali (1823–1893). Born in a Delta village into a family of religious scholars, he gained admittance into new schools for training officials and engineers and went on one of Muhammad Ali's student missions to Paris. Unusual for a native Egyptian, he was able to rise fast in governmental service after returning home during the time of Abbas Pasha. He was dismissed by Sa'id but returned to a series of high positions under Isma'il Pasha, directing governmental programs in public works and education as well as *waqf*s until his retirement in 1891. He played a major role in developing Egypt's industry, agriculture, and education. His stress on love of homeland helped create Egyptian nationalism. He published an encyclopedic 20-volume study of Egypt.

Muhyi al-Din [Mohieddin], Khalid (1922–). Born in 1922 into a prominent landowning family in the Delta, he graduated from the Military Academy in 1940 and from Cairo University in 1951. Although associated with a communist organization during the late 1940s, he may not have joined the group. As an officer in the mechanized cavalry, he played an important role in the 1952 coup and became a member of the Revolutionary Command Council. Allied with Muhammad Naguib in 1954, he went into exile after Nasir prevailed but returned the next year and edited the leftist newspaper *al-Misa* for a while and then *Akhbar al-Yawm*. His Marxist views kept him on the periphery, but he became a member of the Executive Committee of the Arab Socialist Union in 1968. He headed the leftist "pulpit" Sadat allowed to form in 1976 and subsequently became leader of the leftist *Tagammu* Party (NPUP) and has been a member of the People's Assembly, continuing to act as a vocal critic of Sadat's and Mubarak's policies.

Nasir [Nasser], Gamal Abd al- (1918–1970). Leader of the 1952 Revolution and President from 1954 until his death. The son of a minor postal official, he was born in Alexandria but grew up mainly in his ancestral village in Upper Egypt. Admitted to the Military Academy after it was opened up to nonelite classes, Nasir served in Upper Egypt and participated in the Palestine War of 1948. He became the leader of the reformist Free Officer movement that overthrew King Faruq. He pursued a nationalist policy that made him a charismatic figure in the Arab world and came to be associated with pan-Arabism. Though anticommunist, he drew the wrath of Western powers and came to depend on Soviet support. His social reforms evolved into what he called Arab Socialism.

Qutb, Sayyid (1906–1966). Born into a well-to-do agricultural family in an Upper Egyptian village, he eventually became a major influence on Islamic resurgence, inspiring radical tendencies in particular. After attending a Qur'anic school in his village, he continued his education in Cairo, particularly at Dar al-Ulum, where he studied education and English literature. It was his subsequent period of study for a doctorate in educational administration in the United States—where he was shocked by racial prejudice, support for Israel, and outright sexual license even at church events—that turned him from a Westernizer to a proponent of the Islamic alternative to both capitalism and communism and member of the Muslim Brothers. Imprisoned in 1954, he underwent harsh treatment and became further radicalized, now insisting that the Islamic world had returned to the "ignorance" of pre-Islamic Arabia that had to be changed through *jihad*. Released from prison in 1965, he was arrested again soon afterward on charges of plotting to overthrow the government and was hanged the next year. His works include a 32-volume study of the Qur'an and 24 other books, including the widely translated *Milestones*.

Sadat, (Muhammad) Anwar (1918–1981). Born in the Delta village of Mit Abu al-Kum (his mother was Sudanese), he graduated from the Military Academy in 1938. Imprisoned in 1942 because of his contacts with the Germans, he was dismissed from the army but regained his commission in 1950. One of the original Free Officers (and their link to the Muslim Brothers, with which he had been associated), he was chosen to announce the July 1952 coup on the radio. He was one of the members of the Revolutionary Command Council and occupied numerous positions over the years, including Secretary General of the National Union, President of the National Assembly, and editor of the government newspaper *al-Gumhuriyyah*, but seemed to be kept away from the real power structure.

Appointed vice president in 1969, he succeeded to the presidency when Nasir died and surprised almost everyone by prevailing over his rivals, fighting a war with Israel in 1973, and replacing growing dependence on the Soviet Union with an alliance with the United States as well as making peace with Israel before his assassination by Islamic militants.

Sa'dawi, Nawal al- (1930–). An internationally prominent proponent of women's rights, she studied medicine and began her career as a doctor in 1955. In addition to several novels, she is the author of such books as *Memoirs of a Woman Doctor* and *The Hidden Face of Eve*, which publicized the widespread practice of female circumcision. Her criticisms of Sadat's policies got her included among the more than 1,500 people he arrested shortly before his assassination, and her subsequent experiences provided the basis for her *Memoirs from the Women's Prison*. She organized the Arab Women's Solidarity Organization in 1982, which Mubarak banned nine years later because of its opposition to the war on Iraq.

Salah al-Din ibn Ayyub [Saladin] (1137/8–1193). A Kurd born in Tikrit (northern Iraq), he accompanied his uncle, a general sent by the Zangid ruler in Damascus to Cairo to intervene on behalf of one of the claimants to power in the Shi'ite Fatimid Caliphate. Eventually becoming vizier (chief minister) and effective ruler, he formally terminated the Fatimid Caliphate by recognizing the legitimacy of the Sunni Abbasid caliph in Baghdad, thus ending the period of Shi'ite ascendancy in Egypt and beginning the Ayyubid dynasty. He extended his rule into much of Syria and Iraq as well as Egypt. He defeated the Crusaders in 1187 and ended their occupation of Jerusalem, precipitating the Third Crusade, which he prevented from reversing his victory. His humane treatment of vanquished enemies made him a symbol of magnanimity.

Shajar al-Durr (12??–1257). Slave woman of Turkish or possibly Armenian origin who took power in Egypt after the death of her husband, the Ayyubid Sultan al-Salih in 1249 and whose leadership saved Egypt from the invading Sixth Crusade. She covered up his death until the return of his son Turanshah from a military campaign, and then the mamluk (literally, enslaved) troops murdered him and made Shajar the official ruler, her claim to legitimacy bolstered by her role as a mother of one of the late sultan's sons who died in infancy. But when the Abbasid caliph sarcastically sent a message offering to send a man to rule if none was available, she married a mamluk commander, Aybak, and allowed him to be a figurehead (along with a boy from the Ayyubid family) while she kept real power. Intensely jealous of Aybak, she forced him to divorce another wife, and when he married again she had him murdered in his bath. Knowing she was doomed, she ground up her jewelry to prevent others from getting it before a group of slave women beat her to death, making way for the rise of Sultan Qutuz.

Sha'rawi, Huda (1879–). The founder of Egypt's feminist movement, she was born in the Upper Egyptian town of al-Minya, a daughter of the Speaker of the Consultative Assembly of Notables (parliament). She memorized the whole Qur'an by age eight. Her husband (and cousin), Ali Sha'rawi, was a member of the famous delegation visiting Sir Reginald Wingate in 1918. Already devoted to promoting the welfare of children, she led a women's demonstration in the 1919 Revolution. She established the Egyptian Women's Union in 1923 and later started two magazines dealing with women's issues. She was an important force in promoting education for girls. She represented Egypt at numerous international women's conferences. The International Women's Association chose her as vice president in 1935.

Tahtawi, Shaykh Rifa'ah Rafi al- (1801–1873). Born into a family of religious scholars in the Delta town of Tanta, he studied in traditional Qur'anic schools and at al-Azhar, where he was influenced by the innovative thinking of Shaykh Hasan al-Attar. Chosen as imam of the first delegation of students Muhammad Ali Pasha sent to Paris (1826), Tahtawi was impressed with French society, about which he wrote a book as well as several other works on education and Egyptian development. Upon his return to Egypt, he held important positions during the eras of Muhammad Ali and Isma'il in the field of education, introducing innovative ideas such as the education of girls, and headed the new Translation Bureau, which translated more than 2,000 works into Arabic and Turkish. He also edited the official *Egyptian Gazette* and an education journal. He urged rethinking of Islamic ideas in light of modern conditions. His emphasis on devotion to the homeland (*watan*) has given him credit as a founder of Egyptian nationalism.

Ubayd [Ebaid], (William) Makram (1889–1961). Born into a landholding Coptic family in Upper Egypt, he studied law at Oxford and at the University of Lyons. After serving as Justice Minister during World War I, he was a close associate of Zaghlul and became a leading figure in the Wafd Party, of which he was secretary general from 1928 until he broke with it in 1942. He published a *Black Book* exposing its corruption and formed his own Wafdist Bloc Party. He served as a minister in several non-Wafdist governments.

Umm Kulthum (1904–1975). The most beloved Egyptian singer of the twentieth century, she was born as Fatima Ibrahim al-Baltaji into the family of the imam of a mosque in a small Delta village and attended the traditional Qur'anic school. She began her career by singing religious songs at weddings as a little girl. She moved with her family to Cairo in the 1920s, where she received formal training in music and soon was established as a major star. She was noted for the authenticity with she represented her own cultural heritage and the way she never ceased seeing herself as a "daughter of the countryside." Her support for Nasir and his revolution arguably provided one of its important assets. The millions who turned out for her funeral allegedly broke the record set by Nasir himself.

Urabi [Arabi], Colonel Ahmad (1840–1911). The son of a village headman in the Delta, he was one of the native Egyptians accepted into the Military Academy during Sa'id's rule. He led the protest against growing foreign control and the predominance of Turks and Circassians. He became Minister of War in 1982 but was exiled to Ceylon following the British occupation later that year. He returned to Egypt in 1901 but did not subsequently play a political role.

Zaghlul, Sa'd (1859–1927). The preeminent Egyptian nationalist leader after 1918, he was the son of a village *umdah* (mayor) in the Delta and studied in Qur'anic schools and at al-Azhar before becoming a lawyer. A follower of Afghani and Abduh, he was associated with the abortive Urabi Revolution and afterwards was briefly arrested because of this. During the British occupation, he served as Minister of Justice and as Minister of Education and was involved in the establishment of the Egyptian [later, Cairo] University in 1907. He became vice-president of the Legislative Assembly in 1913. Immediately after the end of World War I, he headed a delegation asking to present the case for Egyptian independence in London and later—following exile to Malta—was allowed to attend the Paris Peace Conference to no avail. His exile then to the Seychelles set off the Revolution of 1919. Returning to Egypt after formal independence, his Wafd Party won control of parliament in 1924, and he became prime minister but served less than a year before parliament was dissolved. He later served as Speaker of parliament.

Zawahiri, Ayman al- (1951–). Second-ranking leader of al-Qa'ida and chief advisor and personal physician to Usama bin Ladin. He is believed to have been a major planner of the September 11, 2001, attacks on the United States. Al-Zawahiri was born in Giza in 1951 and reared in al-Ma'adi, a suburb of Cairo in which Americans and other Westerners long have been concentrated. A member of a family of prominent doctors and other specialists in the medical field, he graduated from Cairo University Medical School in 1974, later earning an advanced degree in surgery. His mother was from the famous Azzam family, closely related to the first Secretary-General of the Arab League, Abd al-Rahman Azzam. First arrested at age 15 for membership in the Muslim Brothers, he was imprisoned for three years (and allegedly subjected to horrible torture) for involvement in the assassination of Sadat. After his release, he fled to Saudi Arabia and then to Pakistan and Afghanistan, where he forged ties with bin Ladin during the struggle against the Soviet occupation. He was a leader of al-Jihad and played an important role in the unification of one branch of that organization with al-Qa'ida in the late 1990s. In the post-September 2001 period he was believed to be hiding in the Afghanistan–Pakistan border region.

Zewail, Ahmed (1946–). Born into a locally well-known family in Damanhur, in the Delta, he is the son of a government official and businessman. He studied at Alexandria University and was a teaching assistant there for a short time. Then he received a fellowship at the University of Pennsylvania, where he earned his doctorate in Chemistry. Despite initial plans to return to Alexandria, he decided that there was much greater opportunity to do scientific research in the United States, and he eventually took a position at the California Institute of Technology, where he occupies the Linus Pauling Chair. A brilliant scholar who has discovered much about the basic nature of molecules and chemical reactions, he has earned many international awards, including the Nobel Prize for Chemistry in 1999. One Egyptian postage stamp portrays him as the country's Fourth Pyramid. Among his many works is his autobiographical *Passage Through Time.*

Glossary

Abbasid. Dynasty of caliphs (q.v.) that claimed authority over the Islamic world after 750.

Anatolia. Roughly today's Turkey in Asia.

Arab. Originally referring to the tribes of the Arabian Peninsula but today including all those, Christians as well as Muslims, who have adopted the Arabic language and culture (including virtually all Egyptians).

Arab League. League of Arab States, a regional organization established in 1945, with its seat in Cairo.

Arab Socialist Union (ASU). The single ruling party established in Egypt in 1962.

Azhar, al-. Mosque and university established by the Fatimids in newly founded Cairo in 969 and later the most important center of Sunni Islamic learning.

Basin irrigation. *See* Perennial irrigation.

Bey. An Ottoman military title, lower than pasha (q.v.), given to members of the Egyptian elite until the 1952 Revolution.

Berber. The ancient "Hamitic" peoples of North Africa (west of Egypt), only distantly related linguistically to the ancient Egyptians and Semitic peoples such as Arabs. Most have been Arabized, but others (including those of Siwa Oasia in Egypt) hold on to their identity and language.

Caliph. A successor to the Prophet Muhammad as ruler (real or nominal) of the Islamic world.

Capitulations. Agreements with Western states exempting foreign nationals from local jurisdiction.

Chalcedonian. The main branch of Christianity (recognizing Christ as having both human and divine natures) as opposed to the Monophysite (q.v.) Christianity of Egypt.

Circassian. Member of an ethnic group in the Caucasus region who predominated among the mamluk (q.v.) rulers after 1382.

Condominium. Joint rule, as in the case of the former Anglo-Egyptian Sudan.

Copt. Adherent to the Coptic sect of Christianity that once was predominant in Egypt and to which most Egyptian Christians belong, representing the Monophysite (q.v.) as opposed to the Chalcedonian (q.v.) branch of the faith.

Crossing, The. The offensive against the Israelis across the Suez Canal in October 1973.

Crusade. A Roman Catholic holy war against the Islamic world, particularly with reference to the series of Crusades beginning in 1095 to restore Jerusalem to Christian rule.

Delta. The fan-shaped area north of Cairo that has been created by silt from the Nile; also known as Lower Egypt.

Dhimmi. A "protected person," that is, a Christian or Jew in early Islamic states, tolerated but subjected to certain restrictions.

Faddan. 1.038 acres.

Fallah. Peasant; formerly applied indiscriminately to indigenous Egyptians by the Turkish (q.v.) and Circassian (q.v.) ruling class.

Fatwa. A legal ruling from an Islamic jurist.

Federation of Arab Republics. A loose union of Egypt, Syria, and Libya established in 1971 that soon faded away.

Feudalism. A pattern of decentralized rule over land—particularly in medieval Europe and only imperfectly paralleled in Egypt or other parts of the Islamic world—in which lords and vassals have mutual obligations; loosely used in reference to a landlord-dominated society.

Gaza Strip. The small area of southwestern Palestine (q.v.), including the city of Gaza, that Egyptian forces held at the end of the 1948 Palestine War but was occupied by Israel in 1967.

Hamite. Overall name given to the peoples/languages of ancient northern Africa, including Egyptians, Berbers (q.v.), Somalis, et cetera—loosely related to one another and the Semites (q.v.) in what is more accurately known as the "Hamito-Semitic" family of languages.

Harem. Literally, "sacred"; the area of a building reserved for women.

Hellenistic. The post-fourth-century B.C. period of Greek cultural supremacy, lasting in Egypt in many ways until the Islamic conquest.

Iltizam. Literally, "concession," a portion of land awarded, as in Ottoman Egypt, to a person who collects the taxes (often translated as "tax-farm").

Imam. Literally, "leader," that is, the person who leads Muslim prayer; also, another term for the caliph (q.v.) and specifically used by Shi·ites (q.v.) for those considered rightful leaders.

IMF. International Monetary Fund, an international organization dominated by the rich countries that loans hard currency to countries with foreign exchange problems.

Infitah. Literally, "opening"; used by Sadat for his "open door" to private investment.

Intifadah. Literally, "a shaking off," that is, an uprising, a term that came to be known worldwide following the outbreak of the Palestinian Uprising in 1987.

Iqta. Fief, that is, a piece of land awarded to a person in a pattern that in some ways resembled European feudalism (q.v.).

Islam. Literally, "Submission"(to God); the Muslim religion.

Islamic Group. One of the militant Islamist organizations that emerged in the 1970s and long was engaged in terrorism.

Islamism. Broad name for movements advocating a strictly Islamic state and society, sometimes also known, though less accurately, as "Islamic fundamentalism."

Jihad. Striving (in the way of God); analogous when used in a military sense to the Christian concept of "just war" and recently adopted by militant Islamist (q.v.) revolutionaries. One extreme group in Egypt calls itself Tanzim al-Jihad (the Organization of Jihad).

July (or July 23) Revolution. The overthrow of the old regime of King Faruq in 1952 and the radical changes subsequently carried out by Gamal Abd al-Nasir.

Khedive. A Persian title meaning "lord" given to the rulers of Egypt in the late nineteenth century.

LE (or £E). *Livre égyptiènne,* that is, Egyptian pound; worth less than 20 cents at the official rate in 2003 but formerly valued at $2.30.

League of Arab States. *See* Arab League.

Liberal. The movement that developed in the modern Western world emphasizing liberty in general, including a rejection of traditional restrictions on the individual. In the classical sense (generally used in this book), economic liberalism connotes a market economy unrestricted by government intervention. This is a source of confusion for many, as the economic implication of the term came to be reversed, particularly in twentieth-century America, although "liberalism" (or "neoliberalism") still is used for the "free-market" policies of the International Monetary Fund (q.v.) and other international agencies.

Liberal Party. The political party founded during the Sadat period as a rightist alternative to the governing party.

Lower Egypt. The Delta (q.v.).

Mahdi. The "guided one" who, in Shiʿite (q.v.) and popular Sunni (q.v.) doctrine will come to restore justice to the world.

Mamluk. Literally, "the owned"; an enslaved boy trained as a soldier and then manumitted. The ruling class was largely made up of mamluks from the middle ages until the nineteenth century.

Monophysite. The branch of Christianity—as opposed to the Chalcedonians (q.v.)—represented by the Copts (q.v.) that believes Christ has only the divine nature and no human nature.

Mufti. An Islamic jurist authorized to issue a legal ruling or fatwa (q.v.).

Muslim. An adherent to the religion of Islam (q.v.).

National Assembly. The name of the Egyptian parliament established during the Nasir period.

National Democratic Party. The governing party established by Sadat.

Neoliberalism. *See* Liberalism.

Nubians. The Hamitic (q.v.) people in Egypt's far south and in northern Sudan.

Palestine. A geographical term usually defined to include the area between the Mediterranean on the west and the Jordan River and Dead Sea on the East, now constituting the State of Israel and the occupied territories of the West Bank (q.v.) and Gaza Strip (q.v.).

Palestinians. People indigenous to Palestine (q.v.), some of whom now are citizens of Israel but mostly inhabiting the Gaza Strip (q.v.) and West Bank (q.v.) or living as refugees in other countries.

Pasha. An Ottoman military title, higher than Bey (q.v.), given to members of the Egyptian elite until the 1952 Revolution.

People of the Book. Adherents to religions, particularly Christianity and Judaism, recognized in Islam as based on an earlier revelation and supposed to be given dhimmi (q.v.) status in the Islamic state.

People's Assembly. The name of the Egyptian parliament since 1971; previously known as the "National Assembly" (q.v.).

Perennial irrigation. A pattern increasingly used from the nineteenth century onward whereby water from the Nile is used throughout the year, as opposed to the older pattern of basin irrigation, in which floodwater was collected in basins for the subsequent season only.

PNUP. *See* Tagammu.

Prophet. A person who receives messages from God.

RCC. Revolutionary Command Council, the group of Free Officers who took power in 1952.

Sa'id, The. *See* Upper Egypt.

Semites. The linguistically related peoples originating in southwest Asia, including Arabs, Hebrews, and Phoenicians.

Shari'ah. Islamic law, that is, the body of rules that strict Muslims believe should be applied.

Shaykh. Literally, "old man," that is, elder; title of heads of tribes and villages and also of university professors.

Shi'ite. Adherent to the branch of Islam that accepts a series of hereditary leaders *(imams)* as the rightful heads of the Islamic world after the death of the Prophet Muhammad. Subgroups include Twelvers (the largest), Isma'ilis (e.g., the Fatimids of medieval Egypt), and Zaydis (of Yemen).

Socialist Labor Party. Party founded to represent the "center left" under Sadat and that now has adopted an Islamist program. Its name today is simply the "Liberal Party."

Sufi. A variant on Islam, represented by various sufi orders, that stresses mystical communion with God and often plays down the importance of the Shari'ah (q.v.).

Sultan. A title of rulers in the Islamic world; literally meaning "he with power," this was applied in the Middle Ages for real rulers who accepted the nominal supremacy of the caliph (q.v.).

Sunni. Adherent to the majority branch of Islam (including almost all Egyptian Muslims today).

Syria. A geographical term used historically to include Palestine (q.v.), Jordan, and Lebanon as well as the present Syrian Arab Republic.

Tagammu. The leftist Progressive *(Tagammu)* National Unionist Party, headed by Khalid Muhi al-Din, also known as the PNUP.

Turk. A member of the ethnic group that originated in Central Asia and predominated in the military and ruling class of the Islamic world until modern times.

UAR. United Arab Republic (i.e., the state formed by the union of Egypt and Syria in 1958 and kept as the name of Egypt alone after the secession of Syria in 1961 [until 1971]); also the name of an abortive union of Egypt, Syria, and Iraq in 1963.

Ulama. Learned people, used specifically for Islamic religious scholars (sometimes loosely translated as "clergy").

Umayyad. Dynasty of caliphs (q.v.) that ruled the Islamic world from 656 to 750.

Umdah. Mayor of a village.

Ummah. The worldwide Muslim community, which in Islamic doctrine is supposed to supersede national and ethnic divisions.

UNEF. United Nations Emergency Force, the peacekeeping force that helped to keep the Egyptian–Israeli frontier quiet from 1957 to 1967.

Upper Egypt. The Nile Valley (Cairo to the Sudanese border); known in Arabic as the Sa'id (the "Upland").

Vizier. Minister (Arabic: *"wazir"*).

Waqf. Property held in trust under Islamic law to support a charity or sometimes for private use.

West Bank. The part of east-central Palestine (q.v.), including East Jerusalem, that was annexed by Jordan after the 1948 Palestine War and occupied by Israel in 1967.

Young Egypt. A right-wing organization formed in the 1930s.

Bibliographic Essay

Considering the length of Egyptian history, a short bibliographic essay can hardly do it justice. I am limiting this to books specifically on Egypt, especially those that likely will be available and useful to general readers in the English-speaking world. Space does not permit inclusion of articles or of books dealing only in part with Egypt. Taking into consideration the emphasis of this volume, recent periods receive heavy attention. Pharaonic times, which constitute the vast subject matter of Egyptology, can get only token coverage.

A few works deal with the whole length of Egyptian history. See James Jankowski, *Egypt: A Short History* (Oxford, 2000). On a faith that has survived until today, see Otto F. A. Meinardus, *Two Thousand Years of Coptic Christianity* (Cairo, 1999).

ANCIENT EGYPT

Among many scholarly works on pre-Islamic times, I recommend Ian Shaw, *The Oxford History of Ancient Egypt* (Oxford and New York, 2000). Other examples of broad works include Cyril Aldred, *The Egyptians* (London, 1987); Douglas J. Bremer and Emily Teeter, *Egypt and the Egyptians* (Cambridge, 1999); and Nicholas Grimal, *A History of Ancient Egypt* (Oxford, 1992). Some reference works: Donald B. Redford (ed.), *The Oxford Encyclopedia of Ancient Egypt*, 3 vols. (Oxford and New York, 2000) and John Baine and Jaromir Malek, *Atlas of Ancient Egypt* (New York, 1980).

On the Roman/Byzantine period, I recommend the first two chapters in Carl F. Petry (ed.), *The Cambridge History of Egypt*, Volume I: *Islamic Egypt, 640–1517* (Cambridge, England, 1998). Other works on this period include Alan K. Bowman, *Egypt after the Pharaohs: 332 B.C.–A.D. 642* (Berkeley, Calif., 1986); Michel Chaureau, *Egypt in the Age of Cleopatra: History and Society Under the Ptolemies*, trans. David Lorton (Ithaca, N.Y., 2000); and Harold Idris Bell, *Egypt, from Alexander the Great to the Arab Conquest* (Westport, Conn., 1977). Also see Alfred J. Butler, *The Arab Invasion of Egypt and the Last 30 Years of Roman Dominium*, 2nd ed. (Oxford, 1978).

ISLAMIC EGYPT TO THE OTTOMAN CONQUEST

As the title indicates, Petry's *Islamic Egypt* (see earlier) is mainly relevant to the Islamic period. It is a work of unsurpassed thoroughness representing the best scholarship on each period. Janet Abu-Lughod's, *Cairo: 1001 Years of the City Victorious* (Princeton, N.J., 1972) is an admirable study of Egypt's greatest city. Also see: Desmond Stewart, *Great Cairo: Mother of the World*, 3rd. ed. (Cairo, 1996); Andrew Raymond, *Cairo: City of History*, trans. Willard Wood (Cairo, 2001); and Max Rodenbeck, *Cairo: The City Victorious* (New York, 1999). On architecture: Doris Behrens-Abouseif, *Islamic Architecture in Cairo: An Introduction* (New York, 1989) or Richard Yeomans, *The Art and Architecture of Islamic Cairo* (Cairo, 2003).

On an important connection, see Amnon R. Cohen and Gabriel Baer (eds.), *Egypt and Palestine: A Millennium of Association (868–1948)* (Jerusalem and New York, 1984).

Some old works on medieval Egypt are still useful (and interesting reading), particularly Stanley Lane-Poole's *A History of Egypt in the Middle Ages* (London, 1901; reprint, London, 1968) and William Muir, *The Mameluke or Slave Dynasty of Egypt, 1260–1517 A.D.* (London, 1896; reprint, New York, 1973). Also see De Lacy O'Leary, *A Short History of the Fatimid Khalifate* (New York, 1928).

Recent studies include: David Ayalon, *Gunpowder and Firearms in the Mamluk Kingdom*, 2nd ed. (London, 1978); David Ayalon, *Studies on the Mamluks of Egypt (1250–1517)* (London, 1977); Jonathan Berkey, *The Transmission of Knowledge in Medieval Cairo: A Social History of Islamic Education* (Princeton, N.J., 1992); Robert Irwin, *The Middle East in the Middle Ages: The Early Mamluk Sultanate, 1250–1382* (Carbondale, Ill., 1986); Carl F. Petry, *The Civilian Elite in Cairo in the Late Middle Ages* (Princeton, N.J., 1981);

Carl F. Petry, *Protectors and Praetorians?: The Last Mamluk Sultans and Egypt's Waning as a Great Power* (Albany, N.Y., 1994); Carl F. Petry, *Twilight of Majesty: The Reigns of the Mamluk Sultans al-Ashraf, Qaytbay and Qansuh al-Ghawri in Egypt* (Seattle, 1994); Thomas Phillips and Ulrich Haarmann, eds., *The Mamluks in Egyptian Politics and Society* (Cambridge, 1998); and Reuven Amitai-Preiss, *Mongols and Mamluks: The Mamluk-Ilkhanid War, 1260–1281* (Cambridge, 1995).

Biographies include D.E.P. Jackson, *Saladin: The Politics of Holy War* (Cambridge, 1984) and Yaacov Lev, *Saladin in Egypt* (Leiden, 1999). On another important ruler, see *Peter Thorau, The Lion of Egypt: Sultan Baybars and the Near East in the Thirteenth Century*, trans. P. M. Holt (New York, 1992).

THE OTTOMAN ERA TO 1798

The Ottoman period is covered in W. M. Daly (ed.), *The Cambridge History of Egypt*, Volume II: *Modern Egypt, from 1517 to the End of the Twentieth Century* (Cambridge, 1998). Specialized studies include: Galal En-Nahal, *The Judicial Administration of Ottoman Egypt* (Minneapolis, 1979); Stanford J. Shaw, *The Budget of Ottoman Egypt 1005–1006/1596–1597* (The Hague, 1968); and Michael Winter, *Society and Religion in Early Ottoman Egypt* (New Brunswick, N.J., 1982).

Specifically on the eighteenth century, see Daniel Crecelius, *The Roots of Modern Egypt: A Study of the Regimes of 'Ali Bey al-Kabir and Muhammad Bey Abu al-Dhahab, 1760–1775* (Minneapolis, 1981). Also see Huseyn Efendi, *Ottoman Egypt in the Age of the French Revolution*, trans. Stanford J. Shaw (Cambridge, Mass., 1964) and Stanford J. Shaw (ed.), *Ottoman Egypt in the Eighteenth Century: The Nizamname-i Misir of Cezzar Ahmed Pasha* (Cambridge, Mass., 1964). Continuing into the later period is Peter Gran, *Islamic Roots of Capitalism: Egypt, 1760–1840* (Austin, Tex., 1979).

MODERN EGYPT: GENERAL

Daly's *Modern Egypt* (see previous listing) provides thorough, scholarly treatment of what is usually considered the modern period (that is, the period starting in the late eighteenth century) as well as the earlier Ottoman period. For readable general works, see Arthur Goldschmidt, Jr., *Modern Egypt: The Formation of a Nation State*, 7th ed. (Boulder, Colo., 2004) and Afaf Lutfi al-Sayyid Marsot, *A Short History of Modern Egypt* (Cambridge, 1985). A more detailed study is P. J. Vatikiotis, *The History of Egypt: From Muhammad Ali to Mubarak*, 4th ed. (Baltimore, 1991). Another survey is J.C.B. Richmond, *Egypt: 1789–1952* (New York, 1977). Important specialized studies may be found in P. M. Holt (ed.), *Political and Social Change in Modern Egypt* (London, 1968). Gabriel Baer's *Studies in the Social History of Modern Egypt* (Chicago, 1969) is an important work. For an interesting interpretation, see Amira El-Azhary Sonbol, *The New Mamluks: Egyptian Society and Modern Feudalism* (Syracuse, N.Y., 2000). P. M. Holt (ed.), *Political and Social Change in Modern Egypt* (London, 1968) contains important studies. Jacques Berque, *Egypt: Imperialism and Revolution*, trans. Jean Stewart (New York, 1967) is a massive, brilliant social history from the British occupation to the 1952 Revolution. Also see Tom Little, *Modern Egypt* (New York, 1967).

Reference works include Arthur Goldschmidt, Jr., *Biographical Dictionary of Modern Egypt* (Boulder, Colo., 2000); Arthur Goldschmidt, Jr., *Historical Dictionary of Egypt* (Lanham, Md., 1994); and Joan Wucher King, *Historical Dictionary of Egypt* (Metuchen, N.J., 1984).

For an English Orientalist's classic portrait of Egyptian society first published in 1836 (and based on the 1860 edition), see Edward Lane, *An Account of the Manners and Customs of the Modern Egyptians* (Cairo, 2003).

An important study of ideas as the basis of political community during the nineteenth and early twentieth centuries is Nadav Safran, *Egypt in Search of Political Community* (Cambridge, Mass., 1978). Other valuable studies include Jamal Mohammed Ahmed, *The Intellectual Origins of Egyptian Nationalism* (London, 1960); Charles Adams, *Islam and Modernism in Egypt* (London, 1933; reprint, New York, 1968); and Charles D. Smith, *Islam and the Search for Political Order in Modern Egypt* (Albany, N.Y., 1983). On two important Muslim thinkers, see Malcolm Kerr, *Islamic Reform: The Political and Legal Theories of Muhammad 'Abduh and Rashid Rida* (Berkeley, Calif., 1961). Also see Farhat J. Ziadeh, *Lawyers, the Rule of Law, and Liberalism in Modern Egypt* (Stanford, 1968).

For a study of popular religion, see Morroe Berger, *Islam in Egypt Today: Social and Political Aspects of Popular Religion* (Cambridge, 1970).

On education, see J. Heyworth-Dunne, *An Introduction to the History of Education in Modern Egypt* (London, 1938; reprint, London, 1968) and Donald Malcolm Reid, *Cairo University and the Making of Modern Egypt* (Cambridge, Mass., 1990). Also see Bayard Dodge, *Al-Azhar: A Millennium of Muslim Learning* (Washington, D.C., 1974) and A. Chris Eccel, *Egypt, Islam and Social Change: Al-Azhar in Conflict and Accommodation* (Berlin, 1984). Taha Hussein's *The Days: His Autobiography in Three Parts* (Cairo, 2001) provides a valuable picture of traditional education. Also see Ahmad Abdullah, *The Student Movement and National Politics in Egypt* (London, 1985).

Another important aspect of society is covered by Nazih Ayyubi, *Bureaucracy and Politics in Contemporary Egypt* (London, 1980); Morroe Berger, *Bureaucracy and Society in Modern Egypt: A Study of the Higher Civil Service* (Princeton, N.J., 1970); and Monte Palmer et al., *The Egyptian Bureaucracy* (Syracuse, N.Y., 1988).

Economic studies include Alan Richards, *Egypt's Agricultural Development, 1800–1980* (Boulder, Colo., 1982); Robert Mabro and Samir Radwan, *The Industrialization of Egypt, 1939–1973: Policy and Performance* (Oxford, 1976); and Roger Owen, *Cotton and the Egyptian Economy, 1820–1914* (Oxford, 1969). The labor movement is dealt with by Joel Bienen and Zachary Lockman, *Workers on the Nile* (Princeton, N.J., 1981).

On the countryside, see Richard H. Adams, Jr., *Development and Social Change in Rural Egypt* (Syracuse, N.Y., 1986) and Nicholas S. Hopkins and Kirsten Westergaard, *Directions of Change in Rural Egypt* (Cairo, 2001). Also see Nathan J. Brown, *Peasant Politics in Modern Egypt* (New Haven, Conn., 1990). Other portrayals of village life include Hamid Ammar, *Growing Up in an Egyptian Village* (London, 1954) and Henry Habib Ayrout, *The Egyptian Peasant*, trans. John Alden Williams (Boston, 1963). On landownership, see Kenneth M. Cuno, *The Pasha's Peasants: Land, Society, and Economy in Lower Egypt: 1740–1858* (Cambridge, 1992).

On gender issues, see Soha Abdel Kader, *Egyptian Women in a Changing Society, 1899–1987* (Boulder, Colo., 1987); Qasim Amin, *The Liberation of Women and the New Woman: Two Documents in the History of Egyptian Feminism*, trans. Samiha Sidhom Peterson (Cairo, 2000); Nayra Atiya, *Khul-Khaal: Five Egyptian Women Tell Their Stories* (Syracuse, N.Y., 1982); Margot Badran, *Feminists, Islam, and Nation: Gender in the Making of Modern Egypt* (Princeton, N.J., 1994); Beth Baron, *The Women's Awakening in Egypt: Culture, Society, and the Press* (New Haven, Conn., 1994); Selma Botman, *Engendering Citizenship in Egypt* (New York, 1999); Evelyn A. Early, *Baladi Women of Cairo: Playing with an Egg and a Stone* (Boulder, Colo., 1993); Cynthia Nelson, *Doria Shafik, Egyptian Feminist: A Woman Apart* (Gainesville, Fla., 1996); Huda Shaarawi, *Harem Years: The Memoirs of an Egyptian Feminist, 1879–1924*, trans. Margaret Badram (London, 1986); Earl L. Sullivan, *Women in Egyptian Public Life* (Syracuse, N.Y., 1986); Ghada Hashem Talhami, *The Mobilization of Muslim Women in Egypt* (Gainesville, Fla., 1996); Judith Tucker, *Women in Nineteenth-Century Egypt* (Cambridge, 1985); and Sherifa Zuhur, *Revealing Reveiling: Islamic Gender Ideology in Contemporary Egypt* (Albany, N.Y., 1992).

On minorities: Gudrun Kramer, *The Jews of Modern Egypt, 1914–1952* (Seattle, 1989); Jacob M. Landau, *Jews in Nineteenth-Century Egypt* (New York, 1969); and Edward Wakin, *A Lonely Minority: The Modern Story of Egypt's Copts* (New York, 1963).

FROM BONAPARTE TO THE BRITISH
OCCUPATION

The French occupation is dealt with by Christopher Herold, *Bonaparte in Egypt* (New York, 1962). Other works on this period include Robert Anderson and Ibrahim Fawzy (eds.), *Egypt in 1800: Scenes from Napoleon's Déscription de l'Egypte* (London, 1988) and Percival S. Elgood. *Bonaparte's Adventure in Egypt* (London, 1931).

On the Muhammad Ali period, I recommend Afaf Lutfi al-Sayyid Marsot, *Egypt in the Reign of Muhammad Ali* (Cambridge, 1984). Also see Khaled Fahmy, *All the Pasha's Men: Mehmed Ali, His Army and the Making of Modern Egypt* (Cairo, 2002) and Fred H. Lawson, *The Social Origins of Egyptian Expansionism During the Muhammad 'Ali Period* (New York, 1992). Another excellent study is Helen B. Rivlin, *The Agricultural Policy of Muhammad Ali in Egypt* (Cambridge, Mass., 1961). Still useful is Henry Dodwell, *The Founder of Modern Egypt* (Cambridge, 1931).

A first-rate study that briefly deals with Muhammad Ali but focuses mostly on his successors is F. Robert Hunter, *Egypt under the Khedives, 1805–1879: From Household Government to Modern Bureaucracy* (Pittsburgh, 1984). Ehud R. Toledano, *State and Society in Mid-Nineteenth-Century Egypt* (Cambridge, 1990) is another important study. On European economic penetration, see David S. Landes, *Bankers and Pashas: International Finance and Economic Imperialism in Egypt* (Cambridge, Mass., 1958). Also on the pre-1882 period: John Marlowe, *Spoiling the Egyptians* (New York, 1976) and Michael Reimer, *Colonial Bridgehead: Government and Society in Alexandria, 1807–1882* (Boulder, Colo., 1997).

Important recent studies include Juan R. I. Cole, *Colonialism and Revolution in the Middle East: Social and Cultural Origins of Egypt's 'Urabi Revolution* (Princeton, N.J., 1993) and Alexander Schölch, *Egypt for the Egyptians! The Socio-political Crisis in Egypt, 1878–1882* (London, 1981). Also see Ahmad 'Urabi, *The Defense Statement of Ahmad 'Urabi the Egyptian,* trans. Trevor Le Gassick (Cairo, 1982). For a personal account of developments leading up to the British occupation, see Mary Rowlatt, *Founders of Modern Egypt* (Bombay, 1962).

Scholarly accounts of the British occupation include Afaf Lutfi al-Sayyid Marsot, *Egypt and Cromer* (London, 1968) and Robert L. Tignor, *Modernization and British Colonial Rule in Egypt, 1882–1914* (Princeton, N.J., 1966). An imperialist view may be found in Lord Cromer, *Modern Egypt,* two vols. (London: 1908). On another important figure: M. W. Daly, *The Sirdar: Sir Reginald Wingate and the British Empire in the Middle East* (Philadelphia, 1997). Also see George A. L. Lloyd, *Egypt Since Cromer,* 2 vols. (New York,

1970) and Viscount Alfred Milner, *England and Egypt* (New York, 1970). British colonialism is analyzed in Robert T. Harrison, *Gladstone's Imperialism in Egypt: Techniques of Domination* (Westport, Conn., 1995). For a broader seminal study, see Ronald Robinson, John Gallagher, and Alice Denny, *Africa and the Victorians: The Official Mind of Imperialism* (New York, 1967).

Broader treatment of relations with Britain may be found in John Marlowe, *A History of Modern Egypt and Anglo-Egyptian Relations 1800–1956* (Hamden, Conn., 1965); Peter Mansfield, *The British in Egypt* (New York, 1970); and Keith M. Wilson, ed., *Imperialism and Nationalism in the Near East: The Anglo-Egyptian Experience 1882–1982* (London, 1983). Also see Timothy Mitchell, *Colonizing Egypt* (New York, 1988).

THE "LIBERAL" PERIOD

Studies of the post-1918 period include Selma Botman, *Egypt from Independence to Revolution, 1919–1952* (Syracuse, N.Y., 1972) and Afaf Lutfi al-Sayyid-Marsot, *Egypt's Liberal Experiment: 1922–1936* (Berkeley, Calif., 1977). Also see John Darwin, *Britain, Egypt, and the Middle East: Imperial Policy in the Aftermath of War, 1918–1922* (New York, 1981) and Mahmud Y. Zayid, *Egypt's Struggle for Independence* (Beirut, 1965).

On parties and movements, see Marius Deeb, *Party Politics in Egypt: The Wafd and Its Rivals, 1919–1939* (London, 1979); Janice Terry, *The Wafd 1919–1952* (London, 1982); and James Jankowski, *Egypt's Young Rebels: "Young Egypt," 1933–1952* (Stanford, Calif., 1975). Also see Jacob M. Landau, *Parliaments and Parties in Egypt* (Tel-Aviv, 1953).

On the Islamist movement, see Christina Phelps Harris, *Nationalism and Revolution in Egypt: The Role of the Muslim Brotherhood* (The Hague, 1964); Ishak Musa al-Husayni, *The Muslim Brethren* (Beirut, 1956; Westport, Conn., 1979); and especially Richard P. Mitchell, *The Society of the Muslim Brothers* (London, 1969). Also see Abd Al-Fattah Muhammad El-Awaisi, *The Muslim Brothers and the Palestine Question 1928–1947* (London, 1998).

For another movement that dates back to the "liberal" period, see Selma Botman, *The Rise of Egyptian Communism, 1939–1970* (Syracuse, N.Y., 1988) and Tareq Y. Ismael and Rifa'at El-Sa'id, *The Communist Movement in Egypt, 1920–1988* (Syracuse, N.Y., 1988). Also see Joel Beinin, *Was the Red Flag Flying There? Marxist Politics and the Arab-Israeli Conflict in Egypt and Israel, 1948–1965* (Berkeley, Calif., 1990).

Economic studies include Eric Davis, *Challenging Colonialism: Bank Misr and Egyptian Industrialism, 1920–1941* (Princeton, N.J., 1983); Robert L. Tignor, *State, Private Enterprise, and Economic Change in Egypt, 1918–1952*

(Princeton, 1984); and Robert Vitalis, *When Capitalists Collide: Business Conflict and the End of Empire in Egypt* (Berkeley, Calif., 1995).

Two works by Israel Gershoni and James P. Jankowski, *Egypt, Islam, and the Arabs: The Search for Egyptian Nationhood, 1900–1930* (New York, 1986) and *Redefining the Egyptian Nation, 1930–1945* (Cambridge, 1995) analyze the problem of national identity. Also see Michael Doran, *Pan-Arabism before Nasser: Egyptian Power Politics and the Palestine Question* (New York, 1999) and Israel Gershoni, *The Emergence of Pan-Arabism in Egypt* (Tel-Aviv, 1981). Ties with the Arab world and the question of Palestine are analyzed in Thomas Mayer, *Egypt and the Palestine Question, 1936–1945* (Berlin, 1982) and Barry Rubin, *The Arab States and the Palestine Conflict* (Syracuse, N.Y., 1981).

Fiction portraying this period includes Naguib Mahfouz, *The Cairo Trilogy*, trans. William Maynard Hutchins et al. (Cairo, 2001), a one-volume edition of three important novels *(Palace of Desire, Palace Walk*, and *Sugar Street)*. Or, by Tawfiq al-Hakim: *The Maze of Justice*, trans. Abba Eban (London, 1947).

EGYPT SINCE 1952: GENERAL

For an assessment of changes, see Galal Amin's *Whatever Happened to the Egyptians?: Changes in Egyptian Society from 1950 to the Present* (Cairo, 2000) and *Whatever Else Happened to the Egyptians: From the Revolution to the Age of Globalization* (Cairo, 2003).

For a general survey of the Nasir and Sadat periods, see Derek Hopwood, *Egypt: Politics and Society, 1945–1981* (London, 1982). An assessment that includes the Nasir period and all but the last years of his successor is Raymond William Baker, *Egypt's Uncertain Revolution Under Nasser and Sadat* (Cambridge, Mass., 1979). Also recommended: Mark Cooper, *The Transformation of Egypt* (Baltimore, 1982). On political economy, see John Waterbury, *The Egypt of Nasser and Sadat: The Political Economy of Two Regimes* (Princeton, N.J., 1983). Other economic studies include Iliya Harik, *Economic Policy Reform in Egypt* (Gainesville, FL, 1997) and Mourad M. Wahba, *The Role of the State in the Egyptian Economy* (Reading, Mass., 1994). Also see Clement H. Moore, *Images of Development: Egyptian Engineers in Search of Industry* (Cambridge, Mass., 1980). On agriculture, see Yahya M. Sadowski, *Political Vegetables: Businessman and Bureaucrat in the Development of Egyptian Agriculture* (Washington, D.C., 1991).

Maye Kassem, *Egyptian Politics: The Dynamics of Authoritarian Rule* (Boulder, Colo., 2004) provides an up-to-date analysis of the durability of authoritarian patterns since 1952.

Raymond Baker is the author of two important works: *Egypt's Uncertain Revolution Under Nasser and Sadat* (Cambridge, Mass., 1978) and *Sadat and After* (Cambridge, Mass., 1990). Also see Shaheen Ayubi, *Nasser and Sadat* (New York, 1994).

Useful essays may be found in Shimon Shamir (ed.), *Egypt: from Monarchy to Republic* (Boulder, Colo., 1995).

An eye-opening study of the continuing importance of family ties and other connections in Egyptian society is Robert Springborg, *Family, Power, and Politics in Egypt: Sayed Bey Marei—His Clan, Clients, and Cohorts* (Philadelphia, 1982).

For an important analysis of the Egyptian Revolution's relation to the class structure, see Leonard Binder, *In a Moment of Enthusiasm: Political Power and the Second Stratum in Egypt* (Chicago, 1978). For a Marxist analysis, see Mahmoud Hussein, *Class Conflict in Egypt* (New York, 1975). On the bourgeoisie, see Malak Zaalouk, *Power, Class and Foreign Capital in Egypt: The Rise of the New Bourgeoisie* (London, 1989). Incisive analysis of the old landed bourgeoisie and its resurgence may be found in Saad Eddin Ibrahim, *Egypt, Islam, and Democracy,* 2nd ed. (Cairo, 2002) and in Hamied Ansari, *Egypt: The Stalled Society* (Albany, N.Y., 1986).

THE NASIR PERIOD

Gamal Abdel Nasser [Nasir], *The Philosophy of the Revolution* (Cairo, n.d.) may give even the novice some valuable insight. The same piece was published as *Egypt's Liberation* (Washington, D.C., 1955). Another personal account is Anwar El-Sadat, *Revolt on the Nile* (London, 1957). For a leftist Egyptian perspective, see Rashed Barawy, *The Military Coup in Egypt* (Cairo, 1952). Also see Mohammed Naguib [Muhammad Nagib], *Egypt's Destiny: A Personal Statement* (Garden City, N.Y., 1955) and Khalid Mohi El Din [Muhi al-Din], *Memories of a Revolution: Egypt 1952* (Cairo, 1995).

Among the best broad studies of the Nasir regime are Kirk J. Beattie, *Egypt During the Nasser Years* (Boulder, Colo., 1994) and R. Hrair Dekmejian, *Egypt Under Nasir: A Study in Political Dynamics* (Syracuse, N.Y., 1985). Also see: Harry Hopkins, *Egypt the Crucible: The Unfinished Revolution in the Arab World* (Boston, 1969) and Peter Mansfield, *Nasser's Egypt,* rev. ed. (Baltimore, 1969). An important Egyptian leftist's interpretation is Anouar Abdel-Malek, *Egypt: Military Society* (New York, 1968). Also see Abdel Magid Farid, *Nasser: The Final Years* (Reading, England, 1994). An excellent work on the early period is Joel Gordon, *Nasser's Blessed Moment: Egypt's Free Officers and the July Revolution* (New York, 1992). Miles Copeland's *The Game of Nations: The Amorality of Power Politics* (New York, 1969) provides some insight but should at times be taken with a grain of salt. James Mayfield's *Rural Politics in Nasser's Egypt* (Austin, Tex., 1971) is useful on the structure of the ASU in the countryside. On ideology, see Nissim Rejwan, *Nasserist Ideology: Its Exponents and Critics* (New York, 1974). Also see Gabriel S. Saab, *The Egyptian Agrarian Reform, 1952–1967* (London, 1967) and P. J. Vatikiotis (ed.), *Egypt Since the Revolution* (New York, 1968).

On pan-Arabism during this period, see A. I. Dawisha, *Egypt and the Arab World* (New York, 1976); Tawfig Y. Hasou, *The Struggle for the Arab World: Egypt's Nasser and the Arab League* (London, 1985); Najla M. Abu Izzedin, *Nasser of the Arabs* (London, 1981); James Jankowski, *Nasser's Egypt, Arab Nationalism, and the United Arab Republic* (Boulder, Colo., 2002); Joseph P. Lorenz, *Egypt and the Arabs* (Boulder, Colo., 1990); Elie Podeh, *The Decline of Arab Unity: The Rise and Fall of the United Arab Republic* (Brighton, England, 1999); and Ghada Hashem Talhami, *Palestine and Egyptian National Identity* (New York, 1990).

Important economic studies include Charles Issawi, *Egypt in Revolution: An Economic Analysis* (London, 1963); Robert Mabro, *The Egyptian Economy, 1952–1972* (Oxford, 1974); Patrick O'Brien, *The Revolution in Egypt's Economic System: From Private Enterprise to Socialism* (London, 1966). Also see Gouda Abd al-Khalek and Robert Tignor, *The Political Economy of Income Distribution in Egypt* (New York, 1982).

Recommended biographies of Nasir include Jean Lacouture, *Nasser: A Biography*, trans. by Daniel Hofstadter (New York,1973); Anthony Nutting, *Nasser* (New York, 1972); and Robert Stephens, *Nasser: A Political Biography* (New York, 1972). Also see P. J. Vatikiotis, *Nasser and His Generation* (London, 1978). For a shorter profile, see Peter Woodward, *Nasser* (London, 1992).

On the role of another important figure, see Munir K. Nasser, *Press, Politics, and Power: Egypt's Heikal and Al-Ahram* (Ames, Iowa, 1979).

P. J. Vatikiotis, *The Egyptian Army in Politics* (Bloomington, Ind., 1961) provides a useful analysis of the social origins of the 1952 Revolution. For another view, see Amos Perlmutter, *Egypt: The Praetorian State* (New Brunswick, N.J., 1974).

On relations with the Arab world, one penetrating yet readable study is Malcolm Kerr, *The Arab Cold War: Gamal Abd al-Nasir and His Rivals, 1958–1975*, 3rd ed. (New York, 1971). For insight into Nasir's position vis-à-vis the Palestine conflict, see Elmore Jackson, *Middle East Mission: The Story of a Major Bid for Peace in the Time of Nasser and Ben-Gurion* (New York, 1983). On relations with Africa: Tareq Ismael, *The U.A.R. and Africa: Egypt's Policy under Nasser* (Evanston, Ill., 1971).

On relations with the United States, see Geoffrey Aronson, *From Sideline*

to Center Stage: U.S. Policy Towards Egypt, 1946–1956 (Boulder, Colo., 1986);
Nigel John Ashton, *Eisenhower, Macmillan and the Problem of Nasser: Anglo-American Relations and Arab Nationalism, 1955–59* (New York, 1996); William J. Burns, *Economic Aid and American Policy Toward Egypt, 1955–1981* (Albany, N.Y., 1985); Peter L. Hahn, *The United States, Great Britain, and Egypt, 1945–1956: Strategy and Diplomacy in the Early Cold War* (Chapel Hill, N.C., 1991); Matthew F. Holland, *America and Egypt: From Roosevelt to Eisenhower* (Westport, Conn., 1996); Gail E. Meyer, *Egypt and the United States: The Formative Years* (Rutherford, N.J., 1980); and Muhammad Abd el-Wahab Sayed-Ahmed, *Nasser and American Foreign Policy 1952–1956* (London, 1989).

Relations with the Soviet Union are covered in Karen Dawisha, *Soviet Foreign Policy Towards Egypt* (New York, 1979); Mohamed Hasanein Heikal [Muhammad Hasanayn Haykal], *The Sphinx and the Commisar: The Rise and Fall of Soviet Influence in the Middle East* (New York, 1978); Alvin Z. Rubinstein, *Red Star on the Nile: The Soviet-Egyptian Influence Relationship Since the June War* (Princeton, N.J., 1977); and Ali M. Yahya, *Egypt and the Soviet Union, 1955–1972: A Study in the Power of a Small State* (Washington, D.C., 1989). Also see Mohamed Hasanein Heikal [Haykal], *The Cairo Papers: The Inside Story of Nasir and His Relationship with World Leaders, Rebels, and Statesmen* (Garden City, N.Y., 1978).

Works on the Suez Crisis include: Mohamed Hasanein Heikal [Haykal], *Cutting the Lion's Tale: Suez through Egyptian Eyes* (New York, 1987); Wm. Roger Louis and Roger Owen (eds.), *Suez 1956: The Crisis and Its Consequences* (Oxford, 1989); Kenneth Love. *Suez: The Twice-Fought War: A History* (New York and Toronto, 1969); Donald Neff. *Warriors at Suez: Eisenhower Takes America into the Middle East* (New York, 1981); Anthony Nutting, *No End of a Lesson: The Story of Suez* (New York, 1967); Hugh Thomas, *Suez* (New York and Evanston, Ill., 1967; and Selwyn Ilan Troen and Moshe Shemesh (eds.), *The Suez-Sinai Crisis 1956: Retrospective and Reappraisal* (New York, 1990).

On the 1967 conflict, see Richard Parker (ed.), *The Six-Day War: A Retrospective* (Gainesville, FL, 1996). A recent, heavily pro-Israeli study is Michael Oren, *June 1967 and the Making of the Modern Middle East* (New York, 2002).

THE SADAT PERIOD

For thorough studies of the Sadat period, see Kirk J. Beattie, *Egypt During the Sadat Years* (New York, 2000) and Raymond A. Hinnebusch, Jr., *Egyptian Politics Under Sadat: The Post-Populist Development of an*

Authoritarian-Modernizing State (Cambridge, 1985). For critical biographies, see David Hirst and Irene Beeson, *Sadat* (London, 1981) and G. Shukri, *Egypt: Portrait of a President* (London, 1981). As for autobiographies, see Anwar al-Sadat, *In Search of Identity: An Autobiography* (New York, 1978*)* and Jehan Sadat, *A Woman of Egypt* (New York, 1986). For laudatory presentations, see Joseph Finkelstone, *Anwar Sadat: A Visionary Who Dared* (London, 1996) and Raphael Israeli, *Man of Defiance: A Personal Biography of Anwar Sadat* (Totowa, N.J., 1985). Focusing mostly on the Sadat period is Thomas W. Lippman, *Egypt After Nasser: Sadat, Peace and the Mirage of Prosperity* (New York, 1989). For a readable presentation of the condition of Egypt midway in the Sadat era, see John Waterbury, *Egypt, Burdens of the Past, Options for the Future* (Bloomington, Ind., 1978). See also Doreen Kays, *Frogs and Scorpions: Egypt, Sadat and the Media* (London, 1984).

For interesting accounts of events leading up to the 1973 war and to Sadat's assassination, see Muhammad Heikal [Haykal], *The Road to Ramadan* (New York, 1975) and, by the same author, *Autumn of Fury* (New York, 1983).

A critical assessment by an Egyptian general is Saad Shazly, *The Crossing of the Suez* (London, 1980). Also see Boutros Boutros-Ghali, *Egypt's Road to Jerusalem* (New York, 1997); Moshe Dayan, *Breakthrough: A Personal Account of the Egypt-Israel Peace Negotiations* (New York, 1981); Ismael Fahmy, *Negotiating for Peace in the Middle East* (London, 1983); Martin Indyk, *"To the Ends of the Earth": Sadat's Jerusalem Initiative* (Cambridge, Mass., 1984); Mohamed Ibrahim Kamel, *The Camp David Accords: A Testimony* (New York, 1986); William B. Quandt, *Camp David: Peacemaking and Politics* (Washington, D.C., 1986); William B. Quandt (ed.), *The Middle East: Ten Years after Camp David* (Washington, D.C., 1988); Mahmoud Riad, *The Struggle for Peace in the Middle East* (New York, 1982); Howard Morley Sachar, *Egypt and Israel* (New York, 1981); and Adel Safty, *From Camp David to the Gulf* (Montreal and New York, 1992). Key documents may be found in *The Egyptian-Israeli Treaty: Text and Selected Documents* (Beirut, 1979). Also see William B. Quandt, *Peace Process: American Diplomacy and the Arab-Israeli Conflict Since 1967*, rev. ed. (Berkeley, Calif., 2001).

THE MUBARAK PERIOD

Among recent works on Mubarak's Egypt, I recommend Eberhard Kienly, *A Grand Delusion: Democracy and Economic Reform in Egypt* (London and New York, 2001) and May Kassem, *In the Guise of Democracy: Governance in Contemporary Egypt* (Reading, England, 1999). Other excellent works, though covering only the early Mubarak years, include I. M.

Oweiss (ed.), *The Political Economy of Contemporary Egypt* (Washington, D.C., 1990); Robert Springborg, *Mubarak's Egypt: Fragmentation of the Political Order* (Boulder, Colo., 1989); Robert Springborg, *The Political Economy of Mubarak's Egypt* (Boulder, Colo., 1988), and Charles Tripp and Roger Owen (eds.), *Egypt Under Mubarak* (London and New York, 1989).

For insight into the lives of ordinary people, especially women: Diane Singerman, *Avenues of Participation: Family, Politics, and Networks in Urban Quarters of Cairo* (Princeton, N.J., 1995) and Unni Wikan, *Tomorrow, God Willing: Self-Made Destinies in Cairo* (Chicago, 1996).

CONTEMPORARY ISLAMIST MOVEMENTS

Writings on recent Islamism include Geneive Abdo, *No God but God: Egypt and the Triumph of Islam* (New York, 2000); R. Hrair Dekmejian, *Islam in Revolution* (Albany, N.Y., 1985); Nadia Ramsis Farah, *Religious Strife in Egypt* (New York, 1986); J.J.G. Jansen, *The Neglected Duty: The Creed of Sadat's Assassins and Islamic Resurgence in the Middle East* (New York, 1986); Giles Kepel, *Muslim Extremism in Egypt: The Prophet and the Pharaoh*, trans. Jon Rothschild (London, 1985); Caryle Murphy, *Passion for Islam: Shaping the Modern Middle East: The Egyptian Experience* (New York, 2002); Barry Rubin, *Islamic Fundamentalism in Egyptian Politics*, updated ed. (New York, 2002); David Sagiv, *Fundamentalism and Intellectuals in Egypt, 1973–1993* (London, 1995); Emmanuel Sivan, *Radical Islam: Medieval Theology and Modern Politics* (New Haven, Conn., 1985); Denis J. Sullivan and Sana Abed-Kotob, *Islam in Contemporary Egypt: Civil Society vs. the State* (Boulder, Colo., 1999); and Mary Ann Weaver, *A Portrait of Egypt: A Journey Through the World of Militant Islam*, rev. ed. (New York, 2000). Egypt provides a major case study for Mohammed M. Hafez, *Why Muslims Rebel: Repression and Resistance in the Islamic World* (Boulder, Colo., 2003). Although it was written in an earlier period, Sayyid Qutb's *Milestones* (Indianapolis, 1993) also is important.

UPDATING

For regularly updated, encyclopedic information, see Europa Publications' *The Middle East and North Africa*, 50th ed. (London, 2004). News coverage may be found in *Middle East Times* (Cairo), the online edition of which includes even censored articles (http://www.metimes.com), and the *Cairo Times*, selected articles from which are available online (http://www.cairotimes.com/). Links to much raw information can be found at the Egypt page (http://www.al-bab.com/arab/countries/egypt.htm) of the al-bab.com site (An Open Door to the Arab World, http://www.al-bab.com). Some of the most objective and perceptive analysis of the whole region, including Egypt, may be found in *Middle East Report* (Washington), many of whose articles, together with other material, are available on the MERIP Web site (http://www.merip.org/).

Index

About the Author

GLENN E. PERRY is Professor of Political Science at Indiana State University, where he has taught since 1970.

Other Titles in the Greenwood Histories of the Modern Nations

Frank W. Thackeray and John E. Findling, Series Editors

The History of Argentina
Daniel K. Lewis

The History of Australia
Frank G. Clarke

The History of Brazil
Robert M. Levine

The History of the Baltic States
Kevin O'Connor

The History of Canada
Scott W. See

The History of Chile
John L. Rector

The History of China
David C. Wright

The History of Congo
Didier Gondola

The History of Cuba
Clifford L. Staten

The History of France
W. Scott Haine

The History of Germany
Eleanor L. Turk

The History of Holland
Mark T. Hooker

The History of India
John McLeod

The History of Iran
Elton L. Daniel

The History of Ireland
Daniel Webster Hollis III

The History of Israel
Arnold Blumberg

The History of Italy
Charles L. Killinger

The History of Japan
Louis G. Perez

The History of Mexico
Burton Kirkwood

The History of New Zealand
Tom Brooking

The History of Nigeria
Toyin Falola

The History of Poland
M. B. Biskupski

The History of Portugal
James M. Anderson

The History of Russia
Charles E. Ziegler

The History of Serbia
John K. Cox

The History of South Africa
Roger B. Beck

The History of Spain
Peter Pierson

The History of Sweden
Byron J. Nordstrom

The History of Turkey
Douglas A. Howard